Applied ICT

GCSE
Double Award

Steve Cushing

Hodder & Stoughton

A MEMBER OF THE HODDER HEADLINE GROUP

APPLIED ICT GCSE DOUBLE AWARD

Orders: please contact Bookpoint Ltd, 130 Milton Park, Abingdon, Oxon OX14 4SB. Telephone: (44) 01235 827720. Fax: (44) 01235 400454. Lines are open from 9.00–6.00, Monday to Saturday, with a 24 hour message answering service. Email address: orders@bookpoint.co.uk

British Library Cataloguing in Publication Data
A catalogue record for this title is available from the British Library

ISBN 0340 850337

First Published 2002
Impression number   10 9 8 7 6 5 4 3 2 1
Year   2007 2006 2005 2004 2003 2002

Typeset by Pantek Arts Ltd, Maidstone, Kent.
Printed in Italy for Hodder & Stoughton Educational, a division of Hodder Headline Plc, 338 Euston Road, London NW1 3BH.

Contents

Acknowledgements

The author and publishers would like to thank the following for granting permission to use copyright material in this book:

Dyson for the photo on p v
Jan Suttle/Life File for the photo on p 27
Emma Lee/Life File for the photos on pp 38, 126 and 142
Chris Priest/Science Photo Library for the photo on p 72
Corbis for the photo on p 103
PA Photos for the photos on pp 134 and 139 (left)
David Ducros/Science Photo Library for the photo on p 152 (top)
AbilityNet for the photos on p 163
Mike Evans/Life File for the photo on p 175

Introduction

You may have woken this morning to the sound of a microprocessor-controlled alarm clock, got up in your microprocessor-controlled centrally heated bedroom. The clothes that you put on and the breakfast you ate were probably produced by computer-controlled machines. Your parents' washing machine, dishwasher, tumble dryer, microwave, telephone and cooker will all probably be controlled by a microprocessor. You will pick up your microprocessor-controlled mobile phone and set off to school or college in a microprocessor-controlled car. We are all users of information communication technology as it can be found in all areas of life; at home and at work, in shops and offices and even out in the street controlling traffic flows. It has changed our society just as the Industrial Revolution changed the lives of people over a century ago.

This book focuses upon a family and how they use ICT in their home and working lives. The family provide case studies you can use to undertake your research for the GCSE or other ICT courses. Throughout the book there are other case studies looking at real people who work as IT professionals. The job of an IT professional is to design and build the systems that we, the users, come across in our daily lives. So let's meet the family the book focuses upon.

Figure 0.1 *Some of the micro-controlled machines in our home*

Meet the Oliver family

Dad's name is **Iain** and he is the manager of a packaging company in Leicester. He will be celebrating his 50th birthday in a few months' time.

Mum's name is **Veena** and she is a nurse at the local health centre. She met Iain 25 years ago when she was nursing in the general hospital, and he was rushed in with appendicitis. He left hospital without his appendix but with a new girlfriend.

Lata is Iain and Veena's eldest child. She is 22 now and is training to be an accountant. She lives at home at the moment but would really like to move out and find her own flat or little house, if she can afford it. Her boyfriend, **Paco**, works for a company that manufactures mobile phones. He is always ready to tell Lata and her family about the latest developments in telephone technology.

Gavin is just 19, and studying engineering at university. He is particularly interested in designing cars and has just managed to save enough money from a summer holiday job to buy himself an old VW Golf. During the second year of his university course, he will spend six months on placement in an engineering company in Leicester. His best friend **Mike** is in a wheelchair after a motorbike accident.

Edward is the youngest child. He is 16 and studying for his GCSEs at school. He likes ICT, but sometimes finds his ICT lessons a bit boring because the teacher has to cope with those of his classmates who don't get on so well with ICT, while Edward would like to be getting on with designing the website that he and a group of his friends are trying to set up. When he can drag himself away from the computer screen, Edward loves going out on the motorbike which he received for his 16 birthday.

Rupa is Veena's aunt, who lives in a flat attached to the family house. She came from India to join them when her husband died three years ago, and she is still struggling with learning English. Her own daughter lives in Sydney, Australia, and Rupa hopes to be able to visit her soon.

The Oliver family live with two cats that their father named Ragtag and Bobtail after a children's programme he used to watch on an old analogue TV with his mother. It was one of the first TVs anyone had, according to Iain.

Through the experiences of members of the family, the book will explore the use of ICT to:

- communicate with friends, customers, suppliers, staff;
- improve business efficiency;
- manage finance (payroll; budgeting/forecasting; transactions, reporting);
- manage stock control;
- market products and services;
- manage information and control systems.

It also examines specifically the uses of ICT in terms of how it affects day-to-day life of the individual family members and the processing of business tasks:

- functional areas of organisations (comparison of the uses of ICT between the Sales department and the Finance department for example);
- data capture and data storage methods (how do input and output screens vary between a retail outlet, for example, and an insurance company?);
- security issues (e.g. data protection, copyright, Data Misuse Act) and the sensitivity of data relating to patients in a hospital, for example, and clients on a commercial database.

ICT tools and applications

This section does not aim to teach you how to use all the hardware and software packages you will need to use, but aims to revise things you should already know and place these in an applied context. You will also learn how ICT tools and applications can be used to develop business documents to meet communication needs, and how standard ways of working are used in ICT. Having developed skills in a variety of applications, you must explore how and why the different applications can be used in different organisations. This is shown in the other sections of the book. You must be able to identify why the type of application is appropriate for the organisation's purposes and what tools and facilities make it appropriate. For example, libraries use databases to track the location of books.

At the heart of any computer is the **hardware** and **software**. Hardware is the name given to the physical computer system itself:

- the monitor
- the keyboard
- the disk drives
- the mouse
- the printer.

Software is the name given to the programs that run on the computer. The microprocessor forms the centre of a computer system. It controls the way the computer calculates and operates.

Computers have memory and operate in binary. This means that they have a number system based on two states – 1 and 0, or On and Off. These 1s and 0s are called bits, and a group of eight bits equals a byte. Now it is common to talk of things in terms of kilobytes (a thousand bytes), megabytes (a million bytes) and gigabytes (a thousand million bytes). So:

8 bits	=	1 byte
1kb	=	1 000 bytes
1mb	=	1 000 000 bytes (or 1000kb)
1gb	=	1 000 000 000 bytes (or 1000mb)

When you mention the words 'Information Communication Technology', most people think about computers. Virtually everything we use today has some computerised component.

All computers are built around a microprocessor. Computers have lots of different parts that work together. The brain of a computer is the

Central Processing Unit (CPU). Everything that a computer does is controlled by the CPU. The main circuit board in a computer is called the motherboard. The CPU and memory are usually on the motherboard.

Computers have two main types of memory: **Random Access Memory** (RAM), which is used by the computer to store information temporarily that the computer is currently working with, and **Read Only Memory** (ROM), which is a permanent type of memory used by the computer for important data that does not change. There are a number of terms you need to understand when talking about memory. **Caching** is the term given to the way a computer stores frequently used data in RAM that connects directly to the CPU. **Virtual memory** is the term used for space on a hard disk that temporarily stores data. Virtual memory can be swapped in and out of RAM as needed by the CPU.

Gavin's **MP3 player** is a specialised computer for processing MP3 files. His Gameboy is a specialised processor for handling games. These processor controlled devices are designed to do one thing whereas his PC is far more flexible.

The microprocessor and the memory both affect the speed of the computer. The other main factor affecting speed is the clock speed. This determines how fast the data in the computer is processed.

Gavin's computer also has a sound card and a graphics card so he can play computer games. The sound card is used by the computer to record and play sounds by converting analogue sound into digital information and back again. The graphics card translates image data from the computer into a format that can be displayed by the high resolution monitor.

Gavin's computer works in a digital world. Sometimes his mother thinks he lives in one. When he is at home, he is always using ICT for entertainment purposes. He is often found:

- going into chat rooms on the Internet;
- sending e-mail to friends;
- texting his friends on his mobile phone;
- downloading games, tunes for mobile phones and music;
- listening to digital songs.

Figure 1.1 *Sound card and graphics card*

Understanding the difference between analogue and digital

All computers use digital data. Everything is either on (1) or off (0). To understand digital technology you need to understand the differences between analogue and digital signals. This is best explained by looking at the digital sound Gavin likes so much.

If you speak your voice produces an analogue sound wave. The wave is continuous.

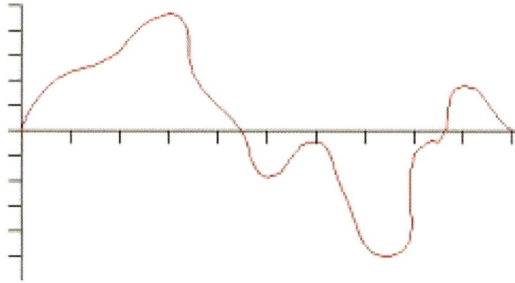

Figure 1.2 *Analogue sound wave*

A digital recording converts the analogue wave into a stream of numbers (1s and 0s) and records the numbers instead of the wave. The conversion is done by a device called an analogue-to-digital converter.

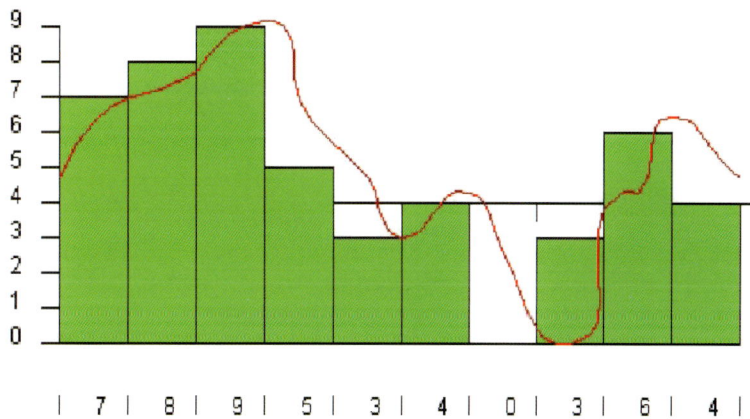

Figure 1.3 *Digital sound wave*

Sounds on a CD or DVD are stored in a number of different digital formats depending on the software. The volume of sound is also stored in digital format. When sound is recorded via a microphone, the sound signal is received by the microphone in analogue format. An analogue signal has a continuous variation between low and high pitch, on a smooth scale. It must be converted into digital format, which is a pitch with distinct steps. Windows uses what are called WAV (short for *wave*) files. WAV files contain a digital representation of sound waves.

The quality and accuracy of a sound file is dependent upon the sampling rate. The higher the sampling rate, the greater the accuracy but the larger the file. It is best to think of sampling rates in a similar way to the resolution of a graphics image. The more dots or pixels in the image, the better its quality. Similarly, the more samples that are taken of a sound, the better its quality.

High sample rates give better quality sound but generate more data to store. There is no point in recording the sound at a higher quality than the human ear can pick up. When Gavin plays the sound back it is converted back into an analogue signal to push through his speakers.

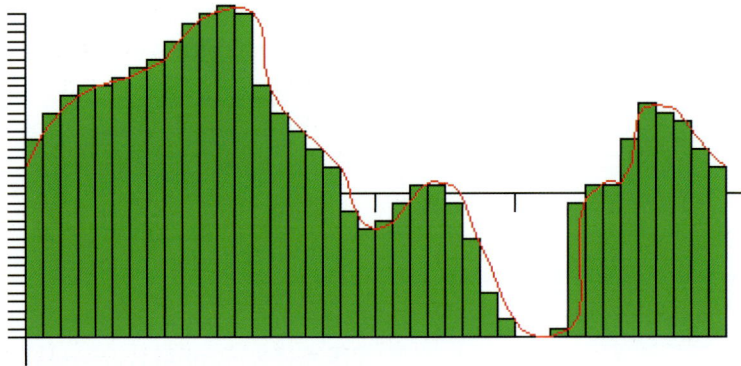

Figure 1.4 *Conversion of analogue sound wave to digital format, showing higher sample rates*

◼ *Data and information*

Computers are very good at any sort of data processing. Searching, sorting and calculating are just three ways of processing data to turn it into information we can all use. We all process data ourselves many times each day. Even such a simple action as recognising your own house involves data processing. The colour of the door, shape of the house, number of windows, position of the gate, position of trees are all pieces of data. Almost without thinking, you take in data and turn it into useful information – 'it's your house'. Without processing this data, you would never arrive at home.

It is important to be clear about the difference between data and information.

Data are the raw values that are entered into, stored and processed by information systems. Examples of data would be the colour of your front door, number of windows etc. Data can be stored in a number of ways.

Information is produced as output and feedback, with a context that gives it meaning. An example of this would be knowing it is your house. Data only becomes information when we know what the data means.

Computers process all information in the form of data. The important difference between a computer processing data and a human brain doing the same thing is that the computer is only a machine and does not understand what the information means. It follows instructions originally given by people through the software program. This is the reason why we say that computers process **data** rather than **information**.

Let's look at another example. The family's digitally controlled washing machine carries out the processing of all the family's washing. Dirty laundry is put into the machine, and it comes out clean. Between these points, the machine carries out a range of processes including heating the water, turning the drum, adding the washing powder, washing, rinsing and then spinning. The washing machine processor follows the data it is given, what to turn on, when, for how long, at what temperatures to switch the heater on and off. Dirty laundry is not much use to us – we need to have our clothes washed before we can wear them again. In the same way the original data is of no use to us unless it is processed into useful information.

So we now know the difference between data and information. But this on its own is of no use to us. We are surrounded by data and information. We have to decide what is important and what is not. As Edward rode his motorbike towards his home one day, he was constantly bombarded with data and information.

Using a number of input devices he could:

- **hear** – birds were singing over the whine of the engine (ears);
- **see** – the sun was shining (eyes);
- **smell** – the flowers and new tar on the road (nose);
- **feel** – the road was bumpy and the power of the engine vibrating the bike (touch sensors);
- **taste** – he had just eaten peanut butter sandwiches (taste sensors).

Edward's sensors were feeding information in the form of data which his brain was turning into information. He was using this information to control his actions; when to turn the handle bars, when to accelerate.

We can design systems using this approach.

- First we select the input devices.
- Then we decide how to process the data.
- Then we decide upon the output.

These are usually represented using the following diagram:

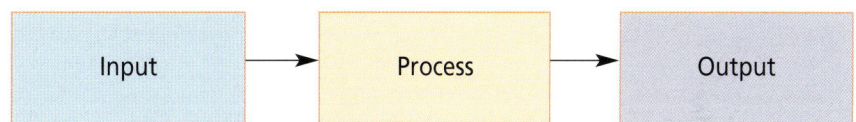

| Input | → | Process | → | Output |

Figure 1.5

In a computer system the input could be from sensors like the washing machine uses or from devices such as keyboards, scanners, digital cameras etc.

A standard computer system that would be used in an office or school situation consists of a number of components: the computer itself, and other hardware devices that are connected to it. These hardware devices are referred to as peripherals. Gavin's computer has a screen, a keyboard, a mouse and one or more additional disk and CD drives.

The whole system can be represented as a simple block diagram.

Arrows show whether a device is an input or output device. Some devices such as disk drives and touch sensitive screens are both input and output devices.

The largest computers are mainframe computers. These are used in situations where vast amounts of processing power and data storage ability are required. Banks, large insurance companies and utility companies such as suppliers of electricity and gas use mainframe computers. All our family members use PCs. Iain uses a PC for his

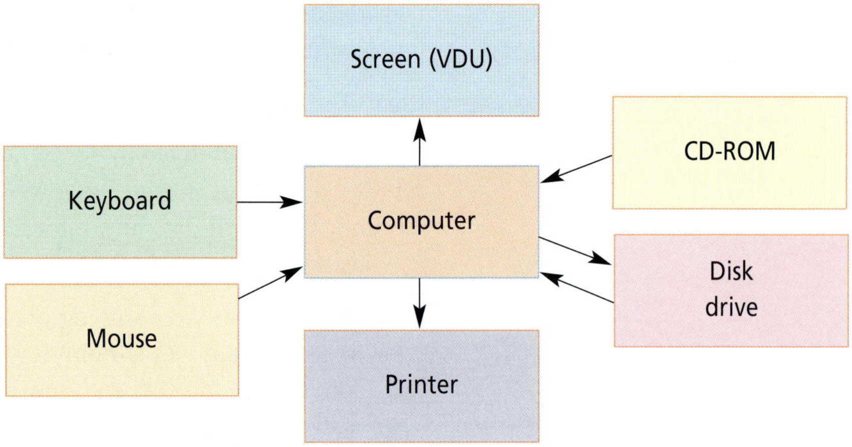

Figure 1.6 *Block diagram of computer system*

company needs. Some very powerful mainframe machines produce considerable amounts of heat. Mainframe computer rooms have to be air conditioned. Some mainframe computers are water-cooled.

Notice how Gavin's computer has four main input devices: a keyboard, a mouse, a CD-ROM and a disk drive. A large number of input devices are described in this book.

Name
Keyboard
Mouse
Concept keyboard
Scanner
Digitiser
Heat sensor
Microphone
Digital camera

Figure 1.7 *Input devices*

Let's return to Edward, still riding his motorbike home. He has only had the motorbike for a few weeks. At first, he could enjoy all of the nice sensations picked up by his sensors and the joy of riding home on a warm sunny day with the cool air blowing in his face. Then suddenly a fast moving van raced into view ahead on the wrong side of the road. Certain pieces of information suddenly became more important than others.

Edward had only seconds to decide:

● Is the van going too fast?
● Should he accelerate?
● Should he apply the brakes?
● Is the van heading for him?

- Is the van slowing down?
- Is the road wide enough for them to pass?
- Is the water in the ditch very cold and wet?
- Is the hedge very thorny?
- What about his new motorbike?

The sounds and smells of the countryside were pushed to the back of his mind. They were no longer important. If he continued enjoying the view, he would soon be asking:

- Will I live?
- Where is the nearest hospital?
- How will my mum know where I am?
- How much will a new bike cost?

He was thinking how he should respond, in other words, his output.

- Swerve into the hedge.
- Swerve into the ditch.
- Cry.
- Shout.

ICT solutions have output devices such as:

Name
Printer
Screen
Speakers
Light bulb
Motor

Figure 1.7 contd *Output devices*

We can represent what happened to Edward on our diagram by adding what is called a feedback loop.

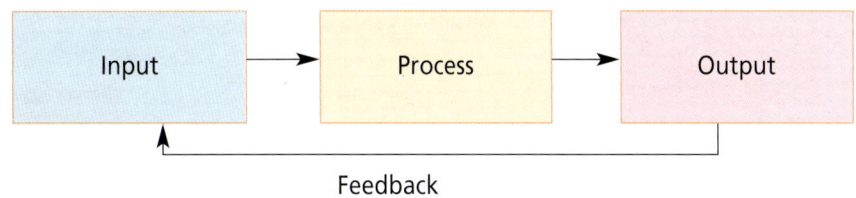

Figure 1.8 *Feedback loop*

The data and information Edward's brain is processing warns him of danger and controls the inputs and processes of the system.

Like Edward, we are surrounded by data and information all the time. Every day, we take in information and data from books, newspapers, radio, television, school lessons, mobile phones, computers, CDs and talking to people. We have to select, from all this, the information we need at the time. We have to select the information that we need to carry out a task or to solve a problem. Before we can design or use a computer system we need first to decide:

- What do we want out of the system?
- What do we need to put into the system?
- In what form do we want the system to process the data?

When you design your own systems you can use a simple system diagram to show what you intend to do. The picture shows a system diagram used by Edward when he designed a web-based advertisement for his father's company. You can read more about this later in the book.

INPUT	PROCESS	OUTPUT
The things that will go into the web page are: clip art from galleries (Internet, MS Office and others) Sound files from the Internet and MS Office) Information from competitor web pages Assignment instructions Views of colleagues Views of person in charge Surveys of potential customers Images scanned	I will change, organise, manipulate and organise using . . . FrontPage features – marquee, scrolling text boxes, hyperlinks, page transition, sound and movement etc. Word-processing of text The manipulation of an image(s) in a print program	The end result can be seen . . . web page(s) on WWW Monitor display of web page on Intranet Monitor display of web page for public to view (e.g. in entrance hall). Use fully or part in a wall poster, flyer, newspaper or magazine advert. Text used in TV Teletext

Let's look at the first case study of a real IT professional and what their job entails. You will notice how important it is to get to know the needs of the business in a systematic way.

Case study

Jo

I did a degree in botany; a lot of the skills I acquired during study for the degree have helped me in my career with IBM, skills such as methodical working, classifying, organisational skills.

I entered IBM as a computer programmer. At the time, I knew nothing about programming. I received training at IBM and found that, although, at the start, I knew less about computers and information systems than some of my colleagues, the skills I already had were very useful to me and I soon learnt programming. If you can cope with cooking a Sunday lunch, you can cope with programming.

Following promotion, I became a solutions architect. This means that I was responsible for designing ICT solutions to client problems. I worked as part of a team, and, in time, became a team leader. If you are working for clients, communication and people skills are very important. I find that mixed gender teams work best – in general, women are good at working through the evolution of problems, while men are good at seeing revolutionary answers. Skills that I use a lot involve:

- Getting to know my customers – understanding how their organisations work, empathising with them. I need to 'get inside' my customer's organisation and see how it feels.
- Questioning – why might a particular idea be useful? What is it useful for? Why is the solution needed?
- Understanding – that what seems to me to be an obvious solution may not be obvious to everyone else; that the simplest, most obvious solutions are often the best; that an ICT solution may not be best in every case; that an ICT solution must be holistic. In other words, although it may not be perfect, it must suit every aspect of the context in the best possible way.

Example: my team was asked to come up with a solution to help a busy workshop organise the jobs that they had waiting. The system they were using was a series of pigeon holes on the wall, into which they put sheets of paper, each bearing the details of one job to be done. The system was inflexible and inefficient, and the working environment noisy and very dirty. The workers in the workshop did not know much about computers and were not very keen on them.

Our holistic solution had to take these factors into consideration:

It was no good designing a user interface that made all the usual beeping noises. They would not be heard in the workshop. All messages had to be visual.

A standard keyboard would have been no use. It would have rapidly become clogged with dirt so we selected a system with a plastic overlay that was easy to clean and did not absorb dirt.

We had to design a system that the workers would be able to relate to, given that they were not very familiar with ICT. Although it was not the most 'sophisticated' solution, we came up with a system of on-screen pigeon holes, like those on the workshop wall, that the workers could quickly understand and use to organise their work.

I have been promoted again, and now manage the Centres for IBM e-business Innovation. I am still helping IBM clients to find solutions to their problems. Typical questions might be:

'How can I retain my existing customer base but extend my activities to sell to new customers?'

'I accept that business is in recession at present, but what steps can I take to ensure that, when business activity lifts out of recession again, I am in the best position to "take off" with new initiatives? Of course, I have to keep my eye on costs.'

My job involves a great deal of co-ordinating and planning. It is a bit like a dating agency – I have to pull all the important elements (teams of people, locations, finance, specialist knowledge) together at the right time. I spend a lot of time making connections between the elements. In each different context, my communication skills are very important, and I must make sure that my methods are suited to the situation. For example, the skills I use when talking face to face to a client are different from those I use when I am sitting in front of a camera for a video conference, or talking to a number of people via a conference telephone call.

I must keep my clients' needs in mind at all times, but I must also meet the needs of my employer, IBM. The solutions I produce must be within budget, and I must make the best use of IBM staff, office space and finance. I am also responsible for the health and safety of IBM staff and visitors, and must make sure that my company does not contravene any regulations or laws. We must always take care that no unauthorised people gain access to IBM's worldwide systems.

We plan on an annual basis. Planning new business for a company as large as IBM is not very different from planning a household budget; the numbers you are dealing with are much larger, that's all.

I do not have a fixed office space, nor do I work a fixed number of hours. My priority, and that of my employer, is that the job gets done in time, and I schedule my work to achieve this. All of my colleagues have access to my working diary, so that they can find me. Even if we are located in different countries, a group of us can get together and talk using conference calls, video conferencing, or web-casting. Sometimes I work from home, which means that I can spend time with my family. I can use my laptop and mobile phone to work while I am travelling on the train. Within IBM, I book rooms to use as I need them. If I am dealing with a confidential matter, for example, or if I really need some quiet, 'thinking' time, I book a small office and shut myself in, switching the telephone to voicemail. Then I can really concentrate, and pick up my messages later. My laptop travels everywhere with me. ICT means that I can achieve this level of flexibility in my work, to get the best end results.

It is very important to me, and to my employer, that I continue my own education, and ICT helps here too. I am undertaking a distance learning MBA course, and work closely with the small group of people who are following the same course. Each of us lives in a different European country, but we can always talk via the telephone or email, and sharing the workload helps each one of us. Within IBM, newsgroups and special interest groups keep me up to date on the latest developments in my working areas, or give me the opportunity to learn about new aspects of ICT.

Communication is a vital part of my job. Also, as a leader and manager, I believe that it is very important that I am seen to be enthusiastic about new technology. I see myself as a kind of evangelist for new ideas, new solutions, but, at the same time, I do not pretend to know all the answers. If someone asks me how to do something and I don't know, I always say, 'I don't know the answer yet, but let's work it out together. That way we will achieve our goal.'

So Jo's job is about understanding the needs of a system before attempting to design one. Looking for the data and information needs of an organisation or process is the starting point for any work in ICT. At the heart of any effective system is organisation.

ORGANISATION

Sunita spent an hour looking for the CD she wanted to play. She was convinced her friend Edward had borrowed it without asking. Finally, she looked under her bed and there it was, buried under a pile of dirty clothes. 'I must get these CDs organised so I can find the one I want,' thought Sunita and, having gathered together all her music collection, she started to put them all into the order in which she had purchased them.

A few minutes later her sister Meera popped her head around the door.
'Whatever are you doing, Sunita?' she shouted above the music.
'Sorting my CD collection,' came the reply.
'How are you sorting them?' shouted Meera.

Sunita emerged from the heap of CDs on her floor, some in cases, some not, and turned the volume down. 'In date order,' she replied.

'Just a moment,' interrupted Meera. 'You haven't stopped to think about what you are doing. How will you remember when you bought a particular CD and where will you write the date on the CD?'

For about 15 minutes, Sunita and Meera thought of lots of different ways to sort the CDs: by recording company, how much they were played, how much they cost, by gender or group. It soon became clear that the easiest way would be to sort the CDs into alphabetical order. Once they had decided whether to sort under first or last names – for example, should Robbie Williams be under R, or W? – the girls were able to begin sorting. Once sorted it was very easy for Sunita to find a particular CD that she wanted to play.

At the heart of good organisation is file management.

■ *Files and file management*

Most people who work with computers quickly generate a large number of files. Without good file management it would be very difficult to find a particular file. Files can be generated in lots of different packages and unlike Sunita's CDs you cannot pick them up and physically look at them. One way of locating files on a computer is to search by file extension. All saved documents are given what is called a file extension.

These are given to identify what type of document your file is:

1. .xls   is an Excel document
2. .doc   is a word-processed document such as Microsoft Word
3. .ppt   is a Powerpoint document
4. .mdb   is a Microsoft database document
5. .html   is a web page document
6. .bmp   is an image document from Microsoft Paint

Without an effective file management system even emails and text messages would not work correctly.

Files are saved on storage media such as the computer's hard disk, floppy disk or CD-ROM.

HARD DISKS

Hard disks and floppy disks are magnetic storage media. Data is held as magnetised spots on the disk surface. Magnets need to be kept away from the surface or they can damage the data stored.

Hard disks are made of metal coated with a magnetisable material. They can hold a large amount of data and are usually fixed inside the hard disk drive of the central processing unit. Each hard disk will usually hold several disks on a single spindle. As each disk surface is able to store data, each surface can have its own read/write head. These can operate simultaneously, which means that data can be transferred and utilised more quickly than by using a single larger disk. This access time is very important because modern software often needs to move data to and from a hard disk. It does not hold everything in RAM all the time.

Figure 1.9 *Hard drive*

Therefore, even if the computer has a fast processor, if access time to the hard disks is slow, the software will not run properly.

Hard disks are used to:

- store the operating system, applications software and user's files for a PC;
- store the operating system, software and files for a local area network (LAN);
- store work awaiting printing.

With all the data a hard disk can contain, finding specific files can be a real problem, especially when you have not given the file its filename.

Sunita's CD collection is small when compared with the number of files on a hard disk.

Because of this, e-mails and web pages work on an internationally agreed file structure.

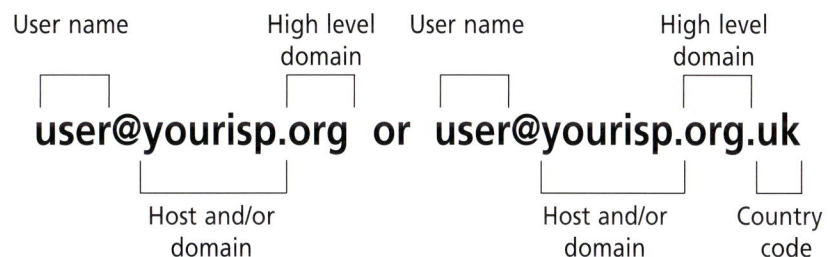

| User name | | High level domain | User name | | High level domain |
| | | | | | |

user@yourisp.org or **user@yourisp.org.uk**

| | Host and/or domain | | Host and/or domain | Country code |

Figure 1.10 *Structure of e-mail address*

@ This is the distinguishing characteristic of e-mail addresses and all e-mails have to have the symbol. It is pronounced 'at'.

USER NAME

This is the part of the e-mail address which is to the left of the @ sign. It is a name that a user selects or has been assigned by a service provider or an e-mail administrator. Often, user names are a combination of a person's first and/or last names. For example, if a user's name is Edward Oliver he could use EdwardOliver or OliverE. As there are probably lots of people with the name Edward Oliver, he may have to add a number or nickname.

HOST AND/OR DOMAIN

The part of an e-mail address to the right of the @ symbol refers to the name of the computer where the mail is to be sent. It can vary, depending on how the computer is named. The computer where the e-mail is sent is called the host. The domain is the network that the computer is connected to. In the example, 'yourisp' is the name of the computer. High level domains usually end in '.com' or '.org'.

Example of an e-mail address: *Sunita@hotmail.com*

When you list any files or e-mail addresses, the computer will automatically list them in alphabetical order, like Sunita's filing system. But as in Sunita's bedroom, there is more than one place the files could be hiding.

Files are usually located on a disk drive. All drives are assigned a letter.

A:\ is assigned to the floppy disk drive.
C:\ is assigned to the computer's hard disk drive.
D:\ is normally assigned to the CD-ROM drive.

To help you find your files there are a number of features of good file management.

Filenames are important. They are often the only way of locating the information stored on a computer. The filename should enable the user to know what the file contains. Most modern software allows you to create filenames over 200 characters long. Always save files with names that clearly indicate their content and remember they will be displayed in alphabetical order by file extension and first letter.

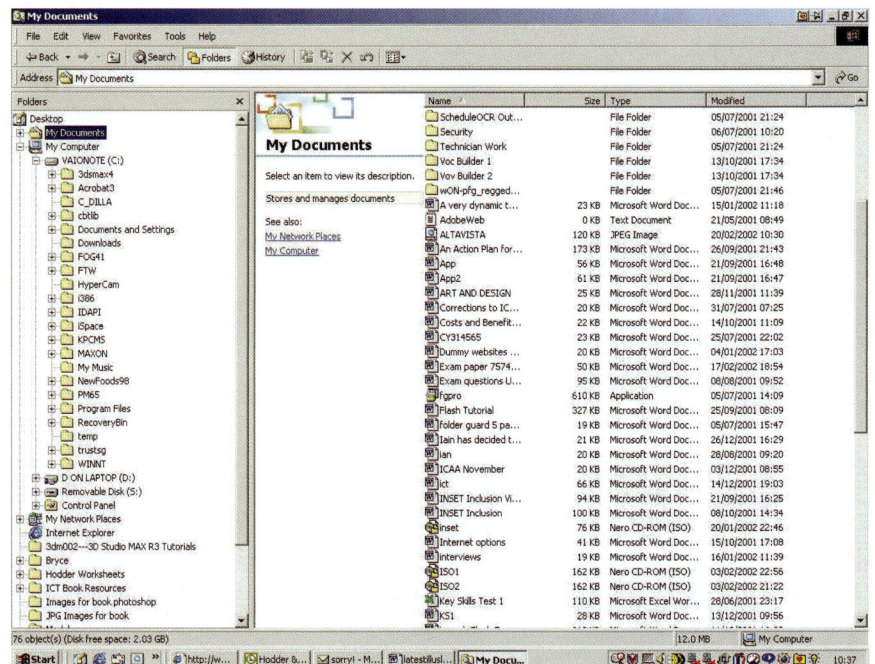

Figure 1.11 *Screenshot of file listings*

Different versions of files should be labelled with version numbers. For example: the first draft of a leaflet could be called Leaflet01, the second draft would then be called Leaflet02 and so on or you could use the number first 01Leaflet, 02Leaflet.

You store files in directories. Another name for a directory is a folder. The name of the folder should also give an indication of the contents of the folder. Folders can be stored inside folders, so it is possible to

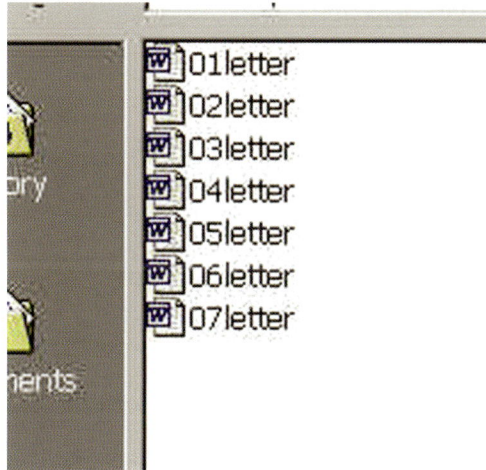

Figure 1.12 *File listings with numbers first*

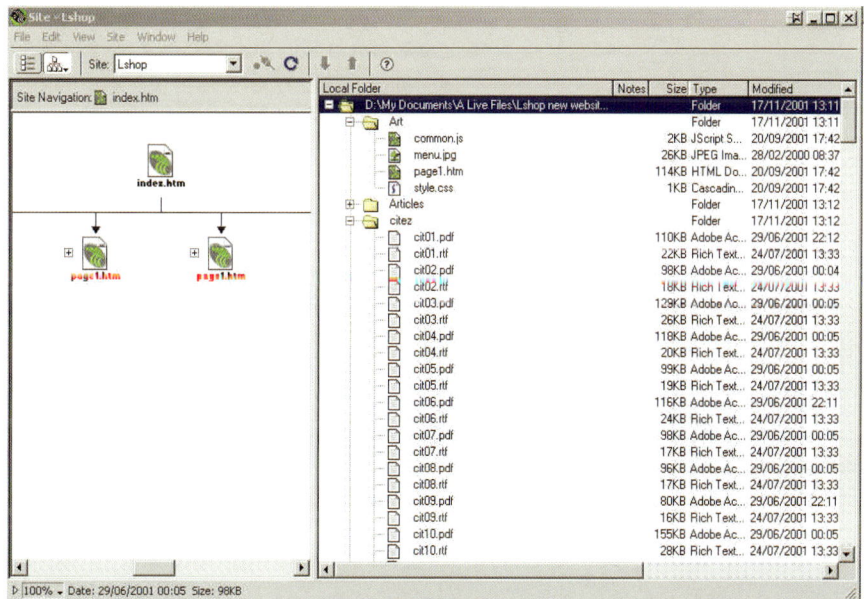

Figure 1.13 *Directory structure*

organise files using an hierarchical system. The user searches down through a series of folders until they find the file they are looking for.

Computers and software can go wrong so you should save open files at regular intervals. Once a file is saved, it is stored permanently in the computer's backing store. When you open a file and work on it, any changes to the file are first stored on the computer's internal RAM, or temporary memory (RAM stands for random access memory). If the computer loses power or crashes while you have the file open, this RAM data is lost forever. For this reason it is important to save work at regular and frequent intervals as you work on a file.

Saving files

While good file management is essential, sometimes you cannot remember the file name you used or where you put your file, just like Sunita and her CD. It can take a long time to find files manually by searching all the places on the computer.

Files are not always kept on the hard disk; sometimes removable media are used. New removable storage devices can store hundreds of megabytes (and even gigabytes) of data on a single disk, cassette, card or cartridge. All removable media work on one of three categories:

- magnetic storage
- optical storage
- solid-state storage.

The advantages of all these types of removable media are:

- you can take your files with you;
- you can make back-up copies of important information;
- you can transport data between two computers;
- you can store software and information which you don't need to access constantly;
- you can copy information to give to someone else;
- you can secure information which you don't want anyone else to access.

Floppy disks used to be the most commonly used removable medium.

Figure 1.14 a, b *Standard floppy disk and super 'optical' disk*

Standard floppy disk

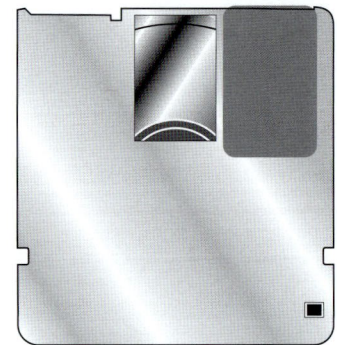

Super 'optical' disk

They are based upon magnetic storage like the hard drive.
Floppy disks are made of plastic coated with a magnetisable material. They are sealed into a protective case with openings to allow data to be written and read. The case can be made of card, but the most commonly used disks have rigid plastic cases. Floppy disks can vary in size, but the commonest is 3.5 inches, which fits into the floppy disk drive of most computers. They hold much less data than hard disks and access is slower also.

They have some advantages:

- They can record information instantly.
- They can be erased and reused many times.
- They are reasonably inexpensive and easy to use.

Before a floppy disk can be used it must be formatted. This creates a magnetic map of the disk surface so that data can be read from the disk or written on to it quickly.

ZIP DRIVES

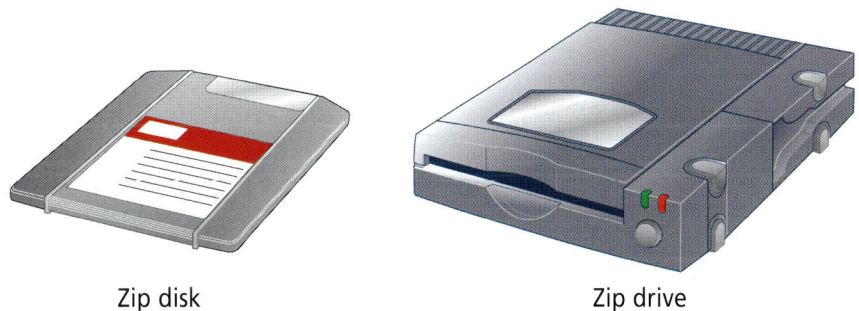

Figure 1.15 a, b *Zip disk and zip drive*   Zip disk   Zip drive

Special high capacity floppy disks can be used in special drives called Zip drives. These are sometimes also used to back up hard drives or data from databases or other applications. These floppies are slightly larger and twice as thick as normal floppies. The main thing that makes a Zip disk different from a floppy disk is the magnetic coating used. On a Zip disk, the coating is of a much higher quality so the read/write head on a Zip disk is significantly smaller than on a floppy disk. The smaller head, in conjunction with a head-positioning mechanism that is similar to the one used in a hard disk, means that a Zip drive can hold more tracks than a traditional floppy. Zip drives also use a variable number of sectors per track. All of these features combine to create a floppy disk that holds a huge amount of data.

EXTERNAL HARD DRIVES

Another method of using magnetic technology for removable storage is simply to take a hard disk and put it in a self-contained case. Completely external, portable hard drives are becoming popular as **USB** technology becomes more common. Lata has a tiny hard drive that is built into a PCMCIA card. It can be plugged into any device with a PCMCIA slot, such as her laptop computer. The name given to this type of drive is a micro-drive.

CD-ROMS / COMPACT DISKS

CD-ROMs are also known as optical disks and work in the same way as compact disks used to store and play music. Data is stored digitally, by changing the way the surface reflects a low energy laser beam. This is explained in more detail later in the book when we look at DVDs. The light is reflected differently according to whether the bit stored is a 1 or a 0. A low intensity beam is used to read the data but a higher intensity beam is needed to write the data on to the disk.

Optical disks have a huge capacity because data can be packed very closely. They are ideal for holding graphics that require large amounts of storage space, such as clip art that can be incorporated into documents. Optical disks are read in the CD drive that forms a standard part of most computer systems. They are more reliable than floppy disks and, because of their great capacity and ease of access, software can be run direct from them without the need to transfer it to the hard drive of a processing unit. If software is held on an optical disk, it does not need to be copied onto another storage medium for back-up purposes.

Figure 1.16 *CD-ROM disk*

CD-R

CD-Rs are recordable optical disks. A user can put a blank disk into the CD-R drive and use it to save data or programs. The disk has the same high capacity as a CD-ROM. Write access is not as fast as to a hard disk, but for many uses, this is not critical.

Figure 1.17 *CD-ROM drive*

Basic CD-R disks can only be written to once. CD-R disks are useful for making back-up copies of data files for archiving. In this case there will be no need to rewrite the disks. CD-RW disks can be used to back up data on a system.

CD-RW

CD-RW disks can be written, erased and rewritten many times. They contain a chemical that changes between reflective and non-reflective forms when heated by a high energy laser beam. They are more expensive than CD-R disks and can be used only in a suitable drive.

CD-R disks cannot be read in a normal CD-ROM drive unless they have been closed to further writing. CD-RW disks can be read only as a read-writer and can never be read on a normal CD-ROM drive.

FLASH MEMORY

A new type of storage device has been developed particularly for small handheld devices. It is called flash-memory. Some storage devices such as CompactFlash and SmartMedia cards have been developed for use in digital cameras and PDAs. Other solid-state memory devices, such as Sony's Memory Stick, are even smaller. Flash memory is a type of solid state memory, which basically means that there are no moving parts

LOOKING FOR FILES

So, after finding where the file you want has been saved, the next step is finding the particular file.

Software usually has a search facility to help you. It is possible to search for files that meet certain criteria or contain certain keywords. Some file management systems allow you to tag information about the file onto it. For example you can write the name of the author and give a description of the file's contents. You can also specify keywords that the file management system will look for.

To find a file in Windows systems, use the Find facility (Start | Find) and then type in the filename you are looking for in the Named text field. You can also tell the software where to look. The default is usually the C Drive, and it will also search all the sub-directories. You can also search using date and file size filters under the Date Modified and Advanced tabs.

If you are unsure of the name of the file you can use wildcards in your search in the filename field. A wildcard is represented by the asterisk '*'. It represents any character that can be used in the file name. For example, if you have the following files on your computer; tea, teatime, tease, and you asked the search command to look for tea* it would return all these files.

If you asked Windows to look for *tea it would find tea. Similarly, if you typed *tea* it would return find all the files which contained the word 'tea' in their filename. The wildcard can also be used in between the filename, for example, 't*a'.

But you will be finding not just your own files, but other people's files on the Internet and CD-ROMs. One of the difficulties here is that we have to guess another person's use of words. Web documents are created from plain text. They contain formatting commands contained in angle brackets (< >) which control the display of text on the web page. The

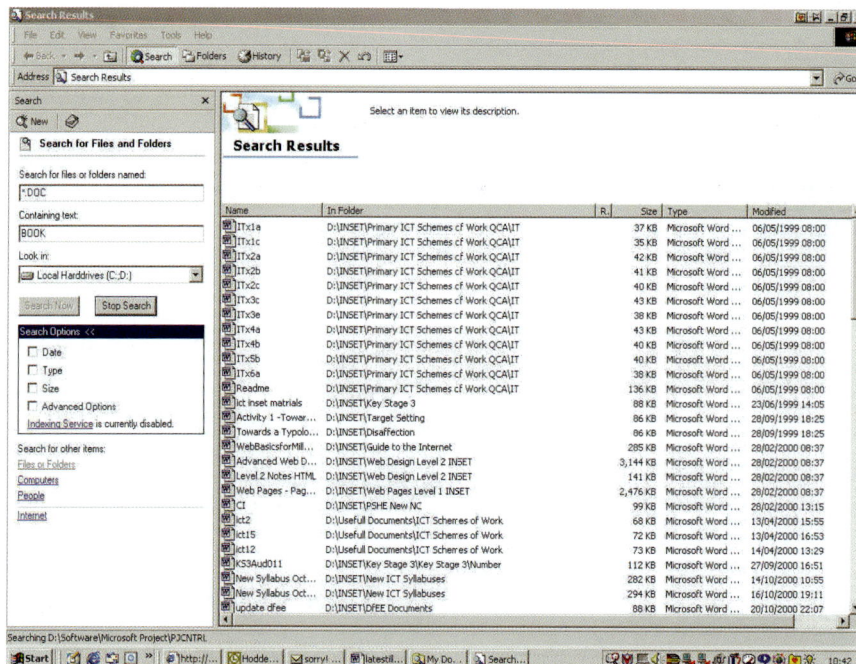

Figure 1.18 *File search*

name given to this is HTML which stands for Hyper Text Markup Language. All HTML commands are contained within angle brackets. We will explore this in a little more detail later in the book.

One way to find a place on the Internet is to type in the filename known as a Universal File Locator or URL. Every web page and every document on the Web has a unique address called a URL. URLs contain letters and numbers understood by the Web. They can be very long and complicated. Understanding URLs will help you grasp some of the inner workings of the Web and the way files are saved using unique filenames. Every item on the Net, whether it be a web page, a graphic image or a sound file, has its own URL.

Protocol · Directory

http://www.lshop.co.uk/links/index.html

Server name · Document

Figure 1.19 *Structure of URL*

Protocol

This indicates which convention a browser will use to access the Net: 'http' stands for web sites, 'ftp' for FTP sites, 'gopher' for gopher sites and 'file' for a file on your computer.

Server name

This typically refers to a physical machine. In URLs for web sites, this portion usually begins with 'www'. Technically, this section ends with a forward slash (/) but you can usually omit it if you are not referring to a specific document.

Directory

This part points to specific directories on a web server where a document is stored. The file may be in a folder buried in the web site. Forward slashes are used to separate directories.

Document

This refers to an HTML document, typically ending in '.htm' or '.html'. If no ending is given the web browser automatically looks for the file index.html. This is the page the browser will find if you just type in the server name e.g. www.lshop.co.uk. The index page is usually the first page of any web site. Once you have located the first page you can use hyperlinks to other pages.

A hyperlink is an instruction to the computer to jump to a new web page. The hyperlink contains the URL of the web page but it could be displayed as something else, for example 'to visit a great site click here'. Hyperlinks in text documents are usually blue and underlined. You can change the hyperlink colours in web design packages.

Once you have found a good site you can use bookmarks or favourites to help you find it again.

'Bookmarks' and 'Favorites' are different names for the same thing. A browser can store the URL of any web site visited. This can be stored and organised rather like a telephone directory. To visit a web site you simply select the Bookmark/Favorite from the list.

The real problem is finding good sites in the first place or transferring good URLs from one computer to another. Remembering URLs is hard and typing them without mistakes even harder. Most people use a search engine to find the files and web sites they want.

Using a search engine

When a member of the family needs to locate specific information relating to a particular topic, he or she uses software called a search engine to speed up the process. Although people call them search engines, there are really two types of search you can do on the Internet using **search engines** and **directories**.

SEARCH ENGINES

Also called 'spiders' or 'crawlers', search engines constantly visit web sites on the Internet in order to create catalogues of web pages. Web pages are indexed and then added to a search engine's database. Search engines 'index' (record word by word) all the words in a web page, as well as those found in the first few sentences of a web document, the website title and other metatag fields. Because they run automatically and index so many web pages, search engines may often find information not listed in directories. AltaVista is an example of an engine.

- *Advantages*: easier to find uncommon words; provides greater coverage than directories as a result of their much larger databases.
- *Disadvantages*: no human classification of documents; you are likely to get too many results because of very large databases.

Figure 1.20 *Alta Vista homepage*

DIRECTORIES

Unlike search engines, directories are created by humans. Sites must be submitted, then they are assigned to an appropriate category or categories. Anticipating searches such as yours, real live people look at web sites and then catalogue them into pre-selected categories, like a library's card catalogue. Yahoo! is an example of a directory as is Google. As a user, you can either browse the directory or enter a search keyword to retrieve documents.

Advantages: Because of the human role, directories can often provide better results than search engines. Directories also have the advantage of accuracy, because people rather than software are cataloging the sites. Good classification makes it easy to find the right information by using relevant searches.

Disadvantages: People are slower than software, so directories offer far fewer sites. Sometimes a topic is less easily classified, making it difficult to understand how the sites were filed and therefore hard to find appropriate sites. Coverage is much less extensive due to cost and time of human labour.

Hybrids

Increasingly, the distinctions between search engines and directories are blurring, as each type is incorporating elements of the other. 'Excite' is a good example of a hybrid, as is the interface of 'AltaVista'. At the front end of a search engine and search directory is a program that is able to search through large quantities of text and other data, according to specific instructions that it has been given.

CONDUCTING A SEARCH

If you type in the key words 'flights Australia', you will search for all documents that contain flights and/or Australia, giving highest priority to those that contain both words. This could result in a long and confusing list of possible contacts.

If only lower case letters are used, the search will find documents that contain the words regardless of whether they are in lower or upper case. If a mixture of upper and lower case is specified, the search will try to find words that match the words exactly – flights Australia.

You can place double quotation marks around the phrase to make sure that the search engine finds only the documents where the words appear in that order.

Search criteria are used to reduce the size of the list of contacts produced, but it will still often be necessary to use more precise search instructions (carry out an advanced search).

ADVANCED SEARCHES

Search engines have slightly different requirements for carrying out advanced searches. The general rules are as follows:

+ and –

- If you put a + in front of a word, documents will be found that contain that word. +traffic+jams will find all documents that contain the word traffic and also the word jams.
- traffic+jams would give a list of documents that contain the word jams but will not necessarily be about traffic.
- If you put a – in front of a work, documents will be found that do not contain that word.
- +traffic–jams would give a list of documents that contain the word traffic but miss out those that contain jams.

And, or, and not

You must learn how to use AND, OR and NOT as part of your search criteria if you are going to use the Search engines effectively.

- The word AND can be used to combine key words. All words joined by AND must be contained in the document for it to be listed in the results of a search.
- OR can be used to combine key words. At least one of the words joined by OR must be contained in the document for it to be listed in the results of the search. OR is often used to link words that have a similar meaning in a search, for example jam OR marmalade.
- AND NOT is also used to combine key words. The search will not include documents containing the word following AND NOT. For example jam AND NOT marmalade would produce documents relating to jam, but not any containing the word marmalade.

Brackets

Brackets are used in searches in the same way as they are used in mathematics. They can group words together to make a more complex search possible. For example, horses AND (dogs OR cats) would produce a list of documents containing the word horses and either the word dogs, or cats, or both.

Wild cards

The character * is called a wild card and can be used to stand for any character or set of characters. For example, typing auto* would produce a list of documents containing words such as automobile, automatic, autogiro, autopsy, and so on.

Titles

Rather than searching whole documents or web sites for key words, a search can be limited to the titles of documents or websites. If the words are important to the document or web site, they may well be contained in the title. The search engine is instructed to do this by typing t: before the key word(s). For example, t: 'fuel shortage' would search titles containing those words, in that order.

EVALUATING THE DATA YOU FIND

Edward was keen to find out about how Velcro worked. He used three search engines to find information but each returned thousands of responses. At last he found what appeared to be the perfect site.

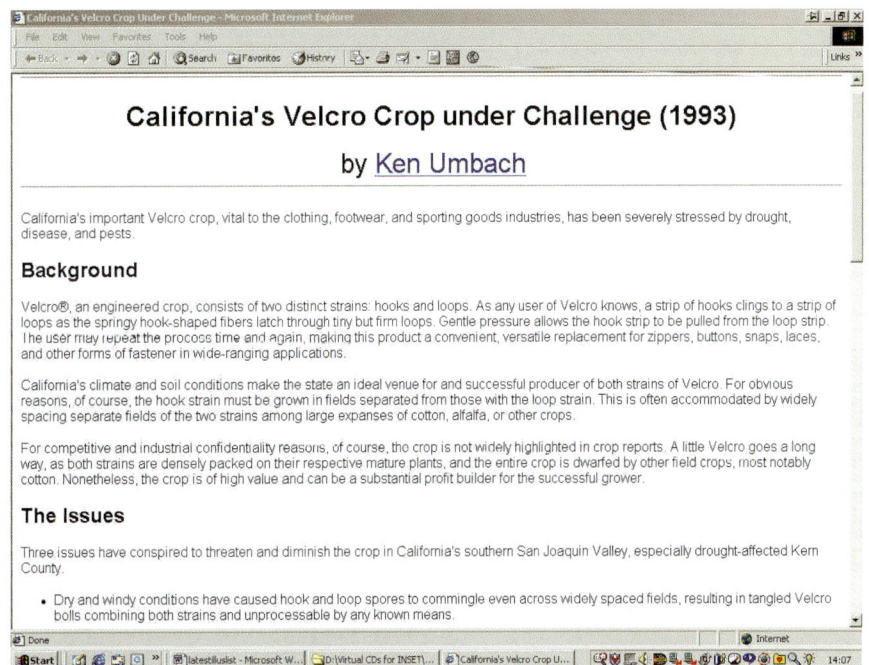

Figure 1.21 *The velcro site*

He was a little confused by the information he found. Was Velcro really grown in California? Were hooks planted in one field and loops in another? Was the crop really under threat? But it must be true; after all it was on the Internet.

Is it true?

Remember that anyone with access to a server can upload anything they want to the Internet. Finding a document on the Web, though, in no way guarantees its quality, accuracy or credibility. Always use a healthy scepticism when evaluating your results.

Evaluation of content

There are three basic areas of evaluation that need to be considered when looking at a website.

Navigation and usability

In order to use a site effectively, and in order to get to the important information you want from it, the site must be navigable and easy-to-use. A site should provide information for all types of learners. Sometimes sites offer hypertext links, so users can jump around although Edward often gets lost unless there is a navigation bar showing him where he is. The Velcro site was at least easy to follow.

Authorship

A site should enable the user to find out easily about the author; where they work, what their qualifications and experience are that makes it appropriate for them to write about the topic. Some sites even have information on how to get in touch with the author for further questions. Who is Ken Umbach? thought Edward. A little further research found what was entitled 'a totally bogus biography'. It said that Ken Umbach is a figure long shrouded in mystery and rumoured to have been born in Ohio. He had invented devices to tell you when your trouser flies were open and had developed genetically modified cats.

Content validity

The most important area to consider when evaluating a web site is the content itself. When you undertake your studies into the vocational use of ICT you need to be able to recognise when a web page is a thinly disguised commercial or opinion page. More importantly, you must realise when each type of page is appropriate for your purpose or task. The site Edward found is clearly a joke page.

Software

Software is fundamental to any communications system. It is at the heart of the processing part of any non-dedicated system. Our family members use a wide range of software in their daily lives. So what is software and what does it do?

Software contains the instructions that tell the computer what to do. There are two ways of giving instructions. One way is to give instructions one at a time, as Edward did to his friend's dad who took him home from school one day: turn left at the next junction, straight on here. Another way is to write down a list of instructions so that another person is able to follow these on their own. The advantage of this second method is that you can be getting on with something else while someone is following your instructions. In a computer the list of written instructions is called a program. If you are giving instructions to someone you must be very accurate or they will end up in the wrong place. It is important to remember that each instruction in the program must be correct; otherwise your result will be wrong. It is just as important to make sure that all the correct instructions are given in the right order. Imagine what would happen if you got the instructions correct but in the wrong order when you gave directions.

So like anyone else, a computer has to be given instructions before it can carry out a task and these instructions must be exact and in the correct order. Computer programs are not magical. They all must be written using the words, numbers, letters and symbols that a computer can understand. In the case study at the start of the book Jo talked about how important organisation skills are. Of course we don't need to give the computer all of the instructions ourselves. We simply install the computer program we want to use. An IT professional has written the instructions in the form of a program for us. We call this program software.

The basic keyboard

The main input device to a computer is the keyboard. A kcyboard is a series of switches, each switch giving a specific response. Keyboards have not changed much from when they were first invented. The name given to a standard keyboard is a QWERTY keyboard. It gets its name from the first six letters on the typing keys. The keys were placed in this awkward way to slow down fast typists. The reason that typewriter manufacturers did this was because the mechanical arms that stamped each character on the paper would often jam together if the keys were pressed too quickly. So even though we no longer have mechanical arms that jam together, the layout on a standard keyboard, designed for typewriters, has not changed. A few extra keys have been added to help navigate the Internet and windows environment but not much else has altered.

The most common keyboards are:

- 101-key Enhanced keyboard
- 104-key Windows keyboard
- 82-key Apple standard keyboard
- 108-key Apple Extended keyboard

Portable computers such as Lata's laptop have custom keyboards with slightly different key positions from a standard keyboard. A typical keyboard has four types of keys:

Figure 1.22 *Keyboard*

- typing keys
- a numeric keypad
- function keys
- a number of control keys.

The numeric keypad was added as computers were used more in business environments. They help speed up numerical data entry. The numeric keypad is arranged in the same configuration used by adding machines and calculators.

The function keys, arranged in a line across the top of the keyboard, can be assigned specific commands.

The control keys provided cursor and screen control. Common control keys include:

- Home
- End
- Insert
- Delete
- Page Up
- Page Down
- Control (Ctrl)
- Alternate (Alt)
- Escape (Esc)

Mice

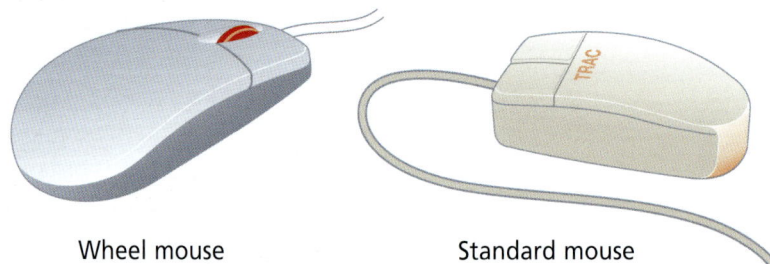

Figure 1.23 a, b *Wheel mouse and standard mouse*

Wheel mouse   Standard mouse

Early computers used punch cards for data entry so they did not need pointing devices. As computers started to do more, arrow keys were added. Light pens were added to a variety of machines. These acted as the main pointing device for a number of years together. Light pens, joy sticks for games and graphics tablets for designers were the main pointing devices until the invention of the mouse.

The first mouse was added to a Macintosh computer. It was an immediate success. Compared to a graphics tablet, joy stick or light pen, mice are inexpensive and take up very little desk space. A mouse is used on the desktop and translates its movements over a flat surface into digital information.

In a traditional mouse the ball underneath the mouse rotates as the mouse is moved, and sensors pick up the movement. More modern mice use a beam of light rather than a ball to monitor movement. The information gained from the movement is fed to the computer, causing the cursor to move on the screen. Mice usually have one, two or three buttons that are used to make selections on the screen.

A mouse is used to select options from a menu or from a set of icons, to position the cursor when editing text or using design software, to select an object in a drawing or a block of text to be copied, moved or deleted. It is ideal for use with a desktop computer, typically in an office situation, but is not as practical for use with a portable computer such as a laptop, notebook or palmtop model.

Publication and presentation software

Organisations use a variety of documents to communicate with different audiences and pass on different types of information. The documents are the output from the system.

In this book most of the family use publication and presentation software.

The two main types of publication software are word processors and desktop publishing (DTP). Publication software is also used in most schools and businesses.

Businesses use publication software because high-quality professional looking documents can be produced. Also:

- Documents can be saved on the computer's backing store. This means large rows of filing cabinets are no longer needed.
- Saved documents can be retrieved and edited to create new documents. This is much quicker than creating a new document from scratch.
- Templates of commonly used documents can be created. An example would be a document containing the business's letterhead, and space to write the letter. The template can then be used to create new letters quickly.

These benefits mean that work can be carried out more quickly, with fewer staff, and using less space than before. This can help to reduce the firm's costs and make the business more efficient. All publication and presentation software has one aim – to communicate effectively.

EFFECTIVE COMMUNICATION

Publication and presentation programs allow companies to communicate by helping them to create attractive page layouts for their documents and websites.

Document	Description
Newspaper	A standard layout type in either tabloid or broadsheet size. Contains a mixture of text and graphics to present news, information and advertisements. A newspaper is dated, and may bear an issue number too. Traditionally black and white.
Agenda	Document given out before a meeting to list what will be discussed at the meeting, and who will lead discussions. Usually simple text on A4 sheet with portrait orientation.
Minutes	Document given out after a meeting to detail what was discussed at the meeting, and any action points agreed on. Usually text on A4 paper with portrait orientation.
Invoice (bill)	When goods are purchased by a customer, an invoice tells the customer how much to pay, and when to pay. It may be sent to the customer after ordering, when the goods are delivered (in this case it will probably accompany a delivery note, providing proof of delivery) or, sometimes, after delivery. An invoice will always be dated, and bear an invoice number.
Flyer (advertisement)	A cheap way to advertise. Often handed out in the street or delivered house-to-house. Usually a single, eye-catching sheet or folded leaflet combining text and graphics, often with bright colour.
Letter	In commercial context, a formal means of communication with well-established formats for presentation. A business letter will normally bear a company letterhead, often incorporating a company logo, and a footer may give details of the company's registered address, VAT number etc. A signature may be printed, or added personally. A standard letter is dated and is normally mostly text.
Fax (facsimile)	A quick, electronic way to send a message, which is message often laid out in a less formal way than a standard letter. Can be a mixture of computer generated and handwritten text. It is normally dated and will bear the fax numbers of sender and recipient. Signature less important than on a letter. Usually sent on A4 paper with portrait orientation.
Web site /	Web site is the presence of a company or an individual web pages on the World Wide Web. Site is composed of pages that do not have to be of a standard size like paper. A mixture of text, graphics, sometimes animation, with buttons providing links to other pages. Company logo is likely to be prominent. Attention will be given to a house style. Designed to be colourful, eye-catching and easy to navigate. The home page of a web site offers a combination of the introduction and contents page of a book – the base point from which to move around the site.

The business world is full of standard types of document that are used for particular purposes. Effective communication starts with accepted practice. It is therefore important that first the user is familiar with standard document layouts.

When designing any of these documents for screen, printout or web site, designers need to consider presentation techniques. Information should be presented clearly as poorly presented information deters readers.

Most presentation and publication software has a number of features to help the user to create effective documents, these include:

layout grids	tables and tab	bulleted lists
templates	upper- and lower-case letters	justification
use of white space	subscript and superscript	columns
titles and headings	graphics	special symbols
fonts and sizes	colour	headers and footers
bold and italic text	borders and shading	charts and graphs
hanging indents	dividing lines	contents and indexes
spell-checkers	thesaurus	word counters

These can be used to help design a document to meet its needs which may be to:

- attract attention – *whose attention is the designer trying to attract?*
- meet the needs of your reader – *is the reader a child or an adult – or someone using English as a second language like Rupa?*
- make your points clearly – *will the target reader(s) be able to follow the document easily?*
- explain details – *the reader(s) must be able to understand what is being communicated;*
- summarise information – *the reader(s) may not have all day – you might need to come to the point quickly.*

Today's software offers lots of possibilities but just because it is possible doesn't mean you should do it. In design, there are rules about what's good and what is not good. We will explore some of these rules later.

First it is important that you understand the differences between these two types of publication software and can decide the best software for the job. This is because, although they are becoming increasingly alike, they still have important differences. These differences mean that it is better to carry out some business tasks on a word processor, and some using desktop publishing (DTP).

WORD PROCESSORS

Word processors replaced typewriters as a way of entering and processing text. Most word-processors are not frame-based. This means that if some of the information on the document is moved, resized or deleted, the position of all the other information will change. This makes them unsuitable for documents requiring lots of graphics.

DESKTOP PUBLISHING

Desktop publishing (DTP) was originally designed to enable users to create high-quality, professional-looking newsletters and leaflets. Most small businesses use DTP to create their publicity material. Most DTP packages are frame-based. This means that when you enter text it goes into a text-frame. When you enter a picture it goes into a picture-frame.

These frames can be moved around the page so that the layout can be improved. Changing the position or size of one frame will not necessarily affect the location of the other frames.

For this reason it is a good idea to use a word processor for documents that are mainly text-based and a DTP package for documents that combine text with a lot of other types of data.

WEB DESIGN SOFTWARE

Although you can create effective websites using word processors and DTP software such as Microsoft Publisher, the software does not have the types of facilities that web design software has and you cannot easily switch between views.

PRESENTATION SOFTWARE

Presentation software produces slides and animation suitable for presentation to an audience either with or without a speaker.

We will explore each type of software separately later in the book.

THE FIRST STAGE

The first stage of designing for publication or presentation is therefore to choose the right software for the job.

The following list gives you an idea of the business documents that can be created using publishing software and what type of software they are usually produced on.

Whichever type of package a company chooses, documents must be carefully planned and the following factors considered if they are to communicate effectively:

- purpose of the document;
- target audience;
- writing style and tone;
- presentation style, e.g. use of colour and images;
- layout, e.g. booklet, poster, web site with frames;
- accuracy, clarity and consistency, e.g. error correction and use of house style.

GENERAL RULES ON PAGE LAYOUTS

Before you start to use any type of presentation or publication software you must think about the documents people read and the places on the Web that they like to visit. For example a web site designer will look at the pages that receive a lot of visitors or attract comment. They will look at their own favourite web sites and those web sites that other people like, especially those relating to the type of web site they are designing.

Document	Business examples	Document usually produced on
Letters	Letters to individual customers or mail-shots to all the firm's customers	Word processor software e.g Microsoft Word .
Notices	Health and Safety notices	DTP software, e.g. Indesign, Publisher, PageMaker
Web site	Customer support and information	Web design software e.g. Dreamweaver, Front Page or Adobe GoLive
Leaflets and posters	Publicity leaflets informing customers of new products	DTP software, e.g. Indesign, Publisher, PageMaker
Reports	Financial reports such as cash flow and profit and loss	DTP Software eg In Design, Publisher, PageMaker
Booklets	Training manuals and a staff handbook	Word processor software, e.g. Microsoft Word
Speaker presentation to an audience	New product launch	Presentation software, e.g. Powerpoint

Designers of printed documents such as posters and leaflets will also look at existing successful solutions. They will think about the magazines and newspapers their customers buy and will explore standard page layouts.

In each case the designer looks for what are called 'hooks'. Things that people want to see or like to look at.

Good design is based upon an understanding of page layout and the use of type and graphics.

But it is not just layout that is important. The writing style should also suit the purpose of the document.

In an advertisement, for example, you would use language designed to get attention, with short, eye-catching phrases.

A contract of employment would have longer sentences with words very carefully chosen because of legal implications.

A children's book will be full of colour and simple words in large print.

Good design also always uses language to suit your reader. For example, if you were writing to Rupa who is learning English, you would use simple words, with short sentences but not use a childlike presentation or she would feel insulted.

Designs can be simple or complex but no matter how simple the design is, there are certain principles that must be applied.

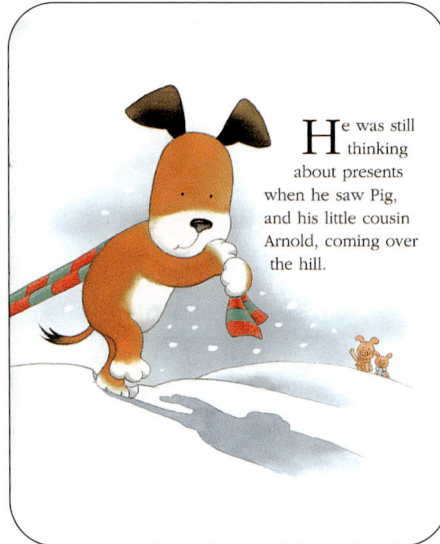

Figure 1.24 *Children's book layout*

Layout is the name given to the process of arranging the text, pictures and other graphics on the page. The amount of space on a page is as important as the text and pictures. It is called white space.

The designer will use white space carefully and will not cram everything on a page as this leads to poor design. White space allows different elements on a page to stand out and be perceived for the meaning and value they offer the reader. A page with no white space at all can be intimidating as the reader doesn't know where to start and stop reading.

White space doesn't have to be white; it can even be black or coloured.

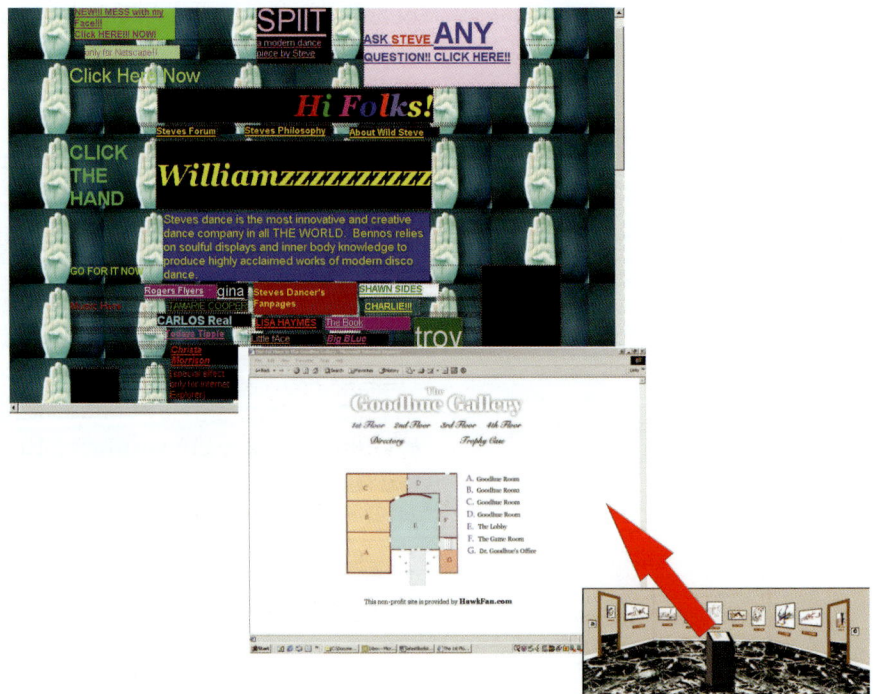

Figure 1.25 *A badly designed page and a well designed page*

BALANCE

At the heart of good design is the arrangement of one or more items of text or graphics so that, visually, they work well together. Every object in nature has structural balance or symmetry.

For graphic design, the visual centre of any typical page is not the actual physical centre but what is termed the **optical centre**. This visual point of balance can be determined mathematically as being located three-eights from the top of the page, five-eights from the bottom.

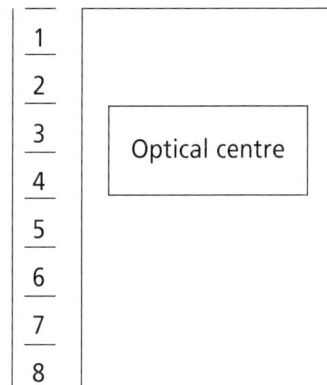

Figure 1.26 *Optical centre of a page*

Mathematical balance

Balance is achieved on a page by establishing what are called margins. Establishing margins requires careful consideration. As we discussed earlier the amount of white space surrounding printed or web-based pages affects both appearance and readability of the document. The default settings of most word processors create automatic margins but designers often increase or decrease margins to improve the appearance of the page. A large amount of margin space indicates luxury or formality; small margins usually indicate business and commerce.

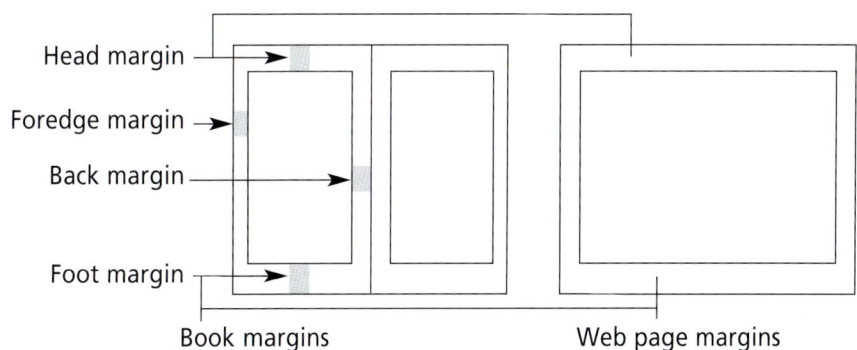

Figure 1.27 *Book and web page margins*

The type and size of margins used depend upon the document being produced. Two facing pages of a book are considered as a single unit; the inside (back) margins are always smaller than the outside (foredge) margins.

Books and magazines are designed differently from single-page documents. When a book is opened, any two pages next to each other must appear to belong together. This book has a larger margin on the left-hand side.

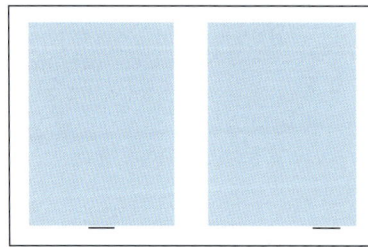

Figure 1.28 *Standard and wide margins*

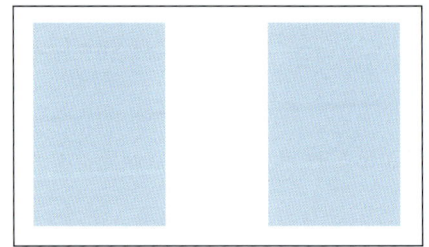

Standard margins   Wide centre margins

Symmetrical balance

By changing the margins and columns, designers can alter the symmetrical balance of the page.

Figure 1.29 *Altering the symmetrical balance of a page*

A symmetrical page layout where both sides are the same produces static, restful design which can appear boring to some readers.

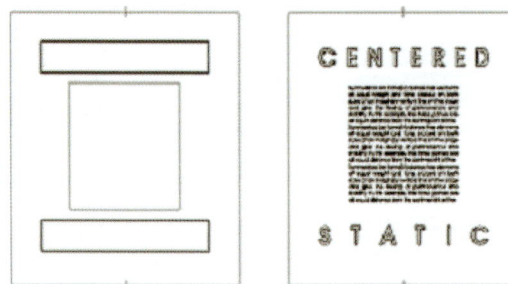

Figure 1.30 *Formal balance on a page*

Formal balance is pleasing but boring.

Asymmetrical

One of the major advantages of an asymmetrical layout is that it is more dynamic. But it can make the reader feel uncomfortable.

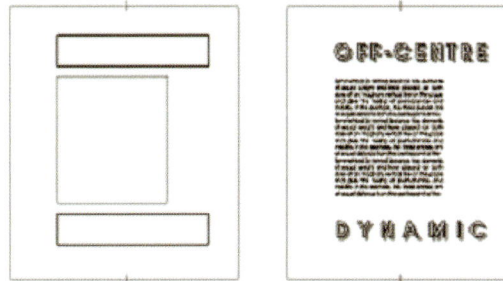

Figure 1.31 *Informal balance on a page*

Informal balance creates visual interest.

COLUMNS

All pages are split into what are called columns. The first column, called the left margin, is usually for the border and the second column is for the text and pictures. Sometimes the text fits into one column like in this book. In a book the third column is also a margin. Often, designers of printed and web based pages divide the page into more than two columns. The illustration below shows a magazine.

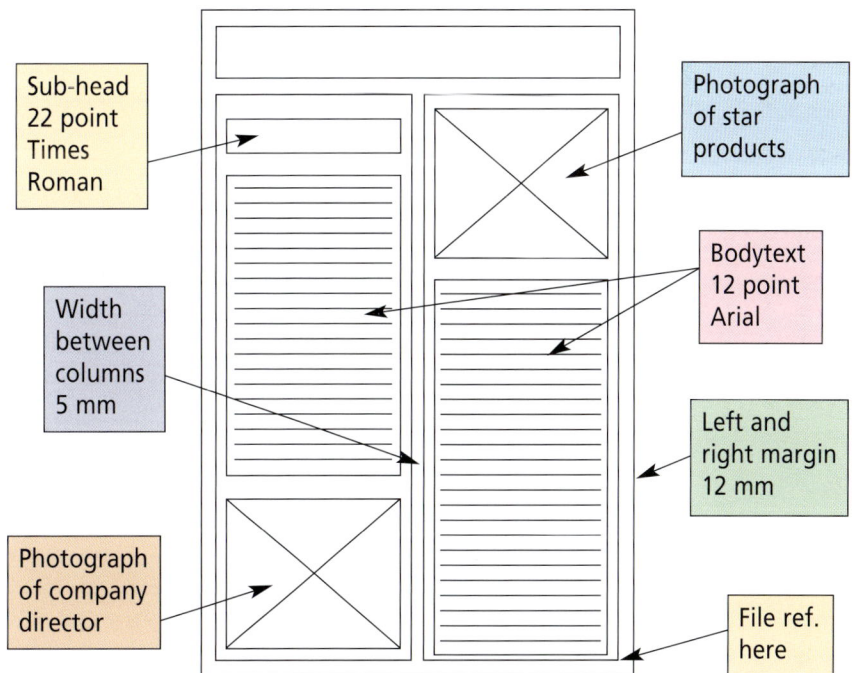

Sub-head 22 point Times Roman

Photograph of star products

Bodytext 12 point Arial

Width between columns 5 mm

Left and right margin 12 mm

Photograph of company director

File ref. here

Figure 1.32 *Page design in a magazine*

Figure 1.33 *Page design in a newspaper*

This example of a newspaper has more columns.

Whether it is a web page or a printed document that is being designed, the designer will need to think about the overall layout and how many columns to use. Web pages are viewed on a computer screen. Although you can scroll down, designers need to consider the overall effect on a page. They usually do this by adding a scroll line.

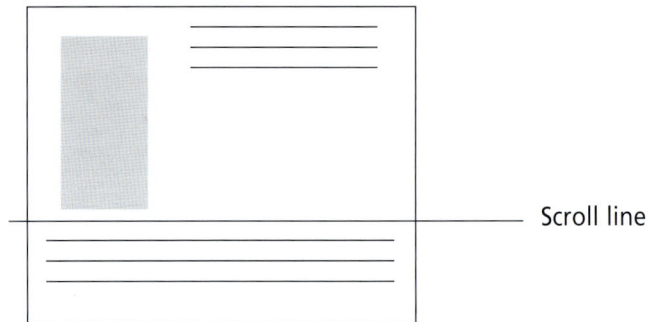

Scroll line

Figure 1.34 *Scroll line on a web page*

It is quite hard to design web pages and digital TV because people have different size and resolution monitors. Designers have to try out their designs at different resolutions.

Figure 1.35 a, b *Designs at different resolutions*

At 800/600 resolution   At 1240/768 resolution

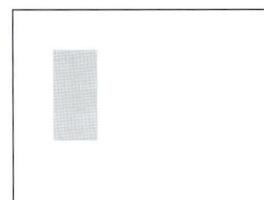

As can be seen the higher the resolution the smaller things are on the screen. This happens to text and pictures.

This two-column layout has an extra-wide space on the left. This is a normal style for web design. A frame of static information, such as a table of contents for the pages on the right, is often included in the left-hand column.

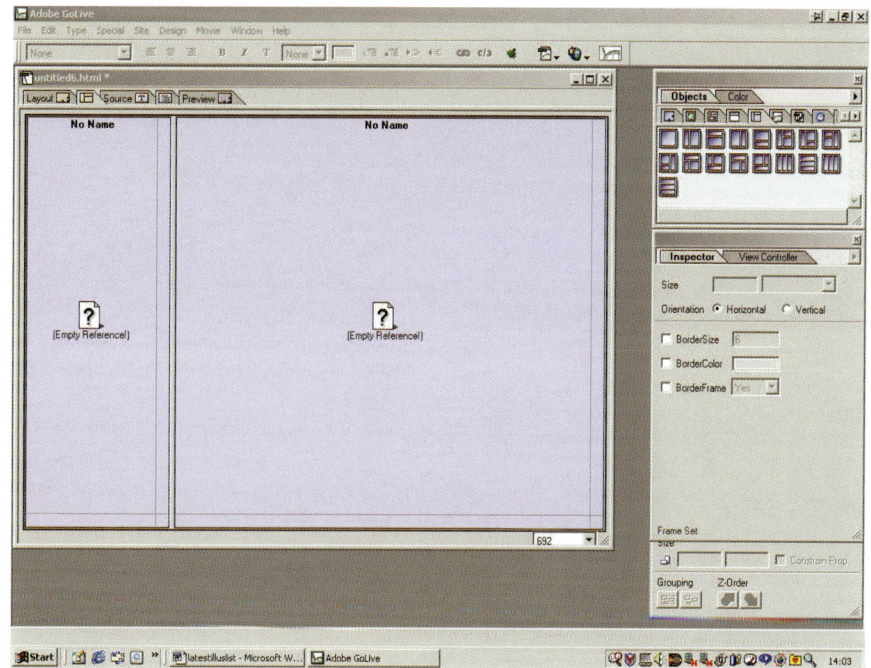

Figure 1.36 *Two-column layout of web page*

Frames enable you to have multiple pages open at the same time. Information about frames is stored in a special web page document called a frame set. Frame sets can include any number of frames, but the more frames you include in a window, the less information will be able to appear in each window. Basically a frame set divides the screen into different pages, each with their own design.

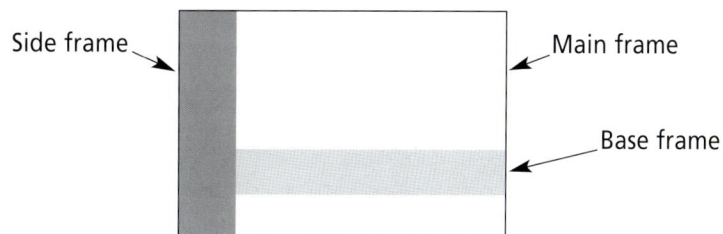

Figure 1.37 *Frameset dividing screen into different pages*

With framesets you can divide the page into as many frames as you want and each can either scroll or not. The menu can stay in the side frame while linked pages are displayed in the main frame. Although framesets

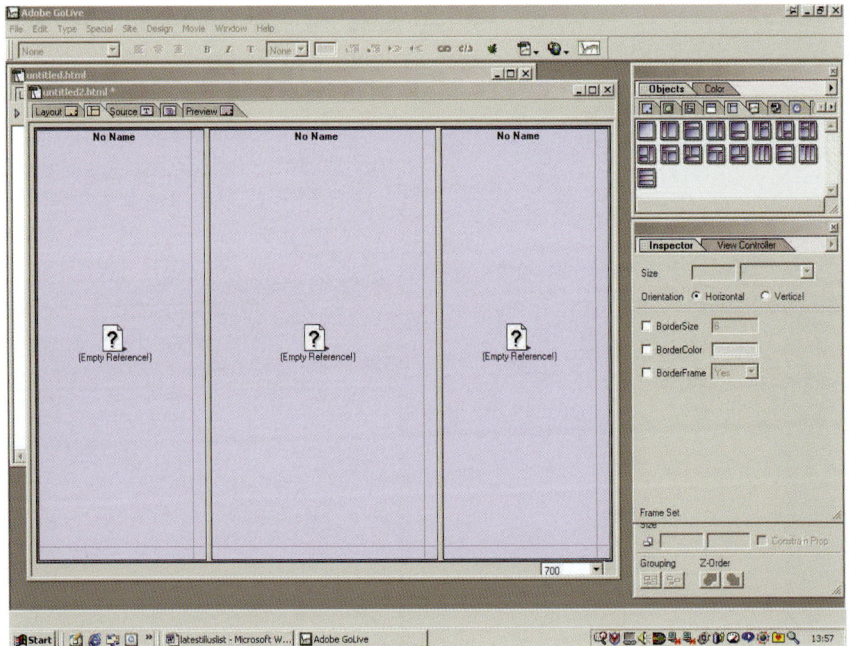

Figure 1.38 *Three-column layout*

make it easy to navigate the site and logos and company names stay on the screen, users can arrive at offensive information in one frame while still having your company logo and name in another. Framesets also limit the screen window that the main screens are viewed in.

This three-column layout is often used for annotations, images, even web frames. The middle column is centred and its size can be increased or decreased as needed. Again this is sometimes achieved using frames.

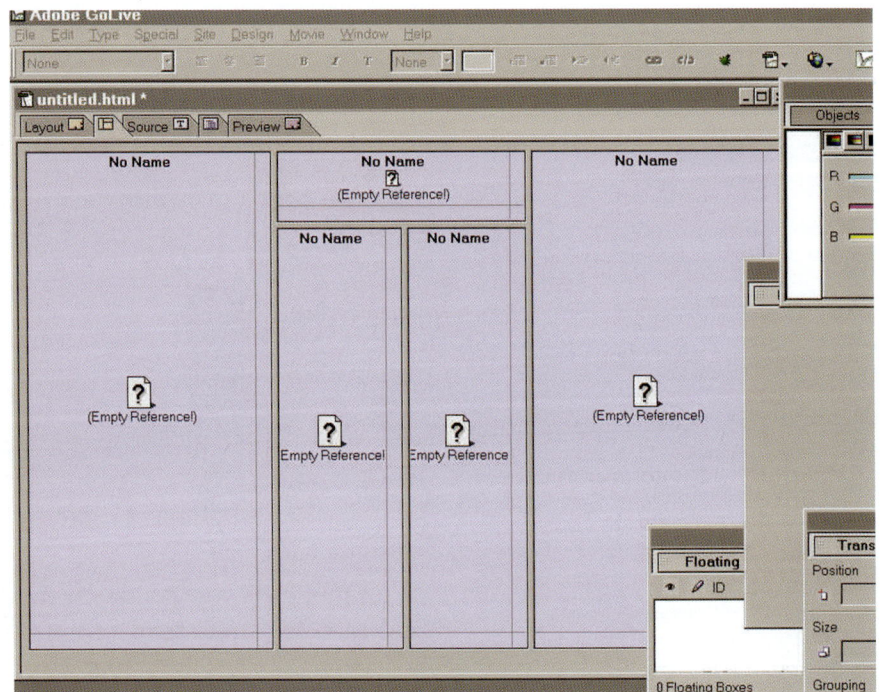

Figure 1.39 *Four-column layout*

Four-column layouts are often used in newspapers and magazines but it is unusual to find this layout on a web site. The layout is quite complex and can combine elements as described in the two previous grids.

ACHIEVING CONTRASTS

We now know that pages can have any number of columns and these columns can be any width. All the columns can even be different widths. But columns don't even have to be square on the page or even have parallel sides.

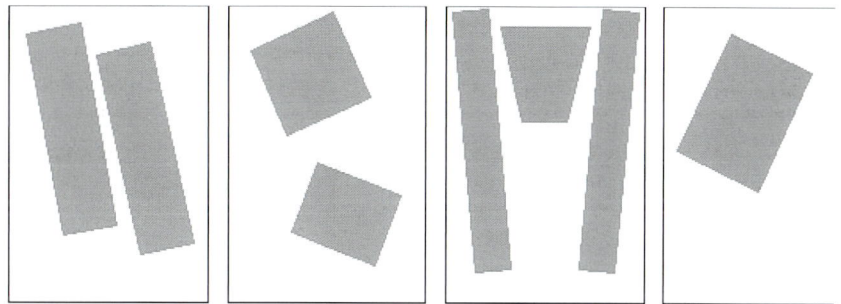

Figure 1.40 *Slanting columns*

The very act of placing any design style (formal or informal) on the slant will cause the design to be in visual contrast to the normal horizontal position. As a general rule, the placing of such designs on a slant is not a desirable practice, although in some cases it can prove to be very effective.

Just remember someone has to read what you put on your page. It is hard to read upside down or on a slant.

Contrast in shape

Trying to put a square peg into a round hole is an impossible task because the shapes fight with each other. This principle can be incorporated into a design where the visual elements are deliberately arranged to be in conflict with each other.

Contrast in colour

A good designer will not limit his or her concept of contrast in colour to the narrow perspective of natural colours, i.e. red, blue, purple, green, yellow etc. Certainly, the use of colour opposites will achieve contrast in a design, as for example the use of a colour opposite, together with a colour that harmonises with the background.

Colour contrast should also be considered in relation to the colour of the typesetting, i.e. the degree of blackness that hits the eye. Careful selection of type, both size and weight, will give a distinctive visual colour to the overall design.

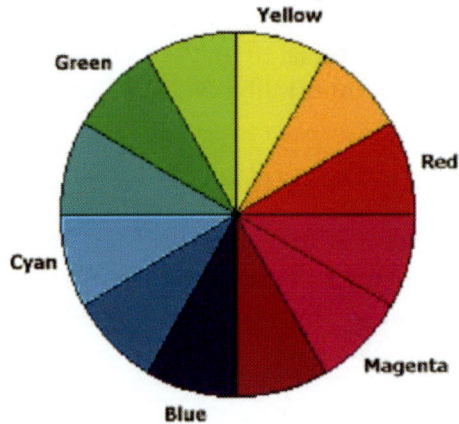

Figure 1.41 *The colour wheel*

PLACING PICTURES AND OTHER GRAPHICS

Once we have our general layout we can think about placing pictures and graphics alongside our blocks of text. Pages that are dense with too closely packed text are often unattractive and off-putting to the reader. A picture can be worth a thousand words, but too many pictures will slow the download time of a web site, and can be a distraction in a printed document, especially if they are not related to the text, a common mistake made by people who use clipart.

How many pictures to use, how large a picture to use and where to place it on the page is an important part of achieving the balance we talked about earlier.

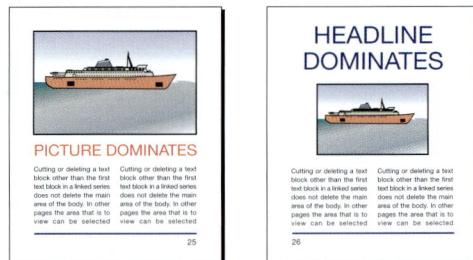

Figure 1.42 a, b *Text and picture: where picture dominates and where text dominates*

A designer should be careful not to clutter up pages with too many pictures, boxes and screens when they are not needed for readability. The design considerations of multi-page formats such as magazine pages are different from those for an advertisement produced on a single page or on a website.

Designers always use sketches to explore different layout ideas. Of all the design principles, contrast is probably the next most important. Contrast creates interest in the web site or document by providing variety in the design. This is similar to normal speech where people will use expression or hand movements as they talk to emphasise a word or phrase. Rupa is always raising her voice to add meaning to what she is trying to say. These changes in speed and tone add

Figure 1.43 *Examples of page layouts*

expression and life to the words spoken. We can do the same thing with text by making it bold, adding colour or making it larger.

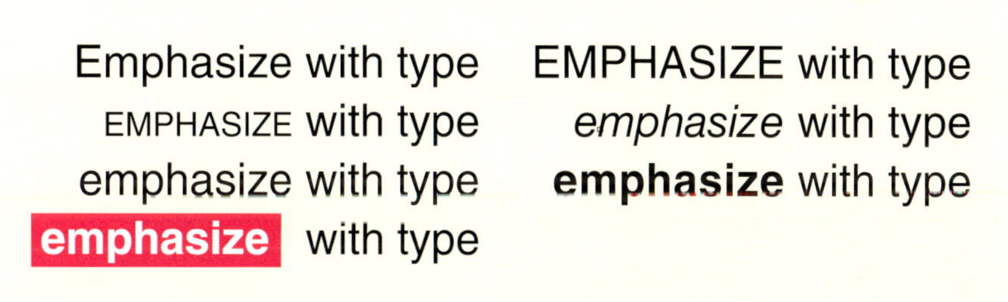

Figure 1.44 *Use of italic, bold, small caps and highlighting in word-processing*

Word processing

Word processing software allows the user to produce and edit text for uses such as letters and reports. You can do a number of things with word processing that are common across all presentation and publication software.

Word processors allow simple entry and editing of text, and correction of errors. They are used for letters, memos and a number of long documents. This book was written in a word processor although it was produced in a DTP package.

In a word processor you can do a number of things with text. You can highlight text and then use the copy function to allow the software to take a copy of the text. You can then go to another place in the document, or to another document, and paste that same text in. In the same way you can highlight text and use the cut function to remove it from one position, but then paste it somewhere else.

www.buy a gift .com

A great site to visit for
free competitions and
imaginative gift ideas.
Hot air balloon flights,
parachuting, paintball
days etc.
Buy a gift is easy to
use, fun and has over
150 inspirational gifts
to choose from

INVITATION

You are invited
to spend a weekend
in a top class hotel
in the Cotswolds

RSPV

ADDRESS BOOK *date*

A message to
everyone in your
address book and a
built in calendar
means that there's
no excuse for
forgetting birthdays

GARAGE SERVICES

All types of repairs
undertaken. MOT work,
servicing, tuning and
accident repairs

Figure 1.45 *Justified text, centre justified text, right justified text and left justified text*

Balance can also be achieved by what is called justification. Full justification arranges the text in a straight line on both the left and right-hand margins. Centre justified text is ragged on both sides but symmetrical in the centre of the page. Left justified will be straight only on the left, leaving the text ragged on the right. This has the advantage of producing more regular word spacing, but full justification often has a better visual effect overall.

Text can also be formatted in various ways.

This is a numbered list:

1. List 1
2. List 2
3. List 3
4. List 4

This is a bulleted list:

- List 1
- List 2
- List 3
- List 4

You can change the way both numbers and bullets are shown in most word processors.

This information is displayed as a table:

Table cell 1	Table cell 2	Table cell 3
Table cell 4	Table cell 5	Table cell 6
Table cell 7	Table cell 8	Table cell 9

You can also use special effects in a word processed document, such as: Clipart and Wordart.

Figure 1.46 *Clipart*

Figure 1.47 *Word art*

You can use drawing tools to create circles, ovals, arrows etc.

Figure 1.48 *Shapes created with drawing tools*

These shapes can be filled with colour, resized, rotated or the line colour changed.

Paragraphs can also be enclosed in text boxes or have shading applied.

We have explored the way that type can be laid out in different ways using margins and other graphic elements. The placing of graphics and text on a page helps to make the text readable and to communicate meaning. The format of text can also be changed and improved by features such as underlining, bold and italics. There is a choice of fonts, font sizes and colours. Bullet points and tables can be inserted to organise text.

We can change the lettering in all presentation and publication software. Types of lettering are called typefaces: just like you can have a different face, lettering can also have different faces. There is a huge selection of fonts or typefaces, but 'because they're there' is not a legitimate reason to use several different typefaces in one design. Each typeface should complement every other element in a design.

Designers usually restrict the number of typefaces they use, employing italics, bold and size to highlight key points, rather than different typefaces. This makes text styles consistent throughout a document.

An important factor in the production of a web site or printed document is the selection of the correct typefaces. While you may have the typeface installed on your computer, others may not. This will not be a problem with printed documents but web sites could be a real problem and spoil all your hard work. Choosing the right type face makes clear the sense of the message and imparts that atmosphere or sense of environment which enables it to be more easily understood by the reader.

Because there are so many type designs to choose from, it is easier first of all to choose a general type style or classification to suit a graphic design, and then look for a particular typeface that relates to that classification.

Typefaces can be described in a number of ways, two of the main categories being

- Serif
- Sans serif.

Serif characters have a line crossing the free end of a stroke. This style face, said to have been invented by the Romans, is also commonly referred to as 'Roman'. It is the one most often used and also one of the most legible styles.

Figure 1.49 *Serif letter shapes based on ancient Roman lettering*

ABCDEFGILM
NOPQRSTVX

SANS SERIF

The name describes itself (*sans* meaning *without*); it has no serif or line at the end of the letter.

Sans serif typefaces are popular for all classes of publicity and advertising work due to the large variety of weight and styles available and because their structure suggests newness and attention-awakening appeal to a remarkable degree. They possess simplicity and neatness since there is little variation in the thickness and weight of the letter strokes.

Like the Oliver family, each font has a family. A family is a group of fonts that have evolved from the original.

One of the most popular sans serif font families is Helvetica.

Helvetica
Helvetica Italic
Helvetica Bold
Helvetica Bold Italic
Helvetica Narrow
Helvetica Narrow Italic
Helvetica Narrow Bold
Helvetica Narrow Bold Italic
Helvetica Black
Helvetica Black Italic

Figure 1.50 *Font family*

The majority of fonts in common use have at least four variations in their families, e.g. normal, italic, bold and bold italic. The popular type design Helvetica has a family of over 50 variations.

CHANGING FONT APPEARANCES

With both sans serif and serif typefaces we can change the appearance easily using other members of the same family such as italics, bold, altering size and changing colours. This keeps consistency throughout the document.

Italic

Italic (Roman)
Italic (Lineale)
Italic (Slab Serif)

Figure 1.51 *Examples of italic type*

Italic differs from Script (see page 48) in that the letters never join, nor do they appear to join. They have a free flowing appearance.

Italics are often used for emphasis, titles, quotes and extracts.

Bold

In bold type the letters are thicker. In the illustration bold has been used to highlight the word bold. Notice how this makes it stand out.

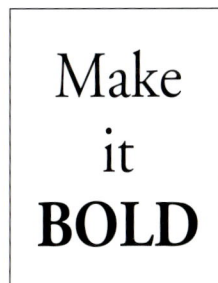

Make
it
BOLD

Figure 1.52 *Examples of bold type*

Script

All script faces are based on different styles of handwriting. Twirls and squiggles are added, sometimes making it hard to read what has been written. Letters of this form are usually highly rounded, slant to the right, and either connect from letter to letter or have a tail on the letters which leads to the next. Decorative and script style fonts do not usually have a range of different variations and are usually restricted to a single font within a family.

Scripts fonts are available in two broad styles:

● *Formal script* is usually based upon classical pen handwriting. This style is used extensively for formal type printing and invitations.
● *Informal script* is more suited to work of a less formal nature: menus, advertisements etc., and is characterised by the looser, less restrained formation of characters. The letters appear to have been casually drawn either by a pen or brush.

Decorative

Decorative typefaces are also known as novelty faces and are primarily designed to be used for a word or words in display or headings and as such are not suited to text setting. They are popular with young people but are not widely used in companies. People either like them or hate them – not a good selection if you are trying to impress.

So we now have two main elements, layout and font. Let's explore this a little further. The illustration below shows fonts, margins, columns and picture positions. It also indicates another common feature in word-processed documents called headers and footers.

Headers and footers are usually added to insert automatic features such as page numbers and dates.

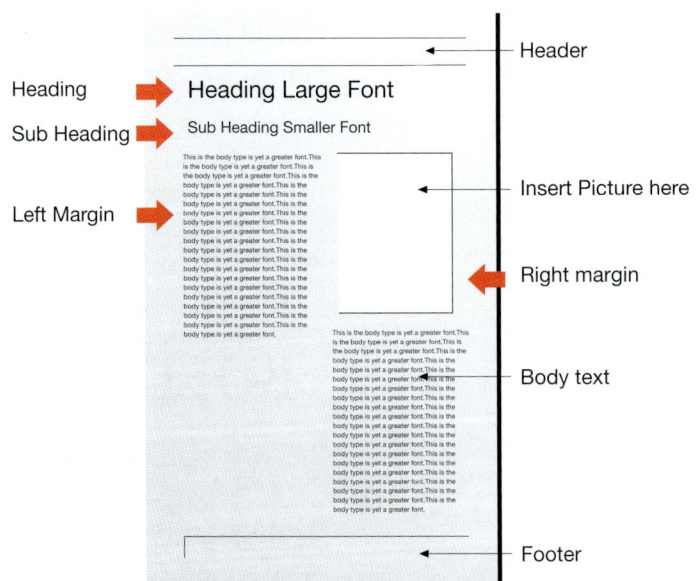

Figure 1.53 *Page layout, showing fonts, margins, columns, picture positions and headers and footers*

In Word they are modified using the View | Header and Footer toolbar.

Word processing software performs a process called word wrapping. This is when, as you type past the end of a line, the cursor automatically jumps to the next line. It rearranges the placement of words as necessary so that no word is split in half. This is very useful because it means that you do not have to hit the return key at the end of every line, and the software automatically evens up the lengths of lines if you add or delete text, or change margins. In most DTP software you can add hyphenated words automatically.

All publishing software can normally check spelling and grammar, and can offer a thesaurus to increase vocabulary choices.

Most DTP and word-processing software can allow a user to highlight words in a text that are to be included in an index, and can then create the index.

You can use search facilities to find specific words in a text and replace them if required.

The software provides facilities for printing and addressing sets of printed letters or memos.

WORD PROCESSING IN PRACTICE

Sunita wants to design the layout of a letter to her friends inviting them to a party.

The first thing she needs to show is that she can design the stationery. She considers page orientation – does she want portrait or landscape? She decides to use a portrait format.

Portrait   Landscape

Figure 1.54–55 *Portrait format and landscape format*

- Justification – left, right, centred or fully blocked?
- Indents – hanging indents or negative?
- Tabulations – use the tab key.
- Line spacing – single, $1\frac{1}{2}$ or double, or greater?
- Fonts – what size? What style?
- Page numbering
- Headers and footers – all reports should contain a footer with information in it.
- Columns.
- Tables.

She decides to draw a block diagram of what each piece of stationery will look like.

Sunita had lots of invitations to send out and it would have taken ages to type them all individually. She decided to use mail merge.

USING MAIL-MERGE FACILITIES

This is a way of quickly producing individual letters to a number of people, each containing the same text, but with each recipient's name and address.

For example, a company could send a letter to all its customers informing them of a new product. The customer's name can be inserted into the letter to make it seem more personal.

We can understand mail merge by asking ourselves what each word means. Mail is obviously something you want to send by post or email. Merge is another word for 'joining' two things together.

Mail merge is the term used for merging a list or database of names and addresses with a standard letter to create personalised letters. These letters can then be printed out and put into envelopes and posted. Sunita had a database of all her friends and a letter she wanted to send inviting them to the party.

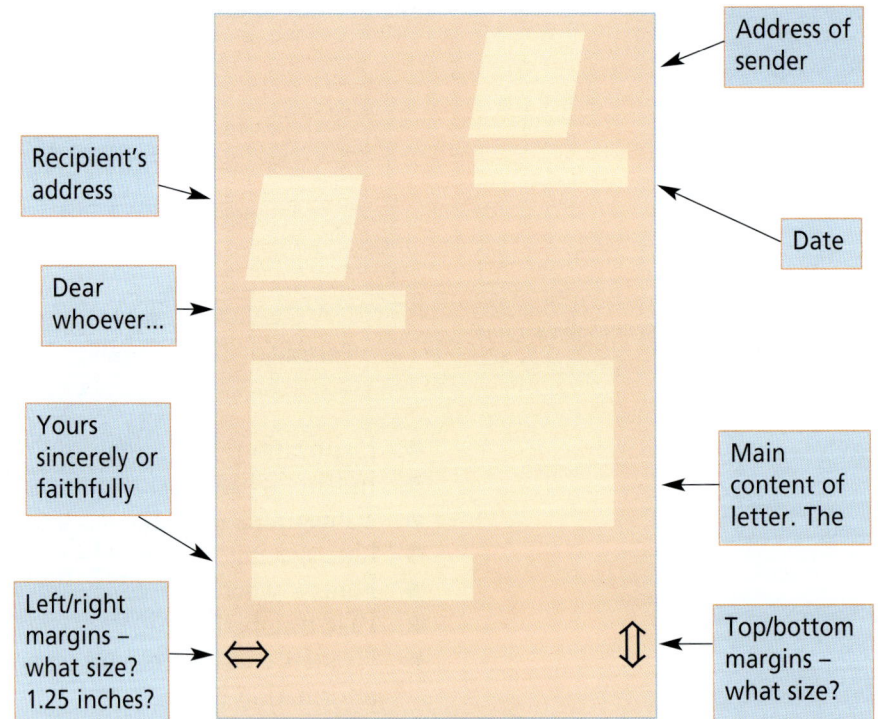

Figure 1.56 *Layout of a standard letter*

Mail merge is a very useful technique whenever you want to send the same or a slightly modified letter to several people, for example:

- to let customers know about a new product;
- to remind members to pay their club membership subscription;
- to chase overdue bills;
- to invite a list of people to an event or party as in Sunita's case.

Instead of having to write out or type a similar letter a large number of times, Sunita simply types the letter once. She then either makes a list of people the letter should go to or links the letter to her friends database in order to merge the letter with the list.

Sunita used a word processor. In Word, special names are given to the letter and list.

- The standard letter is called the **main document**.
- The list of people the letter should go to is called the **data source**.
- A **merge field** (or marker) tells mail merge which bit of the data source to put in what part of the main document.

So Sunita created a standard letter containing the information to go into all the letters and used a separate database to store her friends' personal details (name, address etc.). Codes were placed into the letter where each friend's data was to be inserted. For example the letter could begin Dear

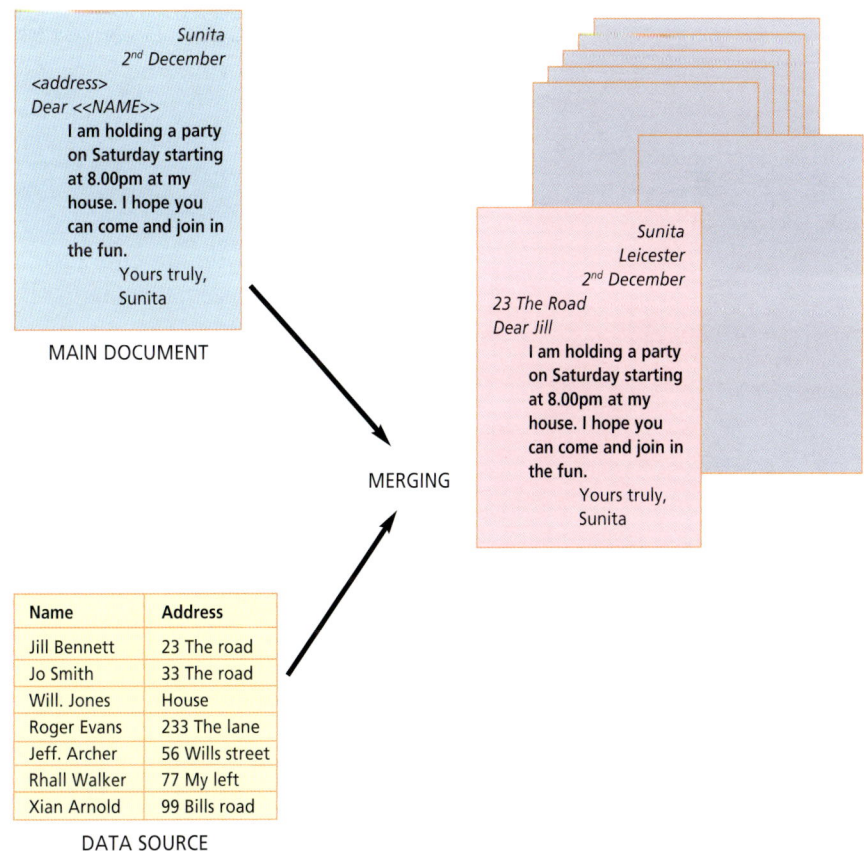

Sunita
2nd December
<address>
Dear <<NAME>>
I am holding a party on Saturday starting at 8.00pm at my house. I hope you can come and join in the fun.
Yours truly,
Sunita

MAIN DOCUMENT

MERGING

Sunita
Leicester
2nd December
23 The Road
Dear Jill
I am holding a party on Saturday starting at 8.00pm at my house. I hope you can come and join in the fun.
Yours truly,
Sunita

Name	Address
Jill Bennett	23 The road
Jo Smith	33 The road
Will. Jones	House
Roger Evans	233 The lane
Jeff. Archer	56 Wills street
Rhall Walker	77 My left
Xian Arnold	99 Bills road

DATA SOURCE

Figure 1.57–59 *Mail merging*

<first name>. The standard letter could then be merged with the database so that each letter was personalised.

Businesses use mail merge all of the time. Example uses are for letters, faxes, memos, books, essays.

Desktop publishing

The latest desktop publishing and presentation software allows the user to produce text, pictures and graphics of all kinds, and organise them into pages. It produces work that is of a quality good enough for publication.

Desktop publishing requires a computer with a high specification. The computer needs a large amount of RAM (random access memory) and a reasonably sized hard disk to store digital pictures in high resolution. The computer system will also need a good quality monitor, high quality colour printer and a range of other devices such as scanner and digital camera.

There are a number of different types of desktop publishing software available. The software takes a number of forms based upon the types of document to be produced.

PAGE LAYOUT SOFTWARE

This type of software is designed for single page layouts or short documents that combine text and graphics. They have extensive typographic control and graphics handling capabilities.

LONG DOCUMENT COMPOSITION

Books and large documents such as stage scripts require a program that can support repeating elements such as headers and footers. They also need a program that can automatically produce tables of contents, indexes, page numbers and an integration of elements such as data from spreadsheets or databases. These packages have extensive text handling facilities, such as pagination and the full automation of repetitive tasks.

DATABASE ASSISTED PUBLISHING

These packages are designed to handle the importing and formatting of external data through what are called 'front ends'. They are used essentially for catalogues, price lists and directories. Most companies that produce catalogues and price lists use this type of software.

CORPORATE PUBLISHING

These desktop publishing packages are particularly suited to high-quality typesetting and document composition. We will explore a context in the second section of the book where Iain uses this type of software.

HOME PUBLISHING

Desktop publishing packages designed for home use contain a large number of templates, design wizards, font ranges and clip-art collections. They do not, however, produce the high-quality typesetting and printouts needed for professional use. They are ideal for home use and producing things like greeting cards, banners, posters and photo albums. They will not allow for automatic colour separation.

USING A DTP PACKAGE

DTP packages make full use of drop-down menus. These are usually controlled by a mouse or pointer.

Before you use a DTP package you have to consider a number of points. What do you want to say? Who will use your document? Where will your publication be read? How many pages? What size of page? How many pictures? Is there a house style you must use? How will the paper be folded?

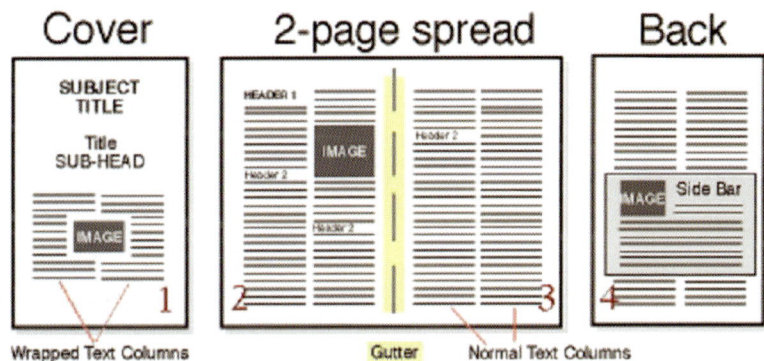

Figure 1.60 *DTP layout*

You can then decide on the software package and hardware you wish to use.

As with word processing you will need to consider the format of the pages:

- titles, headers, columns, font;
- format text;
- where to 'place' graphics and images.

Typical applications of desktop publishing software include:

- to produce newspapers, newsletters, journals, magazines and books;
- to produce reports, brochures and manuals;

- to produce posters and advertisements;
- to add pictures, logos etc. to letters or other documents to make them look attractive.

USING GRAPHICS

Before they are put into the DTP package, pictures taken with a digital camera or scanned into the computer will usually be manipulated in a graphics package. The most common graphics programmes are Photoshop, Corel and Paint.

Software packages that produce graphics can be divided into four main types, according to their function:

- painting and drawing programs
- image manipulation programs
- Computer Aided Design (CAD) packages.
- graphs and charts, sometimes called business graphics programs.

Graphics files in general are of two main types. There are those that represent images as vector graphics, and those that present images as bit maps.

Figure 1.61 *GRAPHICS package*

Vector graphics

With vector graphics, lines are stored in the computer as equations. They are expressed in vector format so they have a starting point, a length and a direction. Vector graphics are easy to change without any loss of resolution. When a vector graphics image is enlarged, the number of

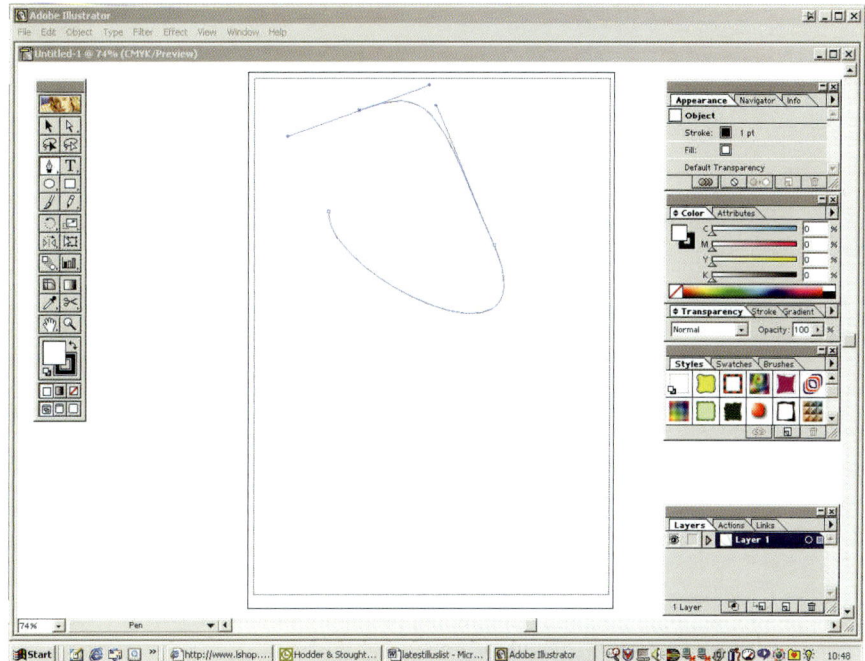

Figure 1.62 *Vector graphics*

pixels used to make up the image increases in proportion, so the detail remains the same.

As well as being used in software for painting and drawing, vector graphics are used in CAD packages.

Bitmap graphics

Bitmap graphics are used in software designed to manipulate images. Such software is often used alongside a digital camera and can change and enhance pictures that have been taken. A bitmap file represents each pixel on the screen as a single bit of information. If the pixel is in colour, additional bits will need to be stored. If the user wants to change a bitmapped image, the software has to alter it one pixel at a time. If the image is enlarged, the number of pixels stays the same and, as a result, the pixels move apart, making the image look grainy and less clear.

Importing from other packages

Most graphics programmes will also import sets of data from a database or spreadsheet.

Some offer a choice of graphs including pie charts, bar charts of all kinds, line graphs and x–y or scatter graphs that can be labelled in terms of both the axes and the data, as appropriate. They offer a range of colours and formats to enhance the presentation of graphs and charts

Almost all drawing programs offer good facilities for freehand drawing, with a wide choice of pens, brushes and drawing styles, and a wide range of colours and patterns. They also offer a range of standard shapes including pictures.

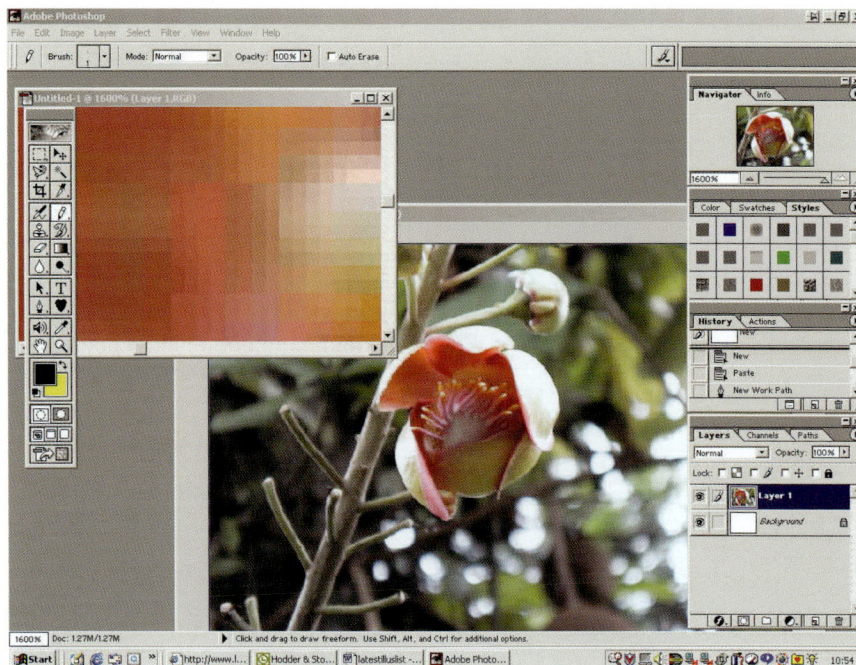

Figure 1.63 *Bitmap graphic*

Choices are made mainly with a mouse and icons and a zoom facility allows you to change individual pixels. Areas can be deleted, copied, resized and moved.

Clipart

Clipart is the name given to illustrations that are copyright-free and intended for use in documents of all kinds, where the user does not want to draw something from scratch. Most professional designers do not use clipart as they do not want their publications to look the same as others. They do, however, use picture libraries to find appropriate illustrations.

Clipart illustrations can be added to all kinds of documents, from word-processed documents, spreadsheets, desktop published documents to graphics. The use of clipart can save time and help to produce a document with a more professional appearance. Disks containing clipart can be bought separately or as part of a DTP or graphics package. Over one million images may be available in a clipart package.

Presentation software

Modern PCs are now equipped with multimedia capabilities. This means that they are able to combine text, graphics, sound, animation, video clips, digital camera images and Internet web pages. Presentation software is used to do this. The end result is usually a set of high-quality slides, which can have a degree of animation, to be used in a presentation to an audience. Powerpoint is a much used presentation package.

Iain had to produce a presentation to the bank. He decided to use Powerpoint which is a multimedia presentation package that allows you to make a slide show of images. Complex images can be constructed and edited.

He started with a blank presentation. Having selected the Slide Layout he decided to use a pre-set design for the presentation. He did this by selecting Apply Design and choosing the backgrounds to give his slide some more colour.

Iain knew the rules for effective presentations:

- Keep the information simple: he should be able to expand on the information on display.
- Use opening and closing slides to set the scene and re-emphasise the important points.
- Avoid using too many slides: each slide should be displayed for between one and two minutes.
- Avoid putting too much information on each slide: use bullet points – no more than four or five per slide.

Iain decided to animate his slides. You can animate most items in presentation software by clicking on the area you wish to work on. This can be text as well as graphics. In Powerpoint he used Custom Animation to animate his slides. Iain knew that he should not add too much animation as this could distract the bank manager from the main message he wanted to give.

Iain did not want all the information to appear on the slide at the same time as he wanted to take his audience through a number of different important points. He set up the software using the animation control so that each point was displayed as a list of bullet points. Each

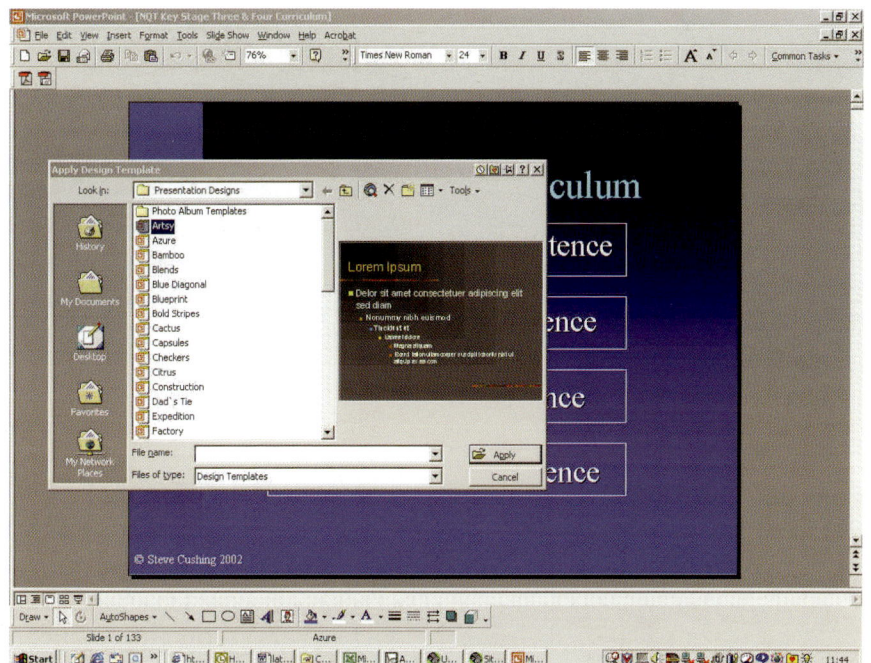

Figure 1.64 *Powerpoint: Apply Design*

new point was added to the list sequentially when he clicked the mouse button. Information could appear and then disappear when it was no longer needed.

When he had made a number of slides he selected Slide Show→View Show to see how they would work when he ran the presentation. Iain finds that one benefit of using presentation software is that it is easy to edit his presentation. Slides can be added or removed, the order of slides could be changed or information on a slide can be edited.

There are an increasing number of companies that use presentation software to enable a person to speak to a group of people. The speaker often complements their speech with a slide show. This can be used to emphasise the main points of the presentation. A benefit is that important information can be communicated to a large group of people. A problem is that the audience mainly listens to the speaker. There is little opportunity for dialogue between the speaker and the audience.

The presentation is usually made via a computer screen, or for better effect, Iain used a large screen via a projector. Documents created using presentation software are normally created in a lower resolution than those created using DTP software.

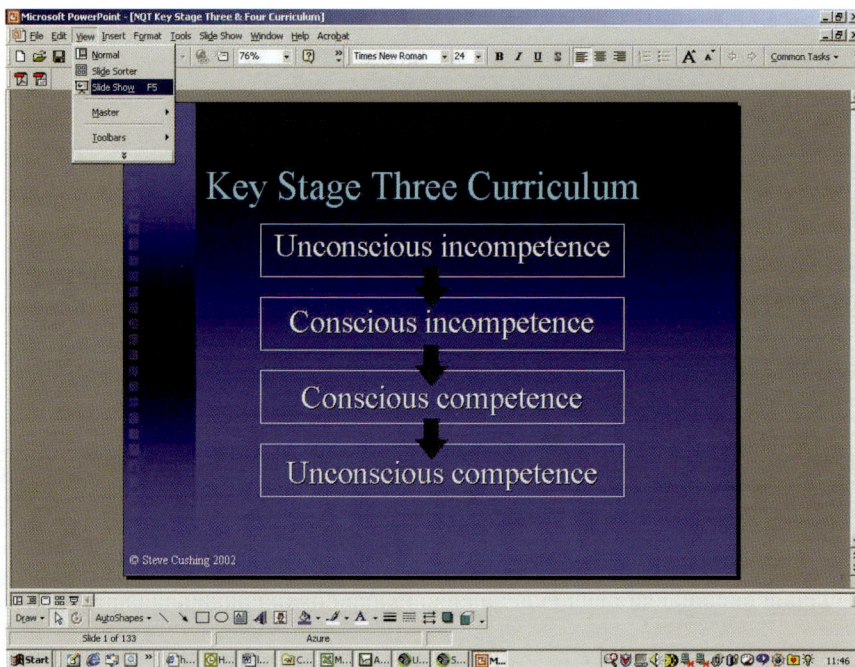

Figure 1.65 *Powerpoint: Slide Show →*
View Show

The LCD projector Iain used works on the same principle as the LCDs people use every day in watches, clocks, calculators and a host of other domestic appliances. LCDs are common because they offer some real advantages over other display technologies. They are thinner and lighter and draw much less power.

LCDs use liquid crystals that are affected by electric current. An LCD can also show the colours red, green and blue. Through the careful control and variation of the voltage applied, the intensity of

Figure 1.66 *Calculator LCD displays*

Figure 1.67 *Microwave and watch LCD displays*

each crystal can change to 256 shades of colour. Combining the crystals creates a palette of 16.8 million colours (256 shades of red × 256 shades of green × 256 shades of blue). Colour displays do, however, need an enormous number of transistors to make them work. For example, a typical laptop computer supporting a 1,024 × 768 resolution needs 2,359,296 transistors.

The projector Iain uses has a bright light to illuminate the LCD panel, and a lens projects the image formed by the LCD on to a screen. The LCD screen is small and backlit by a very bright halogen lamp. The LCD acts very much like a colour slide in a slide projector.

Figure 1.68 *Digital projector*

The latest projectors use a process called reflective technology. In reflective projectors, the image is formed on a small, reflective chip. When light shines on the chip, the image is reflected off it and through a projection lens to the screen.

The quality of this type of presentation can have a very positive effect on the image of the company using it, as it did in Iain's case. The projector and slideshow helped to explain information that was technical and complicated in an easy, accessible way.

The software enables Iain to establish a structure for his document, with a logical navigation route through it. For example, if you are showing a presentation with slides numbered 1–40 and you decide to miss out slides numbers 27–32, you can just skip them. If one of your audience wants to see a particular slide again, you can go straight to it.

The software Iain used offers word-processing features, with a good range of fonts and other format options. Lines, boxes, bullets, borders and colour can be used to enhance effect. Separate components of presentations, and whole documents, can be edited if changes are needed.

Style sheets can be used to help make main text, headings and subheadings consistent. The master page and paragraph styles for a document can be saved as a template to ensure that each page or slide looks the same overall.

THERE IS A DRAWING CAPABILITY

There are good facilities for importing word-processed documents or other files. The software can import data from scanners and digital cameras and utilise this.

Text and pictures can be arranged together in eye-catching ways, and you can change their sizes. Pictures can also be cropped. This is the term for cutting off and discarding part of a picture that is not needed.

Iain used the presentation as a way of communicating information to an audience, in this case the bank. He wanted to make a good impression. Some of the information was informative, where the aim was to let the bank manager make her own mind up about the information. As Iain wanted a loan to buy new equipment for the company, most of the information was persuasive, where the aim was to influence what the bank manager thinks. Ian's slideshow worked, he got the loan he wanted.

Not all businesses use presentation software in the way Iain did. Businesses use presentations for many different reasons. For example, a marketing manager might make a presentation to the board of directors about a possible new product. The marketing manager will try to persuade the directors that the new product will be profitable.

The most common type of presentation is where a speaker talks to a group of people. The information is displayed on a screen using a projector and the speaker gives the presentation standing in front of the display. Presentation software is used to create the display.

Presentation software allows a commentary to be recorded alongside the display. This means that the speaker does not need to be there when the presentation is given. The presentation can, for example, be made available for people to download from the Internet and view on their own computer.

Lata uses a web-based presentation to show how profit and loss can be calculated. Her presentation makes use of the fact that multimedia presentation software allows you to build up the presentation as a series of linked slides, each slide containing information about a particular part of her presentation.

Lata sets the time it takes to display the next part of the presentation (called transition time) automatically. This is useful as the presentation is being given without Lata there.

Spreadsheets

A spreadsheet is a program that allows you to store data that has been organised in some structured way. It is also possible to enter commands that enable the spreadsheet to change or manipulate the data. The result is that the user can see the effects of one change on the data as a whole. Spreadsheets can also convert numerical data into graphs and charts. This makes them particularly useful for generating the data that will go into business reports.

Spreadsheet software allows data and information to be displayed and managed in a table format.

The table is divided into rows and columns of individual boxes called cells.

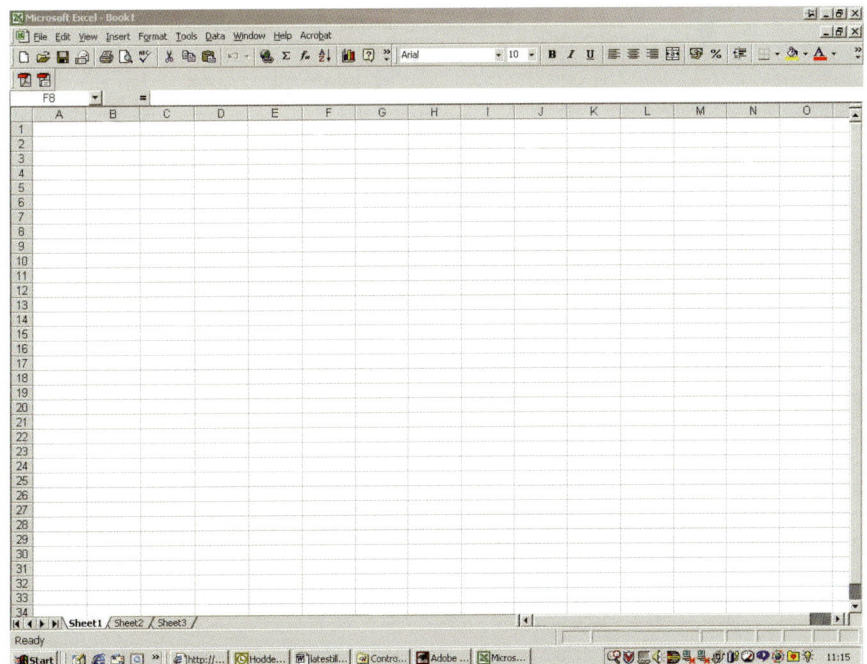

Figure 1.69 *Excel spreadsheet*

The user can enter a number, formula or text into any cell. The power of a spreadsheet lies in its ability to enter formulae. The main symbols used are:

*	Multiply by
/	Divide by
+	Add
–	Subtract
( )	Perform the instruction inside the brackets first

Hence powerful mathematical calculations can be performed on data. The most common functions used in business are the following:

SUM(xx:yy)	Adds together all the numbers in the cells xx to yy
AVERAGE (xx:yy)	Calculates the average (arithmetic mean) of all the numbers in the cells xx to yy
MIN(xx:yy)	Displays the smallest number in a series of numbers
MAX(xx:yy)	Displays the largest number in a series of numbers
IF(xx < 50,"Yes","No")	Displays the word Yes if the data in cell xx is less than 50 or No if it isn't.

(xx = column heading letter followed by row heading number)

The example shows a simple spreadsheet. Sheet 1 shows the input and output data. Sheet 2 shows the formulae used to calculate the results.

1.3	4	=SUM(A1*B1)
2.4	3	SUM(A2*B2)
3.2	3	SUM(A3*B3)
7.3	4	SUM(A4*B4)
=SUM(A1:A4)		=SUM(C1:C4)

1.3	4	5.2
2.4	3	7.2
3.2	3	9.6
7.3	4	29.2
14.2		51.2

Sheet 1   Sheet 2

Spreadsheets are easy to understand if you look at them logically. Edward always explains what he wants to achieve by relating it to real life.

LIFE IS FULL OF LOGICAL POSSIBILITIES

It was Saturday and Edward could get up in the morning or stay in bed. He could eat cornflakes for breakfast or cheese on toast. Alternatively Edward could skip breakfast altogether, stay in bed and wait until 11.10 for a chocolate attack.

A computer views the data it processes in a very logical manner. In spreadsheets you can take advantage of this using functions such as the IF function.

For example, in real life there are always at least two logical possibilities: So if Edward was going to examine this in a spreadsheet he might say…

EITHER	OR
It IS raining at the moment	It IS NOT raining at the moment.

IF it IS raining at the moment, then put the following message on the screen 'Go back to bed!', however, IF it IS NOT raining at the moment, put the following message on the screen 'Get up and go out on your motorbike…' This statement takes care of both possibilities.

USING SPREADSHEETS FOR MODELLING AND WHAT-IF ANALYSIS

A model is a simplified representation of a real-life object or event. Models can be tested to see how they behave and what the results of a particular business decision will be. This knowledge can help the designer to build the real thing.

CAD and other specialised software allow quick visualisation and analysis of manufacturing or architectural designs, even from perspectives other than that from which the design was created. In brief, electronic data processing allows the update, simulation, or manipulation of information in ways that can only be dreamed of with pen and paper or other traditional methods, with far less effort and time.

Computer spreadsheet models are similar to CAD models except that they are based on formulae and functions. For example, Lata is training as an accountant. She often builds a spreadsheet to model the impact of increasing wages on a firm's profits. This information can then be used to help the managers of the business decide on a wage increase that would keep both workers and the employers happy.

The functions and formulae are the 'rules' that govern how the model works. Changing the rules will change the results that the model produces.

All models allow users to carry out 'what-if analysis'. This is true of both CAD based and spreadsheet models. How these models work is quite simple. It means changing either the data fed into the model or the formula, and seeing what happens to the result. For example, an accountant could find out what will happen to company profits if workers have a wage increase of 8% or 10% by simply changing the formula.

The main benefit to businesses of using spreadsheets is that users can create templates of often-used spreadsheets. This means that calculations can be carried out very quickly. The spreadsheet also allows data to be manipulated with a high level of accuracy, as long as the correct data is entered and the correct formulae are used.

Spreadsheets can be formatted like any other document by using various fonts, styles, sizes and colours. Clipart and borders can also be added to spreadsheets.

You can use the data in a spreadsheet to produce charts such as pie charts, bar charts and other types of graphs. The graph below shows Quickpack's profit and loss for 2002. Iain uses a spreadsheet in his factory because calculations can be carried out automatically and less staff might be needed as a result. Spreadsheets allow Iain to build models to find out the effects of taking different business decisions.

A spreadsheet allows calculations to be carried out on cells or groups of cells, both within individual spreadsheets, or across linked spreadsheets.

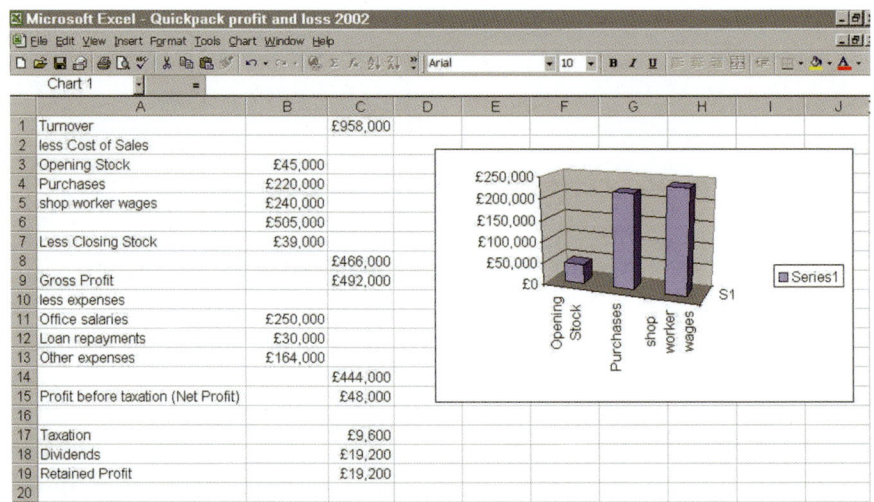

Figure 1.70 *3D bar chart*

Cells can be formatted to display specific types of data, e.g.

- number (you can choose the number of decimal points that will be shown);
- currency(there is a choice of the main world currencies);
- date (you can choose, for example, whether the day or month will appear first, or whether the year is shown);
- time;
- percentage;
- fractions;
- scientific notation.

Furthermore,

- you can insert or delete rows and columns;
- a formula can allow calculations to be carried out in other cells;
- formulae and other data can be copied into groups of cells.

You have the option of using either absolute or relative cell references in a spreadsheet. An absolute reference is a cell address that refers to a fixed location that will not change when a formula is copied to another location. In Lotus 1-2-3 and Excel, an absolute address is indicated by placing a $ sign in front of the column and row information. A relative reference is a cell address that indicates the position of a cell, relative to another cell. If this formula is copied to another location, the address will be changed so that it refers to the cell in the same position relative to the new cell. Lotus 1-2-3 and Excel treat cell addresses as relative unless you have added the $ sign.

A variety of operations can be carried out on rows or columns. These might include functions such as auto-fill, where the spreadsheet automatically enters data such as months of the year or days of the week. It can start a table with a certain value and increase the value in subsequent cells in measured amounts, for example, displaying 0 to 100 in steps of 5 each.

A spreadsheet allows the creation of macros. These are series of commands created by the user that the spreadsheet will perform automatically.

The software allows you to produce a range of charts based on data that you specify in a spreadsheet. The facility called Chart Wizard allows you to choose from charts in the form of columns, bars, lines, pie charts, XY (scatter) graphs, radar charts or doughnuts.

Basic functions relate to the appearance of the display, and are similar to those of a word processor. Examples are text formatting, copy/cut and paste, creation of borders, use of colour and spell checking.

You can print whole spreadsheets, or selected areas of spreadsheets.

Databases

All businesses need to store large amounts of information, for example details of customers, employees and financial records.

If Sunita had used a database to store all of the details of her CDs she would have been able to list them using any of the data or even search by date, artist, track etc.

Sunita had only a small amount of data to store. Some companies have huge amounts of data to store. Storing this data without a database can be a problem. Large amounts of paper need large filing cabinets for storage. Documents can be easily misplaced. Finding a specific document can be time-consuming, just like Sunita's CD, and only one person can use the document at any one time. Any reports or calculations that require information from lots of different documents can take a long time to produce.

Computerised databases solve many of these problems. A database is any place where data is stored and organised in a structured way. Computerised databases store the data on the computer's disks. The computer can find and process the data very quickly. As a result, information can be retrieved from the database and reports generated efficiently.

Use	Business examples
Storing large amounts of data	Storing customer records Storing product details Storing a list of all the components needed to make the firm's products
Searching for data that meets certain criteria	Locating a particular customer Finding out how much stock of a particular product the firm has got left Finding all customers who haven't purchased anything this year
Producing reports	Producing a marketing report on where the firm's sales have increased

The benefits to businesses of computer databases include the following:

- large volumes of data can be stored in a small space;
- the database can be searched to obtain specific information very quickly;
- the information remains stored on the database so there is less chance of it being misplaced;
- the database can process the data so that reports and calculations can be carried out;
- it can be possible for more than one user to see and process the data at the same time.

Data type is important. For example, most database programs cannot add together the data contained in two fields containing text.

But it is not just businesses that need databases.

Before databases, libraries used to issue each borrower with tickets with slots in. To borrow a book, you had to hand over one ticket and it would be filed away in a box, along with thousands of other tickets from other borrowers. The book would be date stamped and you could keep it for three weeks. The trouble with filing so many little cards is that some get lost. Librarians would spend hours trying to find some of them.

Now each book has a bar-coded label inside it, and each borrower has one ticket with a bar code on it. The librarian date stamps the book and runs a bar-code reader across both the book bar code and your ticket; the computer does the rest. It automatically records in its database that a particular borrower has taken that book.

When the book is brought back, it is scanned again with a bar-code reader and the computer 'knows' that the book has been returned.

But before any database can be set up someone has to decide what data is required. Data can take many forms: the date of the book, the name of the author, the cost of the book, or your postcode and address in case you forget to return the book.

Main data types

Data type	What it can store	What processes can be done	Example of data
Text	Stores text or numeric information	Search for data beginning/containing a specific letter Sort data into alphabetical order	Surname Town
Numerical	Stores numbers only	Searches calculations, sorting into ascending/descending order	Telephone number Price Age Shoe size
Date	Stores data as a calendar date	As for numerical data but based on a calendar year	Date of birth Date last sold
Linked objects	Stores data created in other programs	Search for specific objects	Photographs of products Personnel photographs

Field length is also important. This controls how much data can be entered into a field. For example, some banks have customer databases that allow a surname of a maximum of 19 characters.

This is because data must be stored on the computer and storage may be limited.

The name Steven G W Cushing needs 18 data entries (including spaces).

Databases can be expensive to build and install as large databases need expensive computer systems to operate them. For example, the national telephone directory for England has approximately 55 million residential and business listings, requiring over 1100 million data entries. Databases also need constant updating, otherwise the information they contain will become out of date.

All databases have the same basic structure. The data is divided up into different categories. For example, details about a customer can be divided into: first name, last name, address, telephone number, account number. The business will hold the same information about all of its customers.

A database program allows the user to handle files, keep records in an organised way, and retrieve information from these records.

A database is a collection of related items of information, which are organised into records.

FIELD TYPES

Data type	Usage
Text	Alphanumeric data, i.e. any letter, number or other character
Number	Numeric data
Date/time	Access can calculate with dates (e.g. find how many days there are between 03/09/2001 and 25/12/2001) but it could not do this if you entered dates as text
Currency	For all monetary data
Yes/No	True/false data when there are only 2 possible answers
Auto/Number	Often used in the primary key field to identify a record uniquely. No two records ever have the same key field data

USING COMPARISON OPERATORS

Sorting records

Records can be sorted into ascending or descending order, alphabetically or numerically.

Making queries

Data in databases can be organised in any way that you wish through the use of queries. For instance, you can find all the records that satisfy certain criteria such as, 'find all the records for all mobile phones that offer 20 free minutes a week'.

Search criteria are listed in the table below.

Search criteria	Symbol	Description
Equals	=	Finds records matching a specific value
Less than	<	Finds records whose value is less than the specified amount
Greater than	>	Finds records whose value is greater than the specified amount
Not equal to	<> or =/	Finds records whose value is not equal to the specified amount
Less than or equal to	<=	Finds the records whose value is less than or equal to the specified amount
Greater than or equal to	>=	Finds the records whose value is greater than or equal to the specified amount

Multiple criteria

You can use several options when designing queries. You can use operators such as 'AND' and 'OR'. For example, 'find all mobile phones with 20 free minutes that belong to the "Orange" and "One to One" networks'.

A simple search will use one criterion. A complex search will use more than one. Complex searches also use Boolean logic to help the computer decide whether a piece of data meets the criteria.

Boolean logic	Meaning
AND	Finds data that meet two sets of criteria
NOR	Finds data that doesn't meet either criterion
NOT	Finds data that meets one criterion but not the other

Reports can also be generated. It is possible to specify which fields the report will show. For example, in the above search you might want to display the surname and telephone number.

Reports can also structure the output data in specific ways. The most common ways are to put the data into alphabetical or numerical order. For example, the report could list data alphabetically by surname (e.g. Cushing before Yeomans) or numerically by account number.

There are two main types of database: a flat file database and a relational database.

FLAT FILE DATABASES

In a flat file database all the data is stored in a single file and the sorting, searching and printing of reports is all done in this single file.

Flat file databases are:

● easy to use;
● suitable for small amounts of data.

RELATIONAL DATABASES

In relational databases, the tables of data exist independently from the programs that may use them. Relational databases use database management systems (DBMS) to link independent files together. Sometimes different users will have access to different data stored. Some users will not be given permission to look at all the data. Data is stored in the form of records. For example, if the database is about people, each record would contain all the data relating to one individual.

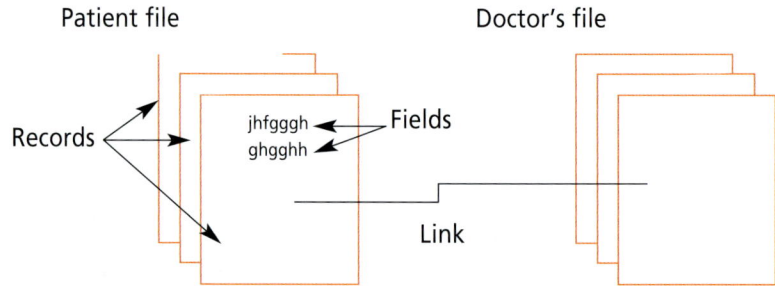

Figure 1.71 *Relational database linking patient file and doctor's file*

You can define how records will be organised by choosing the number of fields and their names, the size of each field and type of data it will hold (e.g. text, currency, date, time), the way records are displayed on the screen. (A field is an area of a record reserved for one particular type of data item. Each field contains one data item.)

VERIFICATION CHECKS

The patient data at Veena's health centre has to be accurate, or incorrect medicines could be given causing illness and even death. Each time data is entered, a verification check is used to make sure that data that has been entered, or copied from another software package or input device, has been transferred correctly.

Sometimes, when Veena enters data using a keyboard, her assistant is asked to enter the same data. The two versions are then compared by the software. If they match, the data is stored. If not, the source document is looked at to see where mistakes were made. Any mistakes are then corrected and stored. Veena thinks that this type of verification checking is a waste of time because they both have to enter the same data.

Veena is always keen to check her own work. She displays the data she has typed on the screen and verifies it by reading through it very carefully to se if it is correct. The doctor assures her that while she is a very good and diligent worker, operators often do not see their own mistakes, or do not believe that they have made any mistakes.

He has recently updated the database to software that uses a parity check. This makes use of the binary code understood by the computer to try to make sure that data is not corrupted during transfer. The way the system works is that when groups of bits (1s and 0s) are being transferred, an extra bit is added so that the total number of 1s is always odd (or, alternatively, always even). This is called the parity of the data. One incorrectly transmitted bit will change the parity, making it possible to detect the error. However, if an even number of incorrect bits has been transmitted, the parity is not changed. Even though not all errors are detected, Veena is warned by those that *are* indicated and can check the data more thoroughly to locate others.

The new software also carries out validation checks.

VALIDATION CHECKS

Validation checking is carried out by the software to make sure that data is sensible and will not cause problems when it is processed. For example, if Veena enters a date of birth that makes someone over 150 years old, the software asks if she is sure she has entered the birth date correctly. This is called a range check and makes sure that data is inside a fixed set of values. For example, date of birth might have to be between 1900 and the present date. A range check can be used with letters as well as numbers. A set range of letters can be specified. For example, authors of books on one shelf rack in the medical library might have names beginning with any letter from N to S.

A presence check makes sure that a value has actually been entered in a particular field. This type of check is used where certain vital data must be entered. An example would be a patient's blood group where a hospital has to give a blood transfusion.

Bar codes

Some of the medicines that Veena has to record on the system have bar codes on them to make it easy for her to enter the data. The bar codes are similar to those used in supermarkets. Bar codes have what are called check digits on them. The check digit is a single digit number calculated from all the rest of the digits in a data item and then attached to the end of the data when it is stored. Check digits are present in bar code numbers and are also used in account numbers. Check digits are used widely to validate numeric data, especially where numbers with many digits are being entered.

When Gavin took out a library book he noticed that there are even check digits on the bar code in the front of the book. It is even in the ISBN, the unique number that identifies each book that is printed. Bar codes are used in most supermarkets and libraries, in luggage handling systems at airports and for warehouse stock control. Each item of stock is marked with a unique code composed of dark and light bars of different widths. Each code has separate left and right halves which can be read in either direction. The code represents a number, which is the data to be fed into the computer system. The bar-code reader detects the amount of light reflected by the dark and light lines in the bar code, and many readers are now so sensitive that they can read a code from a distance of five metres or more. The use of bar codes has made it much easier for Veena and there is less chance of errors.

It is much cheaper for a shop to use bar codes as staff can change the price of goods by altering the price on computer, without having to re-price each individual product. Only the label on the shelf needs alteration. Once the data has been collected from the shopping, the branch computer searches its stock for the matching EAN number. When it has found it, the computer sends back details of the price and a description of the article to the EPOS till.

It is of course possible for a bar-code reader to misread a bar code, for example if there is a dirty mark on the code, but the check digit notices the error. The scanning system Veena uses beeps when data has been accepted and remains quiet when it has not, in which case the code can be typed in using a keyboard.

Check digits are used to detect transposition errors. They can tell if two digits are entered the wrong way round, and detect changes or losses of digits in numbers. When Veena inputs the number, the check digit is recalculated and the two versions are compared. If they match, the data is correct and can be saved. If they do not match, there is a mistake and the number has to be re-input.

Figure 1.72 *Bar codes*

SCANNERS

Bar codes are read by scanners. Scanners have become an important part of our everyday lives. All of the Oliver family use scanners each day at the library, supermarket and office.

Scanners can be classified into two main groups: handheld devices that are moved across the source material being scanned, and fixed scanners.

Scanners work by sending out infra-red laser beams via a set of mirrors, enabling the bar code to be read at lots of different angles. Flatbed and horizontal scanners are the quickest. When Veena passes the bar code over or under the scanner, the black and white parts are detected by the laser. The black stripes reflect very little light but the white parts reflect the most. This is converted into electrical pulses that are sent along cables to the computer.

Alongside bar codes, other options a designer of a medical system might consider includes Optical Character Recognition (OCR) or Optical Mark Recognition (OMR).

Figures 1.73 and 1.74 *Handheld scanner and flatbed desktop scanner*

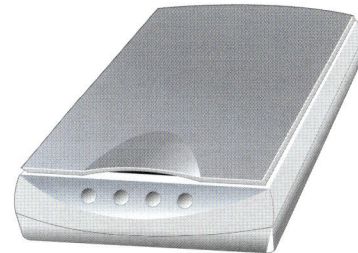

Handheld   Flatbed desktop

There are in fact four main different types of scanner.

- Flatbed scanners are the most versatile and commonly used scanners.
- Sheet-fed scanners are similar to flatbed scanners except the document is moved and the scan head is fixed. Some new printers can also scan documents using this method.
- Handheld scanners use the same basic technology as a flatbed scanner, but rely on the user to move them. They are very useful for quickly capturing text.
- Drum scanners are used by the publishing industry to capture incredibly detailed images.

The basic principle of a scanner is to capture an image and process it in some way. The user then needs to save the captured file on a computer.

Scanners vary in resolution and sharpness. Most flatbed scanners have a resolution of at least 300×300 dots per inch (dpi). Sharpness depends mainly on the quality of the optics used to make the lens, and the brightness of the light source.

As we have explored in a number of places in the book, colour is made by mixing the three basic colours. To achieve a colour image a scanner has to scan a picture three times. It does this with only one movement, as the scanning head has three separate scanning devices, each with a different colour filter.

Optical mark readers and optical mark recognition (OMR)

Optical mark readers are able to sense marks made on pre-printed forms in certain places. Typical uses include multiplechoice answer sheet marking, capturing data from questionnaires, enrolment forms and lottery tickets, and the checking of football pools coupons.

Gavin used an OMR for his Key Skills examination. He had to use a dark pencil mark in the space provided for the answer he thought was correct.

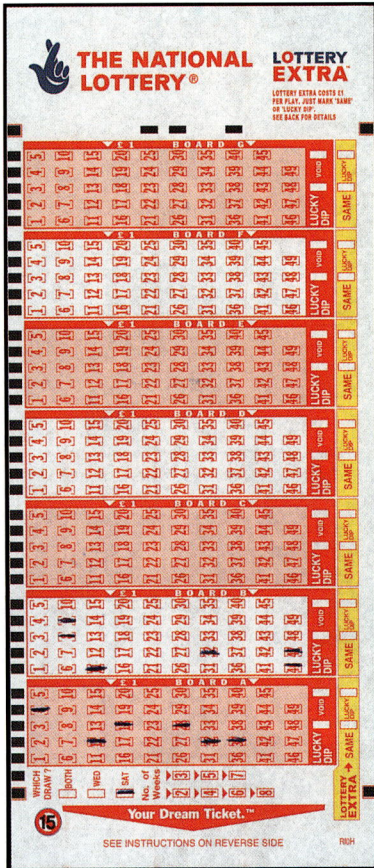

Figure 1.75 *An example of an OMR data capture form*

There was printing already on the form but it was in very pale ink called fade-out ink. This is not detected by the mark reader, which will pick up only the dark pencil marks. It does this by detecting the amount of light reflected from different parts of the form. The dark marks reflect less light. The mark reader transmits data about each space to the computer, and the software works out whether answers are right or wrong, and adds up the total mark.

In Veena's heath centre, data capture via OMR forms is an important part of the system. A large amount of the data required by the system is captured in this way.

Optical character readers and optical character recognition (OCR)

An optical character reader also uses a scanner to detect the amount of light reflected from a sheet of paper. The pattern of data from the reflected light is compared with stored patterns for different characters. The best match is selected and the code representing the character is stored. As each individual letter has been recognised on its own, it can be edited later using word processing software.

Veena sometimes uses OCR technology to capture medical information from traditional paper-based records. She would like it to be able to read the doctor's hand written notes on the patient cards, but it is not able to recognise the difference between the doctor's S and a 5, or a B and an 8. It works if the text is typed, and in a standard font. Different fonts, type sizes and upper and lower case letters all pose problems. In the case of the patient notes, lots of people have written on the record cards. Teaching the system to recognise everyone's handwriting would take Veena longer than typing it all in using a keyboard.

QUALITY OF DATA – ACCURACY, TRUTH

It is important to remember that although Veena uses verification checks to ensure that data is copied correctly, and validation checks to pinpoint data that has numerical or character errors, there is no way of making sure that the data entered into the system is either accurate or true. Sometimes even the patient gets their postcode or telephone number wrong. Sometimes they even lie to her about their name and what drugs they are already taking.

Nobody has yet written software that can act as a lie detector. It is up to the user to make sure that data entered is accurate, otherwise outputs from the system will be wrong.

It is true that if you put rubbish in to a system, you will get rubbish out.

As we explored in the first section of the book, the question of truth is a difficult one, particularly in relation to the Internet. Web pages are innocently used by thousands of people as electronic reference books, but there is no check on the quality of information displayed on them. The user can only hope that, if the site is provided by a reputable organisation, the information offered can be believed.

SAVING DESK SPACE

Every desktop computer, most portables, electronic calculators and mobile phones have a display screen of some kind. On a desktop computer, the screen is often known as the monitor, or as a VDU (visual display unit). Screens are available in various sizes. Display screens used in ICT applications are called monitors. Veena uses a flat screen monitor.

Figure 1.76 *Flat screen monitor*

Standard VDUs on desktop computers work in the same way as the screen on a standard television set, but this technology is too bulky for portables or the other handheld devices. It is also too big for Veena's desk. Handheld devices use liquid crystal displays, made from flat plates with liquid between them. Although this system takes up much less space, the disadvantage is that these screens can be viewed only from a limited angle. This is not a problem to Veena , but space is. As the technology improves, flat screen panels are becoming available for desktop computers too.

Screens provide the Oliver family with lots of ways of receiving information. Through the television screen and VDUs they view parts of the world they would never be able to visit. Gavin watches lots of sports events that he would otherwise not see. Traditional televisions offer a limited choice of information that they can receive. The Oliver family use digital interactive television. With digital interactive televisions they can obtain information such as the weather forecast whenever they want it, at the touch of a button. They can order goods and pay for movies at the time they want to watch them. All ICT devices use some sort of screen for display.

A screen display is either monochrome, or colour. Monochrome does not necessarily mean black and white. They may have orange or green text on a black background, the significant difference being that they do not provide the range of colour of a colour screen.

Monochrome screens are suitable where they are used only to provide text displays. Colour is considered to be more restful to the eye, easier to read and is necessary to show detail of graphics, or to highlight error messages, menu options etc. in word processing. However, the use of colour takes up more storage space and requires more processing time.

The monitor display is the most used output device on any computer. The display provides Veena with instant feedback by showing text and graphic images. Before Veena had a flat screen monitor, her desktop display used a **cathode ray tube** (CRT). Iain's laptop uses a liquid crystal display (LCD). Most portable devices use LCDs, light-emitting diodes (LEDs), gas plasma or other image projection technology. Because of their slimmer design and smaller energy consumption, monitors using LCD technologies are now replacing the cathode ray tubes on many desktops. Of course the health centre had to take into account more than just desk space when they upgraded Veena's monitor. When purchasing a display, there are a number of decisions to make.

They considered:

● the cost of the monitor;
● the maximum resolution of the monitor;
● the viewable area of the display;
● the aspect ratio and orientation (landscape or portrait) of the display;
● the amount of power consumption.

The maximum resolution on a monitor depends on the number of colours displayed. Veena's monitor supports 16.8 million colours at 800×600, or 65,536 colours at 1600×1200. The resolution of a monitor, or screen, is very important. This relates to the clarity of the image on the screen and is defined by the number of separate units of light (known as pixels) across and down the screen that can be displayed. A pixel is square in shape and represents the smallest area of the screen which the computer can change. For some applications, such as computer aided design (CAD) and desktop publishing, a high resolution screen is required, or images will not be sufficiently clear.

The higher the resolution of a display, the more pixels are used. This takes up more storage space in the computer. High resolution images also take longer to process and a fast processor is required to animate a high resolution picture smoothly. All monitors use a projection surface, commonly referred to as a screen. Screen sizes are normally measured from one corner to the corner diagonally across from it. This diagonal measuring system actually came about because the early television manufacturers wanted to make the screen size of their TVs sound more impressive. Each screen has a maximum resolution. This is measured by the number of individual dots of colour, known as pixels, contained on a display.

But it is not just the number of pixels that give a screen its resolution. Monitors also have what is called a **dot pitch** which is how much space there is between a display's pixels. The closer together the pixels, the higher resolution the display will have. It is possible to use a method called interlacing to produce a screen image that seems to have a higher resolution than the screen can display. However, this results in more screen flicker than a display that has not been interlaced.

Veena's display can support a maximum resolution of 1280 by 1024 pixels. It usually also supports lower resolutions such as 1024 by 768, 800 by 600, and 640 by 480.

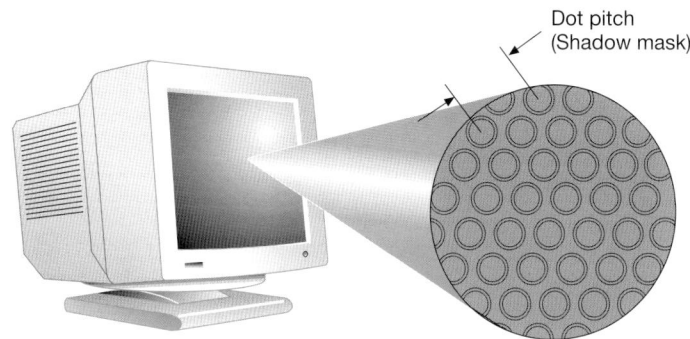

Figure 1.77 *Monitor, showing dot pitch*

Veena can change her monitor settings easily through her Windows control panel.

The health centre that Veena works in is very concerned about environmental issues. CRTs are very power-hungry when compared to LCDs. As the monitor accounts for over 80% of the electricity used, they were keen to reduce electricity costs.

The doctors in Veena's practice use touch-sensitive screens. These are screens through which data can by entered into a computer by touching it with a finger. Items are selected as they would be with a mouse or light pen. Touch-sensitive screens work by means of criss-crossing beams of infra-red light just in front of the glass. When the doctor touches the glass two sets of rays are blocked giving an X and Y axis. Most interactive whiteboards work in a similar way to this.

Touch-sensitive screens are ideal for doctors, who have to select information about patients quickly. They are also useful in theatres, museums, shops and Internet booths. They are easy to use. They are used in Gavin's university, which has a number of information kiosks. The advantage of a touch screen is that no extra peripherals are needed except the monitor, although this has to be adapted to respond to touch. The touch method is very useful in situations where a keyboard or mouse could become dirty or wet, and where users are standing and moving about and where limitations on the number of options available are required.

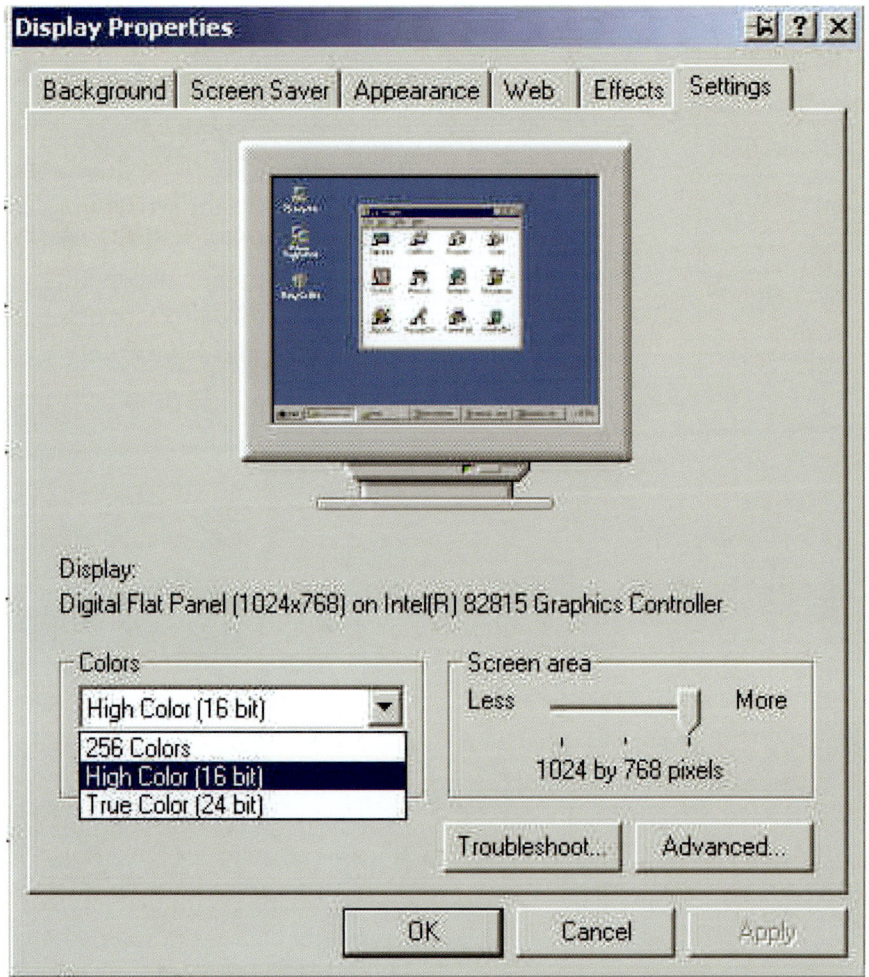

Figure 1.78 *Changing monitor settings in control panel*

ESTABLISHING RELATIONSHIPS BETWEEN DATA FILES

Database software allows you to establish a relationship between fields in two different tables. For example, a database system might contain an employee file that lists what job each employee does. A separate file for each job could contain information on rates of pay for that job, and work schedules that apply to all the workers doing that job.

Database software can carry out a counting function. For example, it could count the number of employees who have been with a company for over five years. It can also perform calculations, such as totalling how much each employee has been paid so far in the year.

The program provides facilities to sort data into different levels of importance.

It provides facilities for information retrieval. You can carry out search, and sort, operations in a database. It can produce lists of all records that meet certain criteria, and it can calculate statistics for groups of records.

It can combine results into a report.

Typical applications of databases are:

- creating and maintaining personal lists such as:
  - details of customers' names, addresses and accounts;
  - details of patients' names, addresses and medical or dental records;
  - student or pupil records;
  - lists of suppliers to a company;
- allowing access to large stores of information such as:
  - an encyclopedia stored on CD;
  - details of books currently in print, with authors, publishers and contents summaries;
  - details of properties for sale;
  - details of careers available with qualification requirements.

Multimedia

AUTHORING SOFTWARE

The layout and graphic design features of good presentation software carry over into authoring software. This is the name given to software packages that are used to produce multimedia or hypertext presentations.

The feature that makes authoring software different from presentation software is its ability to allow you to create different paths through the material. A hypertext presentation is an electronic document that presents information that can be read by following many different connections, instead of just reading one word after the other, as in a printed book. The World Wide Web is an example of hypertext. So are Windows Help files, CD-ROM encyclopedias and interactive displays.

A hypertext document typically starts with a computer screen full of information in the form of text, graphics and/or sound. The user has different options as to what related screen to go to next. The normal way to choose an option is to mouse click over a button that is hyperlinked to the next piece of text. Authoring software gives you the tools to create these hypertext links.

The common thread between desktop publishing, presentation and authoring software is good communications. Their purpose is to present information, in a variety of forms, in the best possible way.

ANIMATION

Sunita watched in horror as the cat caught up with the mouse and the large hammer began to fall. The mouse had seen it too. Looking fearfully over his shoulder, he turned and ran faster and faster but the cat went faster too. There was an awful whooshing noise and a scream. Sunita put her hands over her ears as a hammer fell on the mouse in a great rush of air. The mouse tried to dodge out of the way, but it was too late. The hammer hit him with a sickening thud. Sunita screamed and closed her eyes. Poor Jerry. Good job it is only a cartoon, thought Sunita.

Sunita was very familiar with cartoons and some of the films she had seen in which human beings play little or no part. A number of her favourite pop videos used a combination of puppetry, animation and real film. She really liked *Who Framed Roger Rabbit* which was the first major film to be based on this new technology.

Characters like Donald Duck, Tom and Jerry and Wallace and Grommit are better known to Sunita than many human actors and actresses. All cartoons rely on the fact that our brains can be fooled into seeing movement when there is none. If we are rapidly shown a series of pictures of Tom and Jerry in slightly different positions, they really seem to move. This is called *animation*. There are a number of specialist puppetry and animation companies producing animations such as Morph, Wallace & Grommit, Chicken Run, Toy Story, Toy Story 2 and Bill & Ben.

So moving images are really only fixed images redrawn many times per second. Of course this means that even a few seconds of moving video can take up as much storage space as dozens or hundreds of still pictures. For this reason, data is usually stored on CD-ROMs or DVDs. As access to the pictures needs to be fast if the animation is to run effectively, CD-ROM access speeds and times become very important. Each picture in an animation is known as a frame.

Another important factor is the size of the picture files and the amount of redrawing that has to occur in each frame. Almost all animation programs work on the basis of layers. In effect, layers are like a stack of acetate sheets or panes of glass. Each item in the animation is stored on a different layer. This enables the animator to create a snapshot

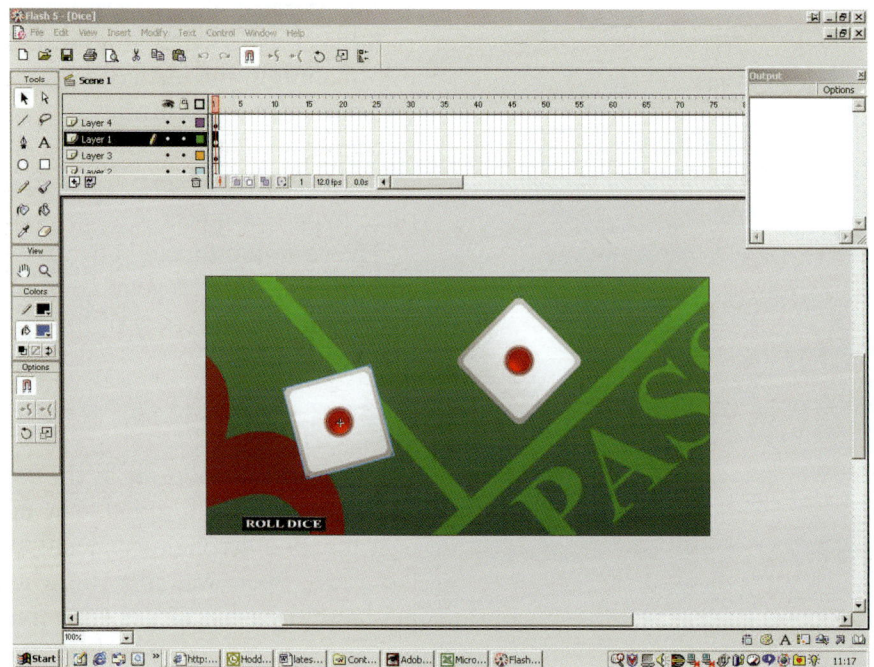

Figure 1.79 *Layers in animation program*

of movement for each object in the animation separately. The first position is created and recorded, the next frame in the sequence is then created by moving or changing the object until the complete animation sequence for that layer is achieved. Computer game animators achieve a reduction in picture size by fixing a common background and changing only small objects against this background layer in each frame.

Most animation programs have a number of tools to help the designer. One of the most important tools is what is called the between or 'tween' tool. This allows an object to be altered between the first and last frames and then automatically generates the position or shape of the object on all of the frames between the first and end frame. This tool, sometimes also referred to as a morphing tool, saves hours of work redrawing. Some packages will even allow you to mark out a path that you want an object to move through and will then generate the necessary movement.

Animation packages are available to enable you to design in both two and three dimensions. The easiest packages to use are those that generate two dimensional animation. The three-dimensional packages use wire frame objects in a similar way to three-dimensional computer aided design packages. When colour and texture are added to three dimensional animations (called rendering), the images are very large.

Systems used for three-dimensional animation need a large amount of computing power.

EDITING MOVING PICTURES – VIDEO DIGITISERS

ICT can be used to edit moving pictures in a similar way to editing still pictures. A video digitiser is used to convert an analogue video picture into a digital computer image. A video camera is used to produce a picture. The digitiser, a combination of hardware and software, converts the analogue video signal into a digital signal in the computer's memory. Each frame from a video is converted so that it can be played back or printed in any required sequence. The stored image can be used in the same way as any other graphic.

Video digitising is used to capture a frame from a video sequence so that it can be printed in a document or magazine, and in making television adverts and pop music videos.

Once a digital video signal has been captured, it can be manipulated and changed, and special effects can be added. There are a number of software programs now available for home and commercial use. Moving pictures require a large amount of memory. The development of DVDs has enabled the storage of over 4.7 gigabytes of digital information on a single disk. Larger capacity disks are being developed all the time.

Moving images are usually stored on DVDs in a format called DVI (digital video interface).

Veena has just purchased a DVD player for the Oliver family's digital TV. Some DVDs can store the equivalent of 26 CD-ROMs. DVDs can be used to store applications software, multimedia programs and full-length films. Gavin is pleased as nearly every movie produced is now available on DVD, and the picture quality is so much better than on the normal video. The manufacturing and distribution costs for DVDs are much lower than standard video, making them much cheaper to produce. DVDs are bringing very good picture and sound quality to Gavin's favourite films and are doing for movies what CDs did for music.

A DVD is very similar to a CD, but it has a much larger data capacity. A standard DVD holds about six or seven times more data than a CD. A DVD has enough room to store a full-length, MPEG-2-encoded movie, as well as a lot of other information.

A DVD can hold:

- up to 133 minutes of high-resolution video using MPEG-2 compression.
- soundtrack presented in up to eight languages in Dolby digital surround sound;
- subtitles in up to 32 languages.

DVD can also be used to store almost eight hours of CD-quality music per side.

DVDs are of the same diameter and thickness as CDs, and they are made using some of the same materials and manufacturing methods. Like a CD, the data on a DVD is encoded in the form of small pits and bumps in the track of the disc but the pits and tracks are smaller on DVDs than on standard CDs. Because of this, single-sided DVDs can store about seven times more data than CDs.

To increase the storage capacity even more, a DVD can have up to four layers, two on each side. The laser that reads the disc can actually focus on the second layer through the first layer.

Figure 1.80 *DVD player*

Even though the storage capacity on a DVD is very large compared with a CD, the uncompressed video data of a full-length movie would never fit on a DVD. If you think back to the section on animation, you will remember how a movie is a set of still pictures shown in sequence. A movie is usually filmed at a rate of 24 pictures (called frames) per second. This means that every second, there are 24 complete digital images displayed on the screen.

In order to fit a movie on the DVD, the manufacturers use what is called video compression. When movies are put onto DVDs, they are compressed using an encoded system called MPEG-2 format. They are then saved on the DVD disk. This compression format is a widely accepted international standard. The Oliver family's DVD player contains an MPEG-2 decoder, which can uncompress this data as quickly as they can watch it.

The MPEG encoder that creates the compressed movie file analyses each frame and decides how to encode it. The compression uses some of the same technology as still image compression does. It also uses information from other frames to reduce the overall size of the file.

MINIDISCS

Figure 1.81 *MiniDisc player*

Music is now sold in a number of different formats. MP3 and CDs are the most popular although DJs still prefer vinyl, and music tapes are also popular. The Sony MiniDisc is another popular format due to its size. A MiniDisc looks like a floppy disk but is square and smaller. MiniDiscs also use special compression software.

MiniDiscs are like a floppy disk in that you can record and erase files, but they hold about 100 times more data than a floppy disk.

MiniDiscs come in two forms:

- pre-recorded;
- blank and recordable.

MiniDiscs store digital music. Both CDs and MiniDiscs can store the same amount of music. A MiniDisc uses a digital compression technique called Adaptive Transform Acoustic Coding

Web browsers and e-mail

The most important business growth area at the moment is the Internet. There are two main parts to the Internet: the World Wide Web, where web pages are made available, and electronic mail.

WORLD WIDE WEB

Many businesses have their own web site where customers can find out about the firm's products. Customers can browse through the site and download information such as brochures and leaflets. A number of these sites enable on-line shopping to take place. In the next section of the book Edward designs a web site for his father Iain's company. You will have learnt earlier in this book how to search the Internet for information.

There are also a number of Internet-only businesses. These companies do not sell to customers through shops but only via their web site. Businesses that combine a traditional range of shops and Internet retailing are called 'bricks and clicks' companies.

To access a web site a user needs a way of connecting to the Internet. This is usually a modem connected to a telephone line and a piece of software called a *browser*. The browser displays the web pages.

Gavin has convinced his father that the Internet would help his business. He told him that the benefits of having a web site would be:

- customers can find out about the company and order products from home;
- the business can make contact with potential customers anywhere in the world;
- visitors to the site can download information from it.
- the Web will be cheaper to put product details on than send a printed copy of a brochure via the post;
- information on the company web site can be updated quickly and economically;
- online purchases do not need sales staff to take the order.

E-mail

Iain's business uses electronic mail (e-mail) to communicate with customers, suppliers and other employees.

E-mail is a way of sending and receiving computer data across the telephone network. Simple e-mail messages contain just plain text but it is also possible to attach complete files from any other software.

One way that firms use e-mail is to exchange copies of documents. For example, a marketing manager might prepare a draft version of a report investigating the possibility of launching a new product. This draft report is e-mailed to a number of people in the marketing department. They then read the report, add comments to it and e-mail it back to the manager. The manager reads the comments and prepares a final version of the report.

The main benefits of using e-mail are as follows:

- e-mail can be used to send a message instantly to another person anywhere in the world, as long as they have an e-mail address;
- multiple copies of e-mails can be sent to lots of different people; this is much cheaper than posting thousands of copies of a mail-shot;

- businesses can use e-mail to communicate directly to their employees;
- e-mail can be used to send copies of computer files; these are linked to the basic message and are known as attachments;
- e-mail can be much cheaper than using the postal service.

As well as the Internet, a company can use other communications technologies:

VIDEO-CONFERENCING

Also known as teleconferencing, this enables people in different locations to see and talk with each other. The main equipment needed is a video camera and microphone, a display monitor and a modem to transmit the data across the telephone network.

One benefit of video-conferencing is that people no longer need to travel to meetings. They can stay in their office and hold the meeting with different people in different offices.

This reduces business costs because travel and accommodation are not needed.

WEB-PAGE DESIGN

Web pages are a way of presenting information to viewers on the World Wide Web. Most of the rules for good presentations apply, except that a speaker will not be present and different pages can be connected in various ways by using hyperlinks.

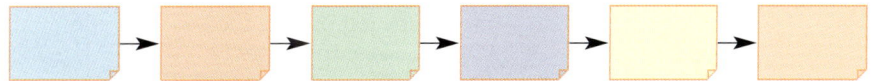

Figure 1.82 *Links between web pages*

The best way to think about a web site is as a series of interlocking pieces of information. This is unlike the way information is displayed in a conventional presentation, where you start at the beginning and sequentially work your way to the end although in reality on a web site, people jump backwards and forwards using hyperlinks.

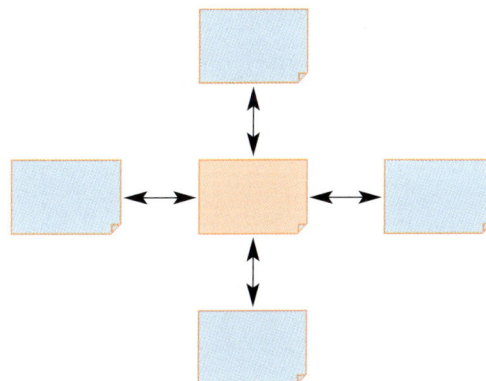

Figure 1.83 *Hyperlinks*

WEB-SITE DESIGN

Main features of web pages	Business examples
Web page: these can display text and images both moving and still	Iain's business website includes text and photographs of its products
Links can be made to animated images and sound files. These are called embedded files	An online music store could let customers hear a short extract from a song before they make a purchase or film company could embed a trailer for the film
Hyperlinks can be added. These are links to other web pages on the web site and elsewhere on the World Wide Web	Could be used to link to pages providing technical information about the product or search engine. Only those people interested in the linked pages need to go there
You can add drop-down menus. These work like the menu bar on most computer software. Selecting the drop-down menu reveals a list of options from which to make a choice	An online computer store can ask customers to choose from a list of add-on software bundles or computer company to design their own computer on-line
Forms can be added; these enable the web site to collect information from the user. They work just like the data capture form on a database.	The customer completes an online order form and can automatically buy goods online
You can use a counter to display how many visitors have viewed the website. Most counters work by depositing cookies onto the user's computer	The business can display how popular its website has been or how many visitors it has had this month or even how many orders for any given product
You can gain information from cookies which are small text files placed by the web site on to the user's computer. These help the web site recognise the user when they next visit the site	The website can customise its appearance for individual users. For example, an online bookshop could display on its homepage special offers in the customer's favourite category of books and CDs

DESIGNING A WEB SITE

You can explore how Edward designed his father's web site in the next section of the book. Most software can be used to create simple web pages containing hyperlinks. These pages must be saved as HTML files before they can be viewed on a web browser. HTML is a markup language that was created with the purpose of displaying documents in the form of web pages. As stated earlier in the book HTML stands for HyperText Markup Language.

SO WHAT IS A MARKUP LANGUAGE?

All software uses markup to say how things will be presented. An easy example of the use of markup is in the word-processing application you looked at earlier in the book. In a word-processed document, there is a page of text. Some of the text might be in bold, italics, or of different sizes from other sections. Somehow the program has to record this when it saves the file so when you open it up again you can display the file on the screen or print out the document. It is markup, which tells the program when each section starts and ends – for example, 'begin some bold red text here' and 'end some bold blue text here'. This information isn't seen by you, but it does control how the document is displayed and printed.

HTML works in the same way, using opening and closing instructions, which instruct the browser how to show, or display, the document. Much of HTML is relatively easy to learn, as many of the 'tags' it uses are easy to understand terms. For example:

<font colour = "blue">

HTML *isn't* a programming language as such as it doesn't need compiling or any special software. To make it you can use any text editor, although it is much easier to use a specialist web design program.

CAD/CAM AND IMAGE CREATION SOFTWARE

Computer Aided Design (CAD) is a system used to create a computer drawn design of an artefact.

Computer aided manufacture (CAM) is a system used to control the operation of production equipment. This enables high quality standardised products to be made.

The two systems are often linked together. CAD produces the design and CAM manufactures the final product.

The main benefits to a business of using CAD software are as follows:

- designs can be drawn much more quickly and accurately than by hand;
- designs can be edited and manipulated quickly;
- drawings can be rotated and resized; this enables the design to be viewed from different angles and distances;
- designs can be saved and reused to help produce future designs;
- designs can be sent to a client very quickly as an email attachment.

Advanced CAD software may also have the following features:

- The CAD software can calculate the cost of an artefact based on the components specified in the design. The effect that changing the design makes to the final cost can then be calculated.

- The software can suggest suitable materials and a design for the artefact. For example it could suggest that a roof of a certain size must have supporting walls of a particular strength.
- The software can simulate the performance of the artefact under certain environmental conditions. For example, it could show whether a building could withstand a hurricane.

CAM software controls the operations of manufacturing equipment. For example, when cutting shapes from a sheet of cloth, the software could organise how to cut the maximum number of pieces with the minimum waste, taking into account the weave and pattern of the cloth.

Other features of CAM software include:

- specifying the size and depth of holes to be drilled; the CAM software will ensure that all holes are cut to within a specified tolerance level;
- specifying speed of production; for example, how many holes can be drilled in one minute;
- order of machine processes; for example, cutting certain pieces before others, or drilling pilot holes before the final hole size;
- carrying out a range of processes one after the other with no need for intervention from the operator; for example, machining a chess piece from a blank of material;
- the ability to work at much higher speeds than manual machining.

MACROS

When designing software systems for companies to use, designers often use macros. Macros can be used in most of the software described in this section of the book. A macro is a sequence of commands and keystrokes that has been recorded and saved by the software. You can easily play back a macro at any time, achieving the same result as if you had entered each command and keystroke individually.

For example, you could create a macro that:

- converts an entire word document from single-spaced to double-spaced;
- goes through a document and formats the first word of each paragraph in 22 point italics;
- saves the document to disk and then prints it in draft mode.

As you can see, macros are very useful as they save time and can be used to maintain a company house style. The simplest way to create a macro is to enter the keystrokes and commands yourself while your software records them just like a tape recorder would do. The only operations that Word for Windows cannot record are mouse editing actions. That is, a macro cannot record the mouse moving the insertion point or selecting text. The operator must use the keyboard for these actions while recording a macro. On the other hand, other mouse actions, such as selecting menu commands or dialogue box options, can be recorded in a macro.

ICT systems in organisations

Case study

Staff at BT

The growth in the use of ICT has led to a number of new jobs. As more companies rely upon the use of ICT it is becoming more and more important to ensure that the equipment and software are working. Any problems with the equipment and software can prevent the business from functioning, costing the companies large amounts of money. The time it takes to fix or repair the problem is crucial.

Sharon

Until very recently, I managed the BT internal Service Desk operation. The Service Desk is like a call centre that can give help to any employee of BT who calls in with a computer, software, or systems problem. The Service Desk is spread over four BT sites, at Preston, Thurso, Liverpool and Exeter, and I am in charge of co-ordinating the entire service. There are about 78 people to answer calls, including four supervisors, and I have to make sure that staff with the right skills are always available. The people phoning in need their equipment or software fixed as quickly as possible, whatever time of the day or night it is. The Preston Desk is open 24 hours a day, seven days a week, and I must always know who is off sick, or away on leave, and what shifts each person can work.

   Not all of the staff who answer calls at the Service Desk are BT staff. Some work for agencies and are on contract to BT, but our policy is to treat each person in exactly the same way in terms of training and team-building. Our target is to answer 86% of all calls coming in, within 30 seconds, and we normally achieve that target. We train each person answering calls to have the knowledge and confidence to answer almost every call without needing to refer to anyone with more specialist knowledge. They need to know about both hardware and software problems. However, if a really tricky problem appears, we have a small number of people called floor walkers who have more specialised ICT knowledge and move around the Service Desk room to give a second opinion if it is needed. The floor walkers also monitor and analyse calls to check that targets are being met and that appropriate solutions are being offered to callers' problems. We find that it is most often hardware problems that have to be referred for a second opinion and may take some time to solve.

Each Service Desk operator is called an analyst, and I would say that the most important skill for an analyst is customer care. You need to know how to deal with frustrated callers, and how to listen carefully. Often, an important business deal may be affected by a computer problem, and the caller may be in danger of losing a lot of money if the equipment cannot be made to work. He or she may be very upset when first calling our Desk.

When a new recruit joins our Service Desk with good basic computer skills, she or he has a period of six to eight weeks' training in the hardware, software and applications used by BT. He or she will work alongside a 'buddy' who is already an experienced analyst, and will gradually begin to take calls as the training progresses. When she or he is finally ready to work independently, she or he will sit near a supervisor at first. The supervisor can monitor progress and offer help as soon as it is needed.

Every analyst has access to our web-based 'Book Server'. This contains information on all procedures and on the 1,040 internal BT applications that people may need help with. The information is updated three times a week so analysts can rely on its accuracy.

I started as an analyst myself. I became a supervisor, then joined our commercial section for a time, before managing the Service Desk. It is easier for me to make decisions about the management of the Service Desk because I understand each aspect of the job.

Whenever BT introduces a new application to its range, analysts will receive a training course to update them. Each Service Desk group is allocated one week's training in three as required for the job. Training may be in house – our analysts take external exams.

The balance of my staff is mixed. All of the supervisors are female, while more than half the analysts are male. The male staff are very interested in technical improvement, while the women are more interested in multi-skilling – the social, people skills as well as the subject knowledge. An important skill is to know your own level of competence, and to have the confidence to ask for help when you need it. Our floor walkers need to be sensitive with analysts. They must be approachable and must not make an analyst feel stupid if he or she does not know the answer to a hardware or software problem.

We monitor all the calls we receive. Part of the aim of call monitoring is to try to reduce the number of calls. We try to spot problems that occur regularly, so that they can be put right before people call in to the Service Desk. We receive 1.8 million calls per year. If a big problem occurs, such as the outbreak of a powerful virus, we put a 'front-end message' on our telephone system that lets everybody know that we are aware of the problem and dealing with it as fast as possible. The 'front-end message' may carry instructions about steps to take. However, despite these messages, many worried callers still want to hear a human voice at the end of the phone to tell them that it will be all right.

Being an analyst is high-pressure work. Each person has a five-minute break every hour, and fifteen minutes each morning and afternoon, plus one hour for lunch. Not everyone is suited to the stress involved in the job, but it can be very rewarding and fulfilling too. I am on call one weekend in four to help sort out problems. A growing number of BT employees work from home, and, for such a person, his or her laptop is 'god' – the whole business depends on it. Our Service Desk has a huge responsibility to help all BT workers to the best of its ability.

I find sometimes that it is very hard to juggle the demands of a full-time job and two young children. Sometimes I have to travel, to visit the Service Desks at the outer BT sites, and I work long hours. The Preston office, where I am based, handles **all** incoming calls after 17.30, so analysts are busy all through the evening and night. My husband and I try to balance our work so that we are not both away at the same time, and sometimes I have to take my laptop home to finish my day's work after I have put the children to bed. BT allow me to work flexible hours, as long as I get my job done, and I get a lot of support from my father and my sisters.

Despite background virus protection running all the time, a new virus can cause real problems for our analysts. Viruses travel from east to west around the world, according to the time zones, so our analysts usually first hear of a new virus during the night, when someone further east informs them. If we are lucky, a 'fix' can be put in place to deal with the virus before all UK offices open in the morning. There was one virus, for example, that deleted the first 50 addresses in the global address list, so the 'fix' that we developed was to insert 50 dummy addresses in front of all the genuine ones, so that the virus deleted only the dummy addresses.

I joined BT as an operator on the Directory Enquiries service after undertaking a two year HNC in Business Studies when my first child was three. I had left school without any particular qualifications. The HNC work was fascinating and involved a project on Manchester Airport that I really enjoyed. I found the assignments hard, with a young child to look after, but my friends helped a lot. Now, my new role within BT involves supervising conformity across all the BT offices. I work out a communication plan that covers the whole year, so that everyone knows the dates for management meetings, team meetings, team briefs and one-to-ones. Good communications skills are vital to me. No matter how good all the technology is, it is the people who make a good company.

Amanda

My job title is Group Commercial Manager for Bespoke Services. BT offers a full computer, systems and software service to commercial customers, and this is called Bespoke Services. A client can call us and tell us their business requirements, and we will then offer the best solution that we can produce. Usually a client will approach BT competitors too, and we have to tender our solution. The best one wins. We offer total support for ICT use including full technical backup to keep the systems working.

I have a staff of about one hundred people, including three managers. One team is multilingual. I have people who can speak French, German, Spanish and Italian, and this can be very useful if we are tendering for ICT support work with European companies. My analysts produce and maintain solutions for our customers, and answer all their queries.

An example of one contract that BT won and now operates takes care of all bookings for a major hotel chain. We have a team of 22 people and a manager in Exeter to support this contract. It is vitally important that the system is kept working. If there are any problem delays in repairing the fault they can cost the business large amounts of money.

My analysts provide support of all kinds at all levels – the customer can have exactly what is required for the best running of the business. Our customers buy Service Level Agreements with BT, that define the level of response that they will get from us, and their priorities, based on the likely impact to their business. For example, it might be vital for one particular company director to have e-mail working all the time so that she or he can remain in contact with offices around the world. Another manager might have a quite different priority. In a retail situation, the manager would want electronic payment systems working at full capacity all the time.

I think that customer skills are most important for my teams. You need to know how to develop a relationship with a client in order to put a contract together. You also need to know how to develop customer loyalty, and to maintain BT's reputation. You want to know that a customer will come back to BT. You need to be intuitive about a customer's requirements, to enable the customer to carry on their business while exploiting the technology in the best possible way. For me, co-ordinating and organising skills are very important too. I work with a lot of other divisions of BT to pull contracts together.

One of my duties is trend analysis. I analyse the nature of calls that we receive and produce a management level report. I recommend training that would help us to provide a better service. Our aim is always to help people to exploit technology. You do not need to know all the detail of **how** it works, but you do need to know how to **use** it.

I have worked for BT for 16 years. I left school and completed a computer programming course. I did not think I was very good at programming, but after my course, I worked in accounts, and then spent some time in Israel, working with horses. Back in the UK, I joined BT as a mainframe operator at first. I used to correct programs and schedule jobs, and then I moved to access control. In a big organisation like BT, the question of who has access to which systems and files is very important. I am now a licensed NVQ assessor and have a three year commitment to looking after a Modern Apprentice. This young person joined BT straight from a local school, and has made great progress under the apprenticeship scheme. When the apprenticeship is finished, she will have a good, well-paid job with BT, with excellent career prospects.

I really enjoy helping people to develop, watching them make progress. With the apprentice, my role is a bit like a work mother. I watch every step she makes in the company, and discuss her progress in monthly one-to-one meetings with her.

I find it difficult sometimes to balance my busy working life with the needs of my home, with two children growing up. I have to travel a lot too, and we have a one in seven rota for being on call when we are out of the office. I find that I have to take some work home with me. For example, I normally write the regular assessments for my apprentice at home.

Communication skills are vital in my job. Being objective is also really important. It is not uncommon for me to receive 100 mail items in a day, and I need to prioritise. I use quarterly staff reviews to motivate my staff and encourage empathy and customer service skills. I undertake feasibility presentations for old and new clients, and service reviews for current clients. Networking skills can be very useful here. Good relationships with people inside and outside BT can lead to better chances for more work for BT. I tell my staff to foster human contact with their customers. I tell them that, even when a contract is running along smoothly, they should still make contact from time to time for a friendly chat. Sometimes I have to counsel people who are feeling very pressurised by their work and I tell my staff that it is always important to have a laugh at the end of the day, to try to see the funny side of things. It would not help our work to be serious all the time.

How and why organisations use ICT

Most organisations use ICT in some aspects of their work. In this section of the book you will investigate how the family members use ICT in a range of working contexts. This will help you to understand how and why organisations use ICT. Companies don't just use ICT for the fun of it. ICT systems are designed to meet particular organisational needs. The ICT aims to help the company function more efficiently. In the first section of this book you learnt how to identify the components used in an ICT system and how to describe their contribution to the overall purposes of the system. Organisations use ICT systems according to their needs. The needs of some organisations are met by the limited use of ICT. However, many organisations have a variety of needs that are met by extensive use of ICT systems.

For example, Veena went to hire a DVD from a rental shop. The shop uses a database system to link customer records to rental records. This means that, for example, fines can be calculated for late returns, DVD rental trends can be monitored and targeted mail shots can be produced. Veena gave her membership card to the assistant who entered the number into the database and asked her security password before checking there were no outstanding DVDs or videos and scanning in the number on the DVD from the barcode. The database system used by the shop is quite simple compared to the complex systems used in Iain's company. Integrated database, spreadsheet and other dedicated software systems calculate pay, profit and loss and a wide range of other important business functions. The company is even considering a web-based ordering system.

In this section of the book you will also learn how to apply the knowledge you have to designing a system for a business need. You will also explore ways of recording your work using system flowcharts.

You should remember from the first section of the book how ICT systems need clear, precise and accurate information presented in the correct order to be able to function effectively. You need to be able to describe the information requirements of a system and design a system of your own drawing upon the information in the first section of the book. To this you will add knowledge about broad characteristics of businesses outlined in the case studies, such as information about production, sales and finances, as well as specific details such as data formats or sampling rates where appropriate. For example, the customer database for the rental shop should include 'Date of Birth' information to prevent customers renting DVDs which they are not old enough to watch, and the detailed design should specify the format of the 'Date of Birth' field.

You will also learn about the main components used to design an ICT system and how to design, implement and test a system and represent it graphically.

DESIGNING SYSTEMS

Edward's design for his father's web site

Designers use a structure to help them to design systems. When you design your own system it is important that you demonstrate the 'Process'. Edward had once been given a guide to designing systems by his teacher. It broke the design process into five important stages.

Stage 1 identify

- Identification is the recognition of a problem or task or aim. Edward needed to carry out a preliminary study to decide exactly what his father's problems/task/aims/objectives were.

Stage 2 analyse

- Edward knew he would have to conduct research relating to his proposed solution – interview the prospective users to find out what they want, list/explain the inputs; list/explain the processes and what would be stored; list/explain the outputs and expand each task by relating your proposed solution to the problem.

Stage 3 design

- The next stage would be to produce a diagrammatic overview (system flowchart) of the site as a whole to show how the layout, inputs, processes and outputs relate to each other then redefine default values such as page orientation, columns etc.

Stage 4 implementation

● Edward knew that the next stage would be to take the design and build it.

Stage 5 evaluation

Edward had to conduct a detailed evaluation by:

● asking a user/an outsider/expert;
● seeing if his work solved the original problem/task/need;
● saying how his solution could be improved.

Edward was designing a website for Iain, his father's, company. He followed his teacher's guidance very carefully. This is how he set about he task.

The first task was analysing the needs of the company.

ANALYSIS

The thing Edward undertook was to describe his father's business/organisation at the moment. He described what it sells, what it does etc. He also stated who its customers/users are. He used a simple layout to present his findings using a word processor.

The second task was describing how the business promotes itself at the moment.

Edward found that his father Iain's company promotes itself at the moment by word of mouth, newspapers, advertisements and leaflets. Most of the business came from regular customers his dad knew very well. The company also used representatives to visit its regular customers.

Edward described all of the other ways his father's company could promote its business.

Edward decided his father's company could get more business if it advised further using mail shots, sponsorship to gain publicity, offering free samples through trade organisations (or other places), money-off coupons to regular customers, specialist trade magazines, telephone calling, billboards and the Internet.

Edward was keen to help his father to focus upon what the company wanted to do in terms of getting better and how this would affect the business.

After visiting his father's company and talking to his dad over breakfast, Edward decided that the business needed to reach a wider audience, keep up with what the competition was doing, sell more, use surplus space/time/facilities, make use of new ICT technology, cut costs etc.

Edward was keen to find out what potential consumers or users wanted from a web site.

Edward interviewed a group of potential consumers/users of his father's business to find out what they might want in a web site. He asked questions about content, colour, organisation of site, features, what would get people to revisit site, how important is changing/up dating site regularly etc.

He explored a range of possible concerns about using the Web.

Edwards father was a little worried about what was going to be on the site. He had to consider the data/information that might appear on the site and how it would be collected through the site. Edward wanted people to join an online community and give membership details, orders, e-mails etc. via the Web, but his father thought some of the data could be very sensitive and valuable to competitors.

'Who will control the web site, who will check that the data is correct, who can access the data that might be collected, how is the data collected to be used, what ways can people make sure that the data the business has on them is correct or is removed when requested?' asked Iain.

At this point Edward explained to his father the basic points of the law entitled the Data Protection Act.

Edward produced a **feasibility** report for his father. He listed the objectives for creating the web site plus points made above. He used a word processor described in the first section of the book and made full use of facilities such as bullet points. His feasibility report stated what he intended to do and not the final result. As part of the feasibility report Edward used the process diagram also shown in the first section of the book.

Input, **process** and **output** – Edward wrote down exactly what he expected each section to do.

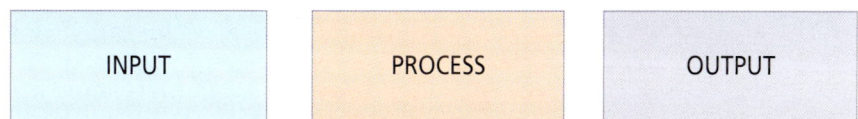

INPUT	PROCESS	OUTPUT

Figure 2.1 *Input–output system*

Edward looked in detail at what parts of the web site would need to be updated regularly and the others that needed infrequent updating.

Edward decided that some parts of his father's web page(s) would need to be updated regularly and some parts of the web page(s) would be changed every so often. He listed the information that was needed on the web site in two columns with these headings.

The next task was deciding the web page 'outline'. He listed what he intended to place on each page, giving a rough idea of the layout, noting the images, text, pictures, links he intended to put in. Based on his analysis of the business/organisation, initial research and his own ideas he listed what he intend to have on each web page.

He told his father where he expected to have problems. In particular, he expected difficulties in obtaining the right images, sounds and text he was looking for. He explored other web sites to get ideas.

Edward stated what hardware and software he would need.

First he stated what **questions** he would use to form the basis for the hardware/software selection needed for this work. He used a hardware/software catalogue to list the software and hardware options, specifying **exactly** what is input, and output. Everything was listed, including mice etc. He mentioned the computer specifications needed to achieve what he wanted to achieve and why. He compared and contrasted the ideal system with what you actually have to work with in his father's office.

He explored a range of different software that could be used to prepare web pages.

He looked at HTML, specific web packages like FrontPage, translation software like Publisher, web authoring sites like Geocities. He also gave the advantages and disadvantages for the systems, remembering there is no **right** or **wrong** way but detailing his reasons for the final selection. Edward discussed the different package(s) that could be used to create the web pages (Word, Publisher, FrontPage, Hotdog, Dream Weaver, Excel, WYSIWYG or HTML editor). Some packages included template ideas but he decided not to use these.

He stated what other packages and peripheral hardware he would use to help with the page construction.

He included packages like Paint Shop Pro and Photoshop, listing the reasons why. He decided he would need a scanner and digital camera and stated why. He outlined other peripheral devices that would be used including a drawing tablet and web cam. As he wanted to copy images from other sites, he explored how to get the permission from those who own images (e.g. trade marks) and how to place links to other sites.

Edward drew up a timetable. He made a detailed timescale to achieve production of the website, dividing the whole process (system) into bits and giving reasons for doing this. His timetable stated what he intend to achieve and by when.

He also stated how he intended to evaluate the finished product.

The evaluation took the form of asking questions to those who might use or view the site.

RESEARCH

Edward spent a long time researching other web sites used by the packaging industry to get ideas on their use of the Internet. He told his dad that looking at the competition was always an early step in the analysis and research part of designing a new site. He wrote down **all** his comments, making a note of the web addresses of the sites he visited.

His notes stated why he liked or disliked that particular site and how what he found could help design his father's site. He looked at sites which people had praised, asking his friends and relations what made them a 'good' site?

Iain wanted to retain the corporate identity of his company. The company had features, colours, shapes, sounds, words and images, which he wanted to maintain as the business customers were used to these things. Edward decided to visit the company to observe, talk to people, take photos, collect leaflets and adverts to help get a 'feel' of his father's organisation.

Once all the research was complete Edward could start to design the system. He did not use a computer yet as this part of the process does **not** require the use of a computer to produce actual pages. He did **not** start the actual web pages until the **implementation** stage. He used A4 and A3 paper plus some squared paper to sketch out the design for the web site based on the research he had done – he produced detailed sketches to present to his father and some of the people he had consulted to get their opinion of the best designs. He was very careful to follow the **specifications** and remember the **purpose** of the task.

He used a table to design the pages after working out the number of cells he needed and which were going to be merged, subdivided, narrowed or widened. He knew that the web page can be longer than the screen size but he had to bear in mind that people have different sized monitors (FrontPage – File Preview in Browser – 640×480, 800×600 and 1024×768).

Edward decided that it would be a good idea to draw a full table first, using light pencil lines for the cells/border, and go over with a heavier pencil to indicate which cells become permanent and which are merged, and draw in new lines to create narrow or subdivided cells. He had to remind himself constantly that the page had to work together and that there should be balance, and that empty space can be wasteful but necessary to give the page a good feel. He had to keep the purpose of the work uppermost in his design as well as the intended audience (in this case more than one person).

He decided to specify:

- what the text will be;
- where he was going to get the text content, 'borrowing' text, prices and dates from other publications **but** making sure he made it fit the intended audience.

Edward annotated his designs using close-up sketches or pictures around the edge of the main design and short notes with arrows explaining his plans and reasons.

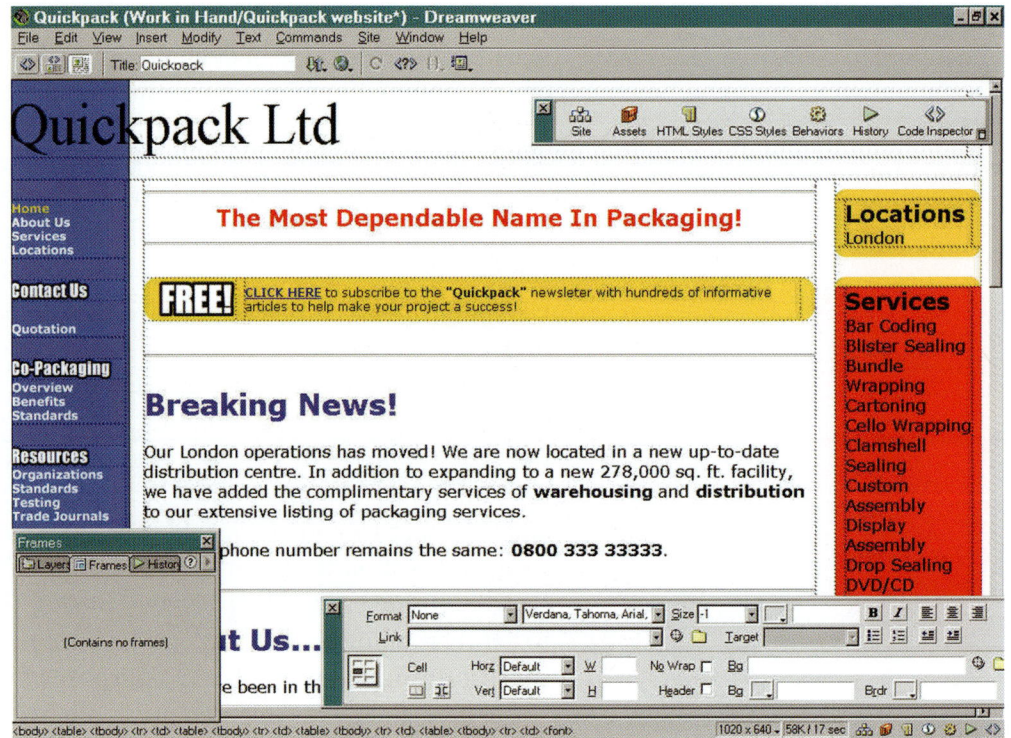

Figure 2.2 *Edward's web page design I*

He used this method to show:

- what background colours he wanted to use;
- what sized text and type of fonts he was going to use, giving reasons for his choice;
- the buttons and boxes he used for the hyperlinks, graphics and scanned pictures for effect.

He also remembered who was going to read the information on the web site – what about people with disabilities – how will they cope – giving reasons.

He stated clearly which parts of the website would be regularly changed. He produced instructions/notes (Word document) for the business/organisation – exploring how much text could go in the space, font, text size, length of line etc.

Once the design was complete and his father was happy with it, Edward started to **implement** the solution. At this stage Edward started to **construct** the site on his **computer** system. He decided to keep a **log** detailing what he did each time he worked on the site.

He entered the necessary information (text, numeric or image), copied information from other documents, used the scanner and digital camera, CD and Internet site.

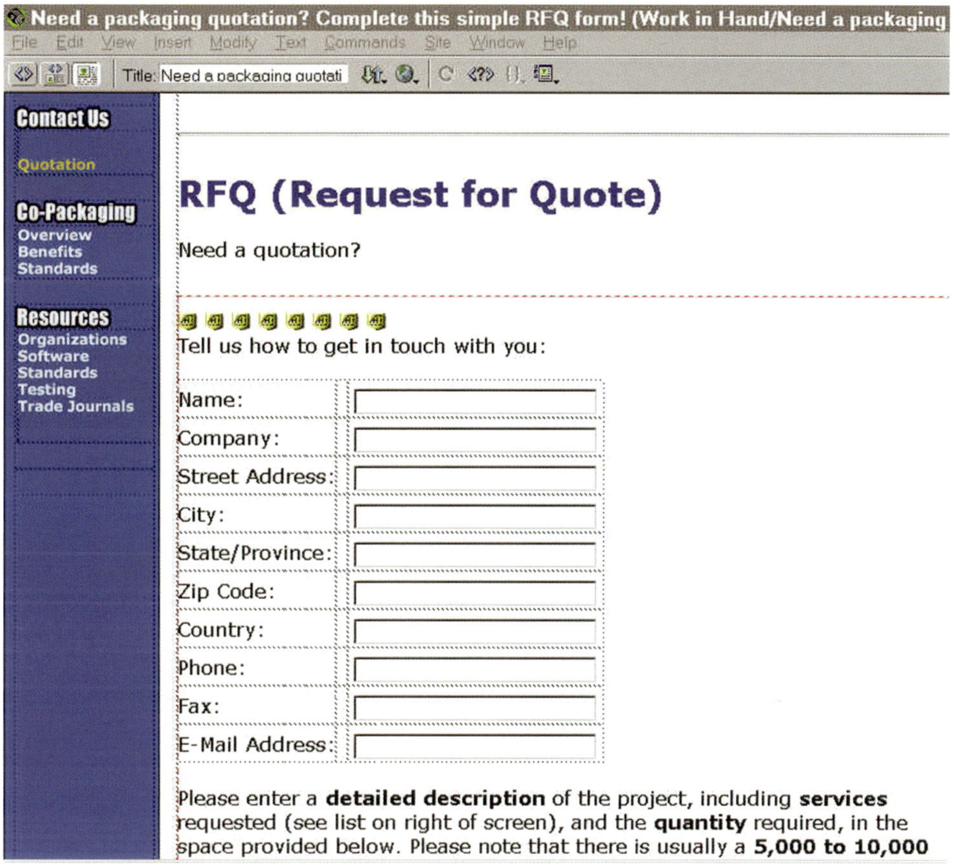

Figure 2.3 *Edward's web page design II*

He used **verification** (checking what was typed in was correct) and **validation** (errors in the data and not typing mistakes) checks to make sure everything was accurate.

He asked his mum Veena to proofread the document. As the work progressed his log showed how he had developed the information collected in the research stage to meet the purpose – changed font, text size and colour, altered or edited the content, added images, made use of web features like a marquee etc. He kept original data and pointed it out in the log, showing how things had been developed to meet the purpose of the task set by his father.

He also used the log to list **all** problems he had (including hardware and software) as he developed the site.

Once completed Edward printed out a trial version. He used **Print Screen** for each web page and then pasted into Word. He then annotated (using AutoShapes) his pages, giving comments as to the good and poor points – getting the views of other people – getting his dad and some regular customers to act as an audience. Each time he wrote down their comments. Then he produced a final version and annotated it.

He then turned his mind to producing **user** documentation for the person/people who would have to **administer** the site. He had to make it as easy as possible as he knew his father's staff did not have much experience in web work. He included **technical** documentation – how he could train the personnel who would administer the site. Finally he produced a report stating how the running of the site could affect the running of his fathers business.

This is what his notes looked like:

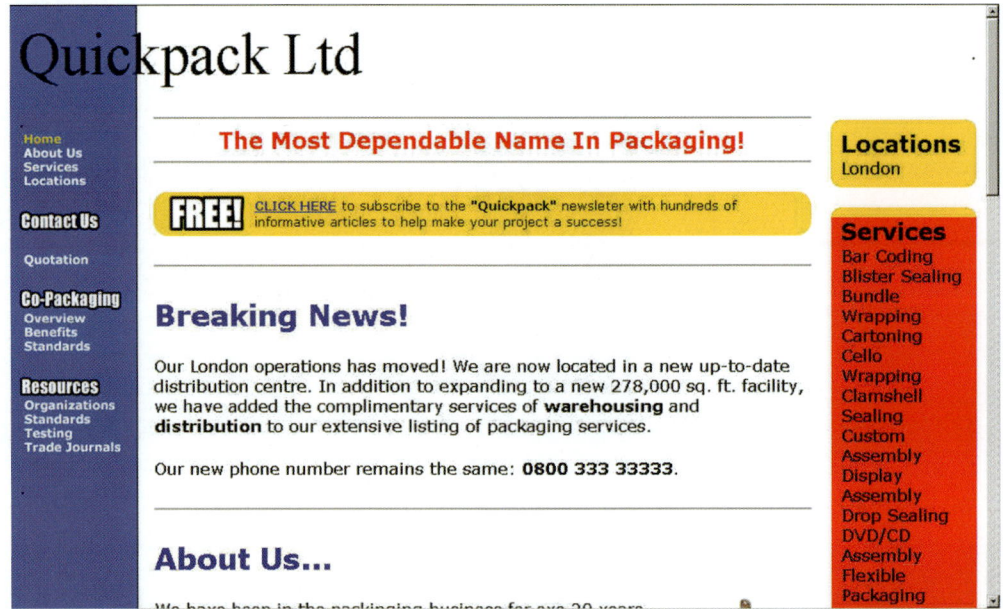

Figure 2.4 *Edward's web page design III*

The final task was an accurate **evaluation**.

Edward produced a report stating how the final product came out at each stage, remembering his original specifications and referring his comments back to them. He knew his dad would not accept comments like **good** on their own. He had to state **why** it was good or bad and relate his final product to the original specifications. He wrote down detailed comments according to his view, stating where the results were expected and where they were not.

Edward used a questionnaire he had constructed to get other people's opinions on the site and collated the answers.

Finally Edward listed what further things could be done in the future to improve the system and how and when the site should be updated.

Edward's father Iain was still worried about the security and confidentiality of the site. He was also worried about the effects the web site would have on his staff. Edward decided he would need to produce a report for his father on these things.

The first part of his report focused upon the changes to the working of the company and what form this could take (i.e. time to develop the site further, location of equipment in the firm, working practices, deskilling, further training for some personnel, need to employ a person who will keep the site up to date etc). He also discussed effects (health and working conditions) on the staff. You can read more about this in the next section of the book. He related all his comments to how **people** in the company would be affected and who could check the integrity of data on the new site. He re-evaluated the possible misuse of data to be put on the site – stating what data cannot be placed there and relating these comments to the **Data Protection Act**. He listed whose permission the company would have to get for using other people's data and images.

ROBOTICS

Of course not every business situation can be solved by an ICT solution. Edward made a good job of the company web site but sometimes got carried away with new ideas.

Rupa's friend Ivy worked at Iain's company, Quickpack Ltd, as a cleaner. She was a short, grey-haired woman, her face lined with years of hard work. In her ten years at the company, Ivy had swept and cleaned in every corner of every room. Edward was keen for his father to try out a new cleaning robot. Edward told his dad that in some situations, robots have a great advantage over people. His father was not convinced that a robot could do all of the jobs of a cleaner. Could it 'sweep floors; vacuum around things; open and close doors; polish desks, not disturbing people who are working; go for a coffee with a colleague, pick up things I have dropped, smile at me, empty bins; go up and down stairs; lock up after itself and deal with any unexpected events, for example close windows if it rains, turn off lights that have been left on, raise the alarm if there is a fire, tell me if something is wrong etc.?' asked Iain.

'Well, not all of these,' said Edward, 'but it can do jobs that are very repetitive. People get bored doing them, and a machine can do them more quickly and more cheaply, as is the case with folding boxes.

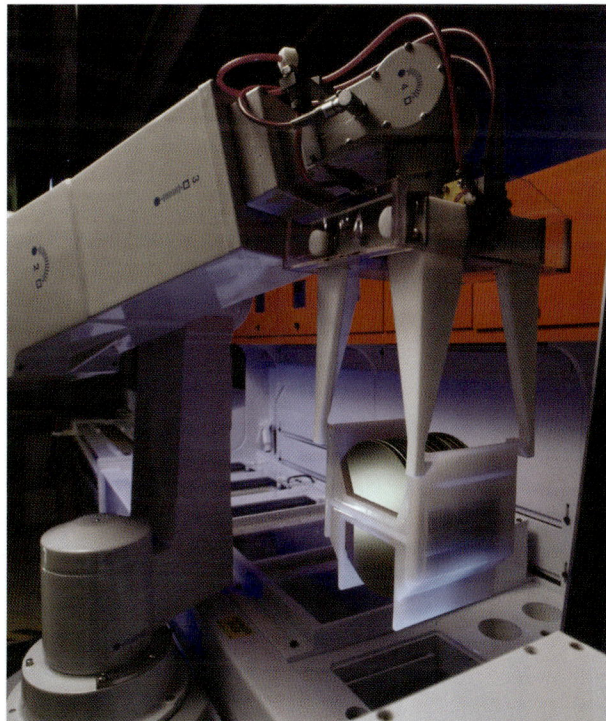

Figure 2.5 *Robot*

'Then there are jobs such as coal mining that are dirty and dangerous for humans,' he added. 'It can do this type of job easily.'

'But I need a cleaner,' stated Iain. 'Robots sound like they are best if they have a limited number of simple tasks to perform. Cleaning needs lots of different tasks in irregular sequences. The more the robot has to do, the more complicated and expensive it will be to build, and this will probably mean it will break down more often. I may look into using a robot in the warehouses to pick up and carry loads from one place to another, but Ivy stays.'

This time, Edward had forgotten the first rule of designing systems – to examine in detail the needs of the situation and the output requirements of any system you design.

To make sure designers understand what is needed they sometimes use a system flowchart.

SYSTEM FLOWCHART

A system can be represented using symbols. This is called a flowchart. Often when designing a system it is easier to work out all of the stages and put them in the right order by producing a flowchart.

There are standard shapes that designers use to represent different operations or actions in a normal flowchart:

Figure 2.6a *Command – an instruction to carry out an operation*

Figure 2.6b *Decision – a point where two or more options are available*

Figure 2.6c *Start or stop – the beginning or end of a series of operations*

In system design a designer can use a number of other standard symbols that represent stages or operations that are particular to using information systems:

Data point

Manual input of data

Card data storage

Multi document
production

Communication

Single document

Manual operation

Data storage

Display results

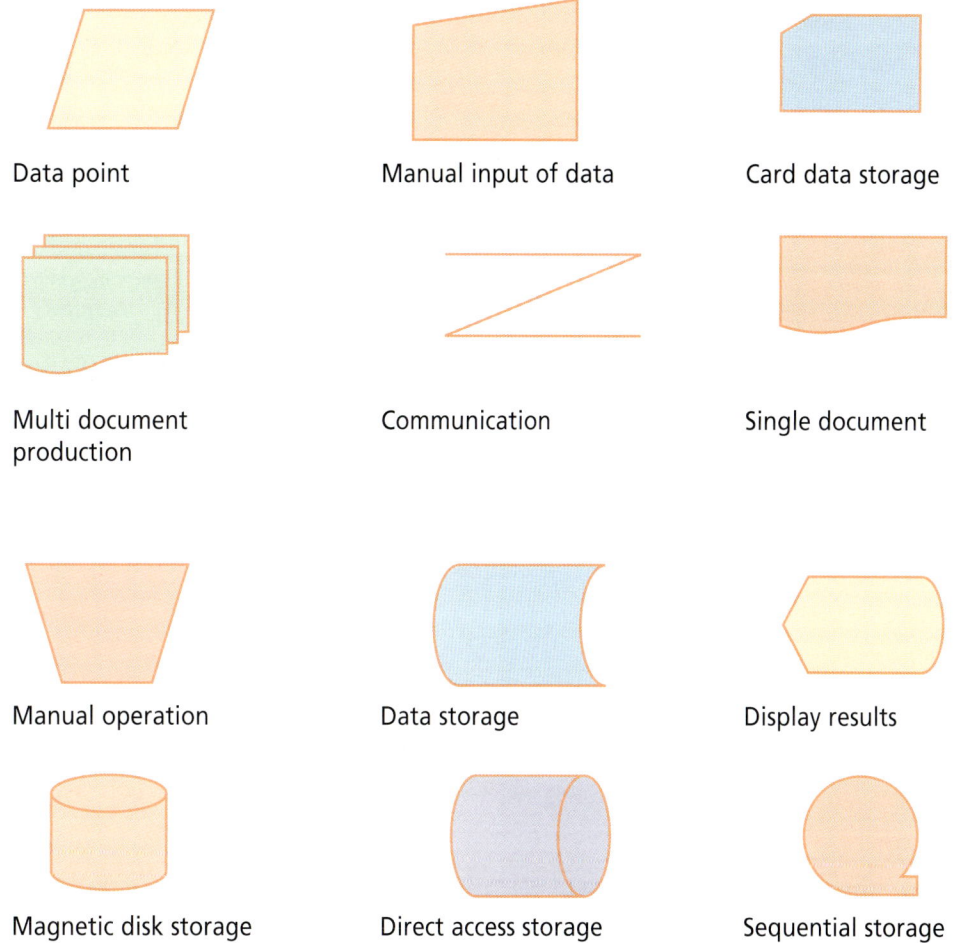

Figure 2.6d *Other standard
symbols for stages or operations
used in information systems*

Magnetic disk storage

Direct access storage

Sequential storage

The system flowchart overleaf shows the sequence of operations
carried out to record information about goods that are delivered to Iain's
company and the arrangements made to store these goods.

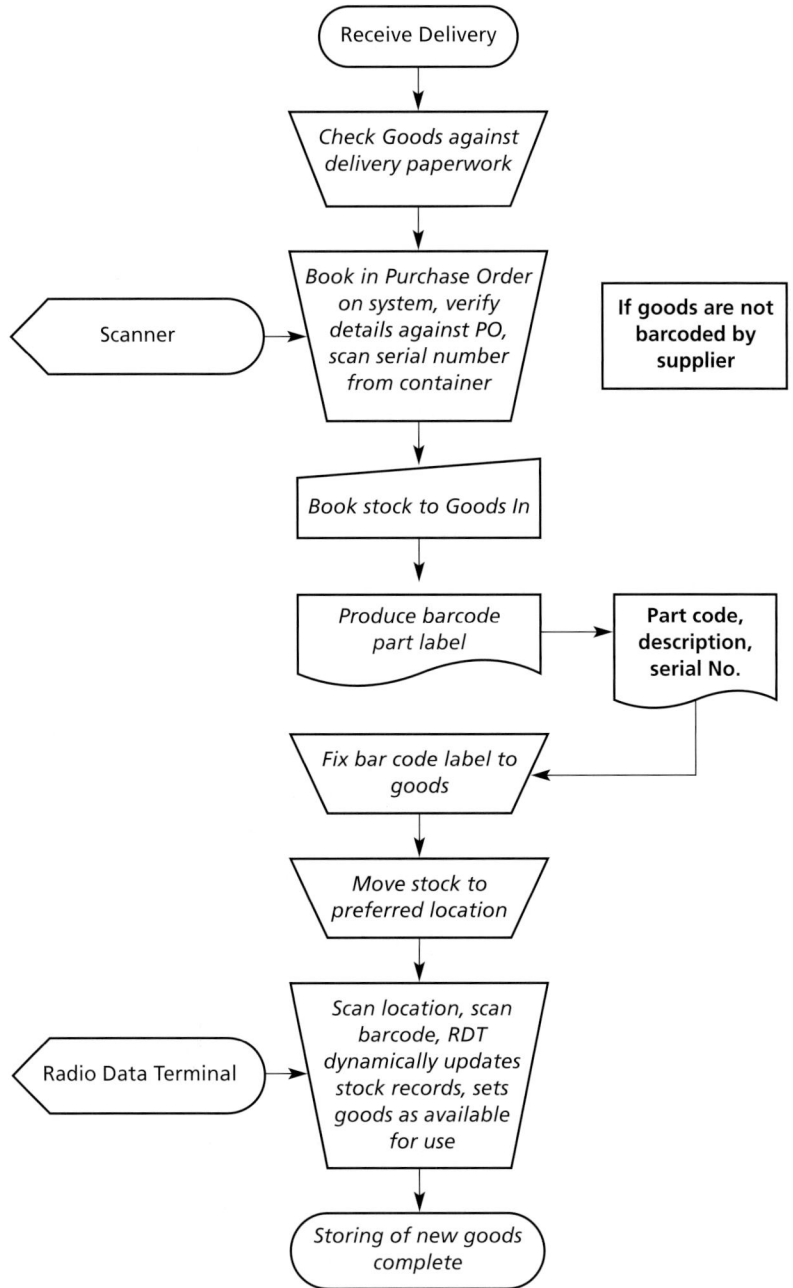

Figure 2.7 *System flowchart showing sequence of operations carried out to record information about delivery and storage of goods*

The operator is involved at various stages, either inputting data to record details of the goods, or to monitor the system itself:

Stage 1	The operator makes a manual check of the delivery note and purchase order against the goods themselves
Stage 2	The operator enters the details of the goods into the information system, and scans the bar code from the goods to keep the records up to date. If the goods are not bar coded, the data is entered manually using a keyboard
Stage 3	The goods are transferred to a holding location ready for dispatch to the appropriate point; details of the location are stored in the information system and produced as a document
Stage 4	The document is attached to the goods, containing a bar code with details of serial number and preferred storage location, for example, refrigerated
Stage 5	The goods are now moved to the preferred location, so that they can be stored until needed
Stage 6	The radio data terminal automatically updates the information system records following a scan of the new bar code. The information about the goods is transmitted to the appropriate users

The above example is relatively simple. It covers a short sequence of operations. Some system flowcharts can become very complicated, with a variety of paths through them depending upon certain situations and criteria.

The following example shows how data is recorded and used for control of a library system.

You will notice that this is made up from three separate routines. Each one can run independently of the other two. However, the strength of the system is how the three work together.

NB. It is important to notice the direction of the arrows in all system flowcharts, as they describe the sequence that operations will follow.

System (i)	
Stage 1	The operator scans the customer details from their swipe card
Stage 2	The book details are scanned from the bar code
Stage 3	The data from these two scans is held in active memory while validity checks are made, for example is the book on request from another customer?

System (ii)	
Stage 1	The customer returns a book and the details are entered into the information system

System (iii)	
Stage 1	Data from other systems are added to the customer file
Stage 2	All data files are stored in backup systems, disk based

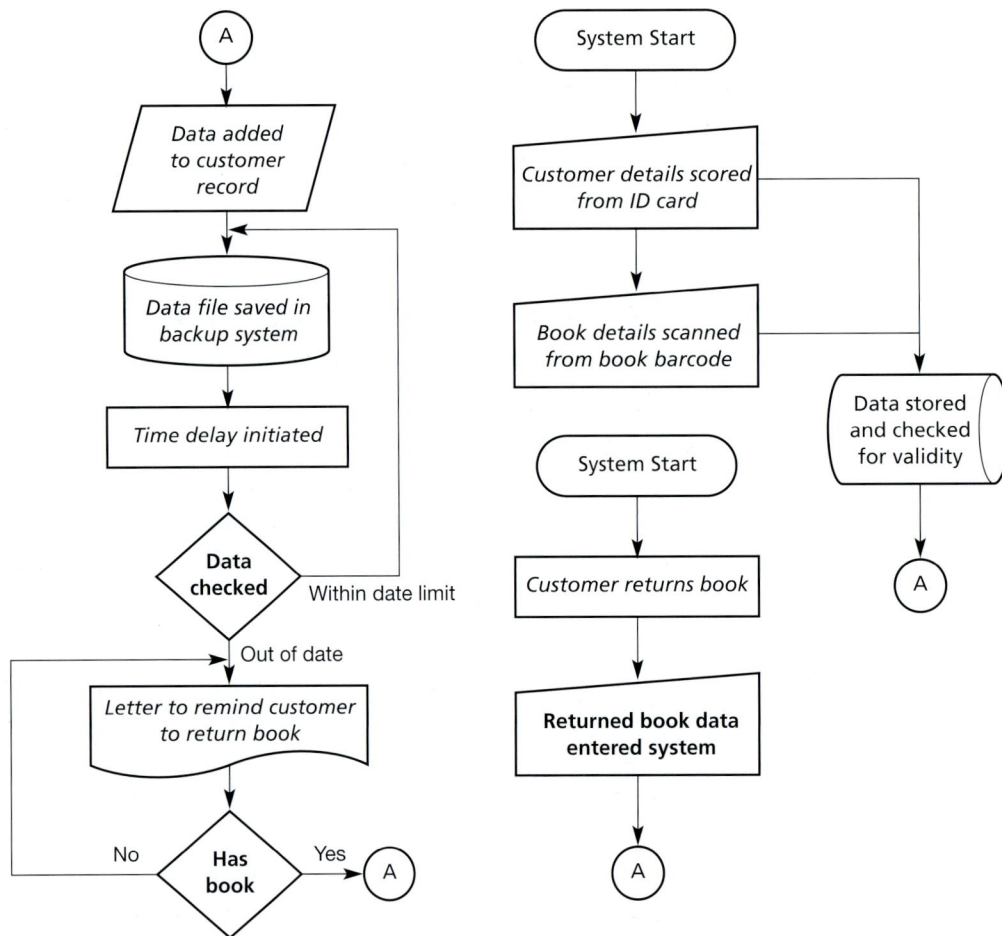

Figure 2.8 *System flowchart showing how data is recorded and used for control of library system*

Stage 3	Time delays are in place to check all files at regular dates, checking customer details and book records
Stage 4	Decisions are made regarding the duration of the book loan and the customer files
Stage 5	If the loan is within permitted time the system runs a loop back to stage 2
Stage 6	If the book is outstanding, a letter is sent to the customer using the data in the files for address and name etc.
Stage 7	A second check is carried out after a delay to check whether the book has been returned
Stage 8	If the book has been returned the data is updated at stage 1 and the system restarts
Stage 9	If the book has not been returned the system automatically sends a second reminder

Throughout these systems it is important that each element is carried out as needed and in accordance with the instructions that would be distributed to the operators. Any system is only as good as the operator that manages each stage.

Good system design often combines a number of operations into one stage. This makes the flowchart much simpler to understand, while still covering the same processes.

Paco's phone company, Mediacom Ltd

Paco works for Mediacom Ltd, a company that manufactures mobile phones. He is the supervisor of a production line. Trying to make sure that the maximum number of phones are made during each working day is always a problem. This is partly because businesses have to balance the needs of a number of interested parties:

- the owners of the company who want as much profit as possible;
- the employees working on the production line who want high wages;
- the suppliers of the parts that go into making up a phone, who want to be paid on time;
- the customers who want good value for money.

Paco is always getting frustrated by missing components, which stop his team from being able to assemble the phones, and by members of the team being off ill, which also disturbs production. Any slow down in production causes Paco stress – the company owners are not getting the financial return they expect, phone prices have to go up to cover the extra costs of manufacture, and there is not enough money to pay the workers the higher wages that they want.

Paco uses a number of ways to motivate his team. This is because, unlike computers and machines, which always work at the same rate, his workers produce far more telephones when they are motivated than they do when they are unhappy. One of the ways of motivating the workers is through pay. Paco knows that the more money they can earn, the better their standard of living will be. Paco uses a computer system to pay bonuses to workers who exceed the work rate, or production targets, while still achieving quality.

Alongside paying bonuses, Paco uses an ICT based bulletin board to improve communication with workers. Through a range of notices and e-mails, he uses the computer system and the company's Intranet to consult and praise members of the team.

Paco also uses the bulletin board system to allow workers to comment on how effective production methods are.

The bulletin board is also used to advertise opportunities for promotion. Paco uses a spreadsheet to rotate workers' jobs so that they do not get bored and under perform as a result of doing the same job all day and every day.

To help manage the production process, Paco uses a computer system. One of the main pieces of software is based on a spreadsheet.

A spreadsheet is organised into rows and columns. Paco and his colleagues use the spreadsheet:

- to decide when to order components and raw materials;
- to produce charts to display weekly production targets;
- to produce charts to show how individual workers are performing; against production targets;
- to perform simple calculations;
- to calculate workers' wages;
- to convert daily production totals into weekly or monthly projected totals.

The name given to the monitoring of workers' production is workflow analysis. Workflow analysis can cover the whole production system, from purchasing of materials to despatch of the finished product. One of the systems used by Mediacom Ltd is called JIT (Just In Time). This is also sometimes called product streaming.

As the components arrive at Mediacom, they are immediately logged into a computer database. The components are labelled with a bar code that contains the information such as date and time of delivery, and where the component is to be stored. Robotic trolleys carry the components to a storage area until they are needed. When they are needed, they are automatically transported to the appropriate area of the production workplace. When stock levels fall below set critical levels, replacements are automatically ordered.

Mediacom also uses the Internet to search for new suppliers. Years ago, they would choose their suppliers by meeting representatives from different companies, who would visit them with suitcases full of sample components. Now, orders are made over the Internet. The name for this is e-procurement.

Mediacom Ltd market their product on the Internet. Using the Internet has enabled the company to compete in a larger market. This is because the Internet has a world-wide audience. The cost of doing business on the Internet is much lower as the company does not need shops, but the Internet is also better for the customer who can compare prices.

CASH FLOW

The main problem faced by Mediacom Ltd is cash flow. The company had lots of orders last year but almost went out of business, as it could not pay the bills. The company was ordered by a court of law to sell some of its assets to raise the cash. Paco and his colleagues hope that the same problem will not arise again. Cash flow is the money that flows into and out of the business on a daily basis. It is needed to pay Mediacom's bills.

Mediacom Ltd got into problems because:

- Customers were not paying for their telephones quickly enough
- Raw materials for the telephones had increased in price
- Mediacom was paying its own bills too early.

In order to try and spot any potential cash-flow problems, Mediacom now produces a computerised cash-flow forecast for the next 6 and 12 months. To do this the Accounts department uses a spreadsheet model. The first step was to create a template. This included all the headings plus the formulae that can be used to calculate receipts, payments and the cash balance automatically. Once the template had been saved, the people in Accounts were able to enter their actual figures and calculate the cash balance.

	C	D	E	F	G	H	I	J	K	L	M	N
	February	March	April	May	June	July	August	September	October	November	December	Total
1												
2												
3												£5,000
4	£3,000	£3,000	£6,000	£6,000	£8,000	£8,000	£8,000	£6,000	£6,000	£6,000	£4,000	£70,000
5	£3,000	£3,000	£6,000	£6,000	£8,000	£8,000	£8,000	£6,000	£6,000	£6,000	£4,000	£75,000
6												
7												
8	£3,000											£8,000
9	£1,200	£1,200	£1,200	£2,000	£2,000	£2,000	£200	£200	£200	£200	£200	£17,000
10	£300	£500	£600	£500	£500	£100	£100	£000	£000	£500	£500	£8,000
11	£300	£300	£300	£300	£300	£500	£500	£500	£500	£300	£300	£4,000
12	£250	£250	£250	£250	£250	£250	£250	£250	£250	£250	£250	£3.000
13	£2,000	£2,000	£2,000	£2,500	£2,500	£2,500	£2,500	£2,500	£2,500	£2,500	£2,500	£28,000
14	£4,250	£4,250	£4,250	£5,950	£5,950	£6,750	£5,550	£5,550	£5,550	£4,750	£4,750	£??????
15												£0
16	£4,350	−£4,500	−£3,150	−£1,200	−£1,350	£700	£????	£4,400	£4,850	£5,300	£6,550	£0
17	−£3,250	£1,750	£1,750	£50	£2,050	£2,050	£2.050	£150	£150	£250	−£750	£5,800
18	£4,900	£3,150	£1,400	£1,350	£700	£1,950	£4,400	£4,850	£5,300	£6,550	£5,800	£5,800

Figure 2.8a *Mediacom cashflow spreadsheet*

In this example Mediacom is going to have a cash-flow problem between February and May. But in general its cash flow looks quite healthy. As a result it could probably convince its bank to give it an overdraft for the first six months of the year.

One benefit of using a spreadsheet is that Mediacom can carry out what-if analysis. One way would be for Accounts to change some of the numbers to try and see how they might be able to avoid a cash-flow problem in future.

LEGISLATION

Mediacom has to ensure that they are complying with a large number of external laws and regulations. A few of the laws they have to comply with are:

- Trade Descriptions Act 1968, which makes it illegal for them to give a false or misleading description of any of the telephones they are selling;
- Customer Credit Act 1974, which gives the company's customers 14 days after signing credit agreements to change their minds and cancel their order;

- Sale of Goods Act 1979, which states that the phones or any other goods sold must do the job that they say they can do, and that the components should work in a way that enables the phones to function correctly; the Act also states that if the phone does not meet these requirements, the customer is entitled to a full refund;
- Supply of Goods & Services Act 1982, which states that any work must be of a reasonable standard;
- Customer Protection Act 1987, which states that the company is liable to the customer for any problems that the customer experiences as a result of sub-standard work.

With all of these laws to consider, monitoring the quality of work is very important to Paco.

CAD/CAM

Mediacom Ltd has just introduced Computer Aided Design and Computer Aided Manufacture. This has made a big difference to the way the telephones are designed and made. In the past, a phone would be designed, and working drawings produced in a drawing office, often on the same premises as the manufacturing department. The drawings would then be passed to the workshop, where engineers would develop a method for producing the desired item.

With the advent of CAD, new phone designs can be produced anywhere in the world. Mediacom has started to use a specialist design company. The design company designs a phone and then converts the design into a computer file. This file is then emailed to Mediacom.

When Mediacom receives the file, it is fed into a computer controlled manufacturing system. The phone is then produced. As the file is specifically aimed at controlling the machines in the manufacturing base, little intervention is needed on the part of the engineers. Once the machines have been set up and the materials prepared, the software takes over. This means that Mediacom has had to re-skill its workforce. They now employ more technicians and fewer traditional engineers. The practical knowledge of manufacturing has been incorporated into the CAD and CAM software.

Iain's company, Quickpack Ltd

PAYMENT SYSTEMS

Iain uses a computer system to calculate the wages of the workers. The company has different workers, working on different payment systems. Most of the office staff receive a fixed salary. For example, Jane, the administration assistant, is paid £12,000 per year, which works out at £1,000 each month. The amount Jane receives is unrelated to her work performance. The benefit to Iain is that he knows exactly how much he has to pay Jane each month, and this helps him to work out his monthly costs.

Employees working in the packing area are paid in two different ways. Half of them are paid on time rates. They are given a set wage based on how many hours they work. The longer they work, the more they are paid. The main problem to Iain with this type of payment is that he needs to make sure that the workers are not lazy, and do not try to extend the number of hours they need to complete a job. The advantage to Iain is that he needs to employ people only for the number of hours needed.

The other half of the packing team are on piece rates. They are paid according to how much packing they do. Each item packed is worth a set amount. Checking the quality of the packing is vitally important to Iain as these workers will try to pack as much as they can in as short a time as possible. The worker may be paid a piece rate of 10p per package. So if the person packs 60 boxes in an hour they would earn £6.

Iain also has two representatives who go out to get new business. They are paid a basic salary which is supplemented by commission and bonuses based on the amount of work they bring in.

Iain also pays bonuses to the workforce. These are one-off payments to reward performance that meets a particular target. For example, if his workforce packs more than the target number set for the month he pays them a bonus of £200 each.

It would be impossible for Quickpack's Accounts department to calculate the wages of all these workers without a computer system.

Wages earned by the workers are called gross pay. Unfortunately, even having calculated the gross pay for the workers, Iain has to deduct income tax and National Insurance contributions before he can calculate how much each worker will take home.

Income tax is the main tax collected by the government and it is taken from everybody who earns a wage above a certain limit. It is even taken from the interest that employees earn from their savings. The most common way of paying income tax is called PAYE (Pay As You Earn). Iain has to use this system to deduct income tax from his workers' wages. Jane's £12,000 salary is taxed as follows:

Tax free allowance £ 4,385.00	Jane pays no tax on all earnings below £4,385.00.
First £1,520.00 of taxable income	Jane pays 10% of this income in tax.
Next £ 26,880 of taxable income	Jane pays 22% of all her remaining income in tax.
All remaining taxable income	Jane does not have to pay this as she does not earn enough money, but if she did, she would pay 40% of this income in tax.

The figures above show Jane's income during the tax year to 2001. Governments change the amounts of tax during budgets, and Iain regularly checks current rates on the Internet at *www.inlandrevenue.gov.uk* to ensure that he is calculating the correct amount of tax for each of his employees.

It is not only tax that Iain has to deduct. He has to collect National Insurance contributions from each worker and pay a contribution himself as the employer. During 2000–2001 tax year, he had to deduct 10% of Jane's gross **weekly** income between £76.00 and £535.00. Any of his workers who earned more than £535.00 paid the same National Insurance contribution, of £45.90 per week, regardless of their income.

Break Even Model

Fixed Cost	Min Number Sold	Variable Cost per Unit	Selling Price per Unit
3,000	0	6	12

Number Increment: 100

Number Packed	Fixed Cost	Variable Cost	Total Cost	Total Revenue
0	3,000	0	3,000	0
100	3,000	600	3,600	1,200
200	3,000	1,200	4,200	2,400
300	3,000	1,800	4,800	3,600
400	3,000	2,400	5,400	4,800
500	3,000	3,000	6,000	6,000
600	3,000	3,600	6,600	7,200
700	3,000	4,200	7,200	8,400
800	3,000	4,800	7,800	9,600
900	3,000	5,400	8,400	10,800

	A	B	C	D
1	Profit and Loss Account			
2				
3	Turnover		£500,000	
4	Less Cost of Sales			
5	Opening Stock	£25,000		
6	Purchases	£120,000		
7	Wages of workers	£100,000		
8		£245,000		
9				
10	Less Closing Stock	£18,000		
11			£227,000	
12				
13	Gross Profit		£273,000	
14	Less office expenses			
15	Office salaries	£130,000		
16	Loan repayments	£15,000		
17	Other expenses	£95,000		
18			£240,000	
19	Profit before taxation (Net Profit)		£33,000	
20				

Figure 2.9 *Iain's system*

Jane has recently had her first baby and is now teleworking from home for four days a week. Teleworking means that Jane uses her own work station at home to undertake the work she does for Iain. She then uses the Internet and email to communicate with the office and transfer files. The system is excellent for Jane as she can work around the baby's needs. To make sure that she is in regular contact with the other members of the office, Jane uses teleconferencing on a daily basis.

With Jane out of the office four days a week, and the representatives out for most of the week, Iain has decided to introduce a system of hot desking. All of the files required for the business are now stored on a computer, not in a filing cabinet. Iain is convinced that the staff do not need their own desks, some of which are empty for most of the week, and computer systems which cost a lot of money sitting idle for most of the week. The idea of hot desking is that people just sit at whichever desk is empty and access their files via the network. While some of the staff are unhappy with not having their own space, Iain believes he is saving the company a large amount of money.

If you are designing a spreadsheet model for Iain's company, remember the stages.

You should include the following in your designs. Remember to make a log of **all** the work you do and the time taken for each part. This is crucial for your **written** report.

(1) An *analysis* of the information needs of your system

You should **evaluate** at least three ideas and write down the advantages/disadvantages for each system and then give your **final** reasons for choosing the selected piece of software. You may need screen dumps or printouts to back this up. Would you need other pieces of software to help you? (clipart sites etc.) Write down the reasons for this.

You also need to consider what **hardware** will be needed for your work. List the pieces of equipment and the reasons for choosing them, and those considered but rejected, also giving reasons. Remember **all** the **input** and **output** devices, including mice, processors, storage, printers, keyboard etc.

Ask yourself the following questions:

- what is the desired **output**?
- what is the desired **input**?
- what is the method of input?
- what is the method of output?

(2) Two hand-drawn spreadsheets. These should show:

- the **layout** of your spreadsheet screens;
- a description to show the size of the text;
- a description to show the style of text and any colour used on the spreadsheet;
- they will show the **formulae** you intend to use, e.g. =SUM(E2:E7);
- they will describe who the spreadsheet is intended for.

If you are doing a spreadsheet about products in a shop, the main spreadsheet will be all the details of the products, purchase price, price sold, quantity sold etc. This must be over a certain period of time, e.g. a week or a month.

So your second spreadsheet could be a summary of the information from the first one, combined with other data. For example, you could take the weekly overall profit from your first spreadsheet, and place that in the second spreadsheet. You could then make up (sample data) figures for other branches of the shop. You could then do some forecasting and predicting.

Alternatively

If you are doing a spreadsheet about football, the main spreadsheet will be all the details of the players, like player name, goals scored, successful tackles etc. This must be over a certain period of time, e.g. a week or a month.

So the second spreadsheet could be adding up all of the goals scored by every player in the team, to work out how many points the team have got in one month. You could then model the top three places in the league and see how high your team would be, on the basis of the goals scored by your players in your first spreadsheet. This could take care of all prediction and forecasting.

(3) Detailed explanation of the formulae you are using for each spreadsheet

E.g. 'At cell F11 I have put the formula "=SUM(F1:F10)". This adds up all of the cells from F1 to F10. The reason for this is to calculate the total number of goals scored in that week. This cell will refer to cell G11 which looks at all the goals conceded…'

(4) Discussion of your chosen inputs, processes and outputs used in your spreadsheets

Processes: You may also produce a user guide. If you do, it must have a contents page. You may wish to add other features, e.g. fonts, colours, cut/paste, formulae, functions, charts, mailmerge.

(5) Describe the charts you are going to use

- Why is it important that we use charts?
- Why is it important for modelling?

(6) Draw a *system flowchart* of the entire design

(7) Construct your system. Remember to keep regular *backups*

(8) *Test* your system yourself by asking other members of your class to test it for you

Remember to record your evaluation using notes/diagrams/tape recorder/questionnaires or any other appropriate means.

(9) *Modify* the system to make it better

Remember to record any changes you make.

■ *Veena's Health Centre*

Veena works with very confidential information. Patient records are protected by the Data Protection Act. You can read more about this in the next section of the book.

It is very important to prevent anyone from accessing the Health Centre's computer files. There are a number of different ways that the Health Centre achieves this.

Many people are worried about computers like Veena's holding lots of personal information about them. As computers have become cheaper and more powerful, more and more large organisations are using databases to store what are called 'databanks' about them. These organisations include health centres like Veena's, dentists, hospitals, banks, shops, government departments and personal individuals.

People are concerned that data may be incorrect, leading to them not getting a loan when they want it, or not getting a job. Incorrect details of their personal bank account could affect their chance of renting or buying a house or obtaining credit from a credit card company or bank. A police record may mean that certain jobs, particularly professional ones, working with children or jobs in which money and valuables are handled, may be closed to them. The data could be incorrect either because a mistake was made by people when the information was first collected, or was typed into the system or could be incorrect simply because it was not updated when they moved house, changed jobs, had children or got married

Other people just do not like data, however accurate, being kept about them, particularly data about their age, sex, marital status, medical condition, country of origin or nationality.

A large number of people are concerned that they don't even know who holds records about them. They would like to know who has these records so that they can check the accuracy of the data and they are also worried that their records could be passed on to other people, without their knowledge or permission.

As we can see, the details stored in a databank can affect a person's life in many ways. Stopping this data from being misused is as important as is checking its accuracy. The data Veena has access to is some of the most confidential to be held on databanks because it includes a large amount of very personal information. Veena has to take every step possible to stop unauthorised people from accessing the data.

STOPPING PEOPLE FROM ACCESSING COMPUTER SYSTEMS

The areas where the computer systems are kept are always locked when not in use. Visitors to the Health Centre are not permitted into areas where computer systems are used. All of the computer hardware in the Health Centre is marked using special ink that is visible only in ultraviolet light. This is to help the police recover any equipment that is stolen.

PREVENTING ACCESS TO THE DATA ON THE NETWORK

The Health Centre has a number of methods to prevent unauthorised people accessing patient details.

These include the use of passwords and user names. Veena uses her mother's name as a user name and has a password that she has to change every month. The password is changed regularly so that if anybody sees her typing it in, it will not be usable for very long.

Veena finds it very hard to remember her passwords, particularly as the rules imposed by the Health Centre will not let her write it down. Veena's user name and password give her total access to all of the patient records, but other people in the practice have more limited access. This is because the system has been set up so that it will allow only the type of access needed for each employee.

Firewalls

Firewalls are used in the Health Centre to keep different parts of the network separate from each other. If an unauthorised user hacks into the system, that user cannot gain access to all of the network. The firewalls also help to prevent viruses from spreading across the whole network.

Data encryption

Veena often has to use the Internet and e-mails to communicate with other parts of the National Health Service. Whenever she sends patients' details or records across the Internet, she uses encryption software to turn the data automatically into a scrambled code.

Any file that is going to be sent via the Internet and contains sensitive data can be protected by codes in a process called encryption. Veena has to encrypt any patient information she sends over the Internet. If a tape or disk containing encrypted files were stolen, or if Internet data were accessed it would be impossible to read it without a decoder.

Encryption is used when important data is being transmitted from one place to another. The data is coded by the source computer before being sent, and decoded at the destination computer. In the Health Centre, the source computer is Veena's computer, and the destination computer might be at a hospital where a patient is being transferred, or at another doctor's practice. The processes are performed automatically by the computers involved. If the data is intercepted en route, it cannot be interpreted or altered.

Veena uses encryption with e-mails to make sure that they reach the right destination, and are not intercepted on the way. Encryption ensures privacy for the sender and recipient of a message, but some governments are not in favour of encryption of emails. They believe that it encourages crime by making it easy for those who want to break the law to communicate with each other.

Security and encryption

The type of encryption Veena uses is not unlike what Edward uses to hide his messages on his mobile text system. Edward often uses his mobile to send secret messages to his friends. He uses a series of letters and numbers that only they understand. At first they used numbers from 1 to 26, one for each letter of the alphabet. The trouble with this was it was too easy for someone to work it out. People have used code in various forms in the past, from Morse code to the secret codes used to send messages during the last world war. The only way to secure financial or any other confidential data, and make it readable only to authorised persons, is to use some sort of complex code.

The way the **encryption** process Veena uses actually works is that, first, the letters of her message are converted by specialised software into a number just like Edward did with his messages. But to make it much harder to break the code, the software performs a complex calculation with the numbers of Veena's converted message, and the recipient's key that is used to break the code. No one else can decode her message without a key that corresponds with her key. Of course, the larger the numbers used to perform the calculation, the more secure the transaction.

Hiding files

Some of the new encryption programs encrypt and then hide files in other files (carriers) so no one knows they are there. This method has the advantage of making the message almost invisible, and considerably increases the work of any experienced code-breaker, who must first find the right carrier, extract the message from it, and only after that (if he/she gets this far) begin the hard work of breaking the code.

The law and encryption

In certain countries, such as the United States, government policy is not in favour of encryption as it believes that the ability to send secret messages would encourage crime. Spain bans it completely. France forbids it without written permission and the Americans have tried to ban export of the most secure systems.

Backup files

Veena regularly has to back up the Health Centre's system files. Once backed up, the backup disks are taken by a security company to a safe and secure location away from the Health Centre. This is to ensure that if there were a fire, patient records would still be available.

Emergency procedures

Veena's Health Centre has very strict procedures that all staff using the system must follow. Staff are not allowed to use their own floppy disks. They are not allowed to use their own family names as passwords, and they have to change their password if they accidentally reveal it to anyone else.

Software security – viruses

One of the greatest threats to the security of the Health Centre's files, and to computer files held on any system that has access to the outside world via the Internet, is the threat of virus infection.

Most viruses are computer programs that automatically copy themselves so that they can 'infect' other disks, email users or programs without the user's knowledge. They are then capable of playing some kind of trick, or of disrupting the operation of the computer, or of a whole system. A virus can be sent via the Internet to any number of computers. When the user of the destination computer opens up the file containing the virus, it is activated and starts to do its damage.

Although all computer infections are called viruses there are many different forms of electronic infection. The most common are:

Viruses – a virus is a small piece of software that infects computer programs. For example, a virus might attach itself to Veena's database program. Each time Veena uses the program, the virus would run too and reproduce itself by attaching to other programs or destroy or modify data within the database.

E-mail viruses – an e-mail virus moves around via e-mail messages. It usually copies itself automatically by e-mailing itself to dozens of people it finds addresses for in the user's e-mail address book. There have been some spectacularly disruptive e-mail viruses including The ILOVEYOU virus, which appeared on 4 May 2000. It contained a piece of code as an attachment and anybody who double clicked on the attachment started the virus working. The code sent copies of itself to everyone in the victim's address book and then started corrupting files on the machines it attacked. The Melissa virus of March 1999 was even more spectacular.

Melissa spread in Microsoft Word documents sent via e-mail. The virus would send itself in an e-mail message to the first 50 people in the person's address book. The e-mail message contained a friendly note that included the person's name. People all over the world opened the document thinking it was harmless. The Melissa virus was the fastest-spreading virus ever seen and forced a number of large companies to shut down their e-mail systems.

Worms – a worm is a small piece of software that uses computer networks and security breaks in Internet based services to copy itself. Each copy of the worm then scans the network for any another machine it can infect, then copies itself to the new machine. Worms have done a lot of damage in recent years For example, the Code Red worm was reported to have copied itself over 250,000 times in approximately nine hours on 19 July 2001.

Trojan horses – a Trojan horse is simply a normal computer program. The program claims to be a game, but instead it does damage when you run it. Some Trojan horses completely erase the hard disk. The good thing is that Trojan horses cannot copy themselves automatically.

All viruses were first written as practical jokes, but it is all too common now for them to be written by people who wish to cause malicious damage to information systems. Because of the virus's ability to copy itself, the scale of the damage can be serious and widespread. Viruses are quite common, and some have become well known to systems users, who have developed methods of dealing with them.

Veena has had special training in preventing viruses from damaging the Health Centre's system. After the ILOVEYOU e-mail virus damaged the Health Centre's e-mail system she was told about how important personal discipline is. She was told that you should never double-click on an attachment that contains an executable that arrives as an e-mail attachment. An executable is a program or installer that will run on its own and adds something to your computer. Executables do not need any other program to run. We looked in the first section at how to identify attachments. Word files (.DOC), spreadsheets (.XLS), images (.GIF and .JPG), are all examples data files that Veena can open as they cannot do damage. Veena is not allowed to open files with extensions like EXE, COM or VBS.

The system in Veena's Health Centre also uses antivirus software to guard against damage by viruses. The software is able to scan through the memory and disks of the Health Centre's computers to detect the presence of any viruses. It can then remove them, in a process that is sometimes called disinfecting. When choosing antivirus software, it is important to compare speeds of checking and buy a package that is suitable for your system.

Whenever new staff join the Health Centre, they receive training about the use of its computer system, and one important aspect of the training covers the regular precautions that all users should take to guard against the threat of viruses.

These precautions are typical of most organisations that operate networked computer systems:

- Obtain all software from a reliable source.
- If you do buy second-hand software, scan it for viruses first.
- Make regular back-up copies of work.
- Write-protect any external disks that relate to the operating system or that contain data that must not be altered. A floppy or zip disk has a tiny write-protect tab in one corner. If you can see through the hole by this tab, you will not be able to write to the disk. (If you close the hole by moving the tab across it, you will be able to read and write data.) CD-ROMs and CD-Rs are automatically write-protected. Files on a CD-RW, or any other files, can be protected by saving them in Read-only format. Files can also be protected with passwords. It is important to remember that files that have been protected with passwords, for example, are no longer protected if you, as the legitimate user, enter the password and open the file.
- Run antivirus software at regular intervals. Most systems are set up so that this software runs automatically when a computer is switched on. It should also check external disks before data is taken from them.
- If a computer has had to be repaired, it should be scanned for viruses before being used again.
- Be wary of downloading software from bulletin boards. They provide one of the easiest ways for people who write viruses to spread them around.
- Be suspicious of all software distributed free of charge. Examples are software and shareware (software that is copyrighted but can be distributed free of charge; users are asked or required to make a payment direct to the author if they use the program regularly) distributed in magazines. These sometimes carry viruses.

Lata's presentation

Lata is preparing a presentation on company costs using presentation software.

She has based her slideshow on Quickpack Ltd. In packaging goods, her father's company has two different types of costs that must be calculated very carefully using ICT.

The first type of costs are known as variable costs. Sometimes these are called direct costs as they relate to the things the company has to pay for to make the product, in this case the packages themselves and inserting the contents. In making the packages, Iain's company has to pay for raw materials, wages of production workers, and the cost of operating the equipment needed to produce the packages. These costs all change according to how many packages are made.

The other costs are known as fixed costs. These are also sometimes called indirect costs, as they are the actual costs of running the business, whether it makes anything, or not. Examples of the company's fixed costs include Iain's and Jane's salaries, advertising costs, rent and rates

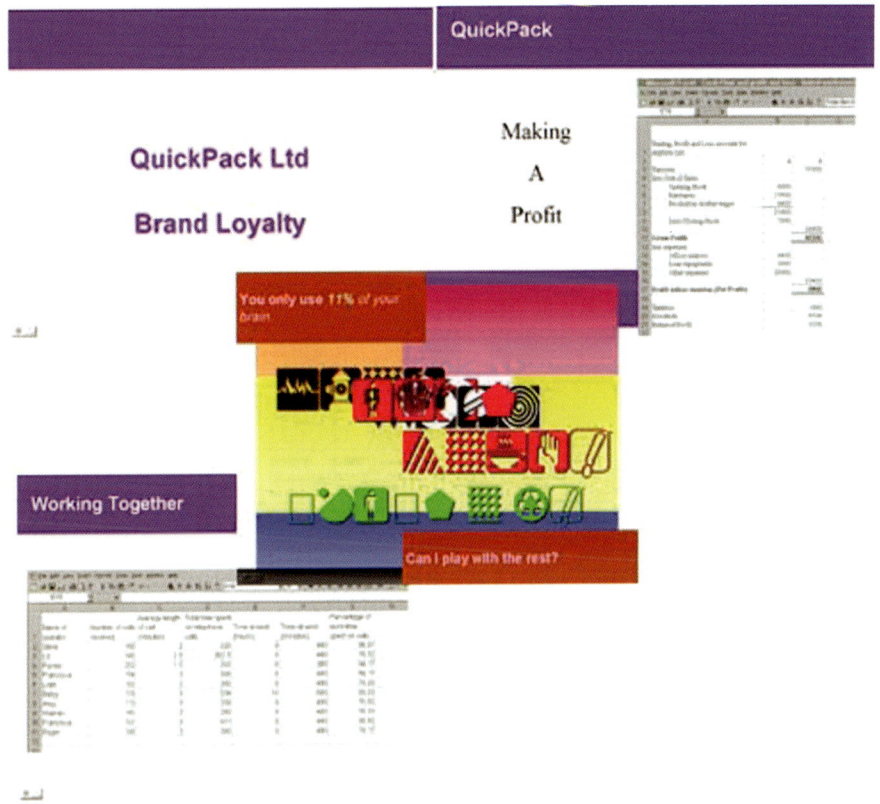

Figure 2.10 *Powerpoint slides on Quickpack Ltd*

associated with the business premises. Quickpack uses a computer model to calculate whether the company is likely to make a profit.

The company's variable costs have to be added to the fixed costs to give the total costs. If Iain knows the company's total costs and the level of production, he can calculate its average costs, otherwise known as unit costs.

The following example gives the costs and revenue (income) data for Quickpack Ltd:

Output	Fixed cost £	Variable cost £	Total cost	Total revenue	Profit
0	1500	0	1500	0	−1500
10000	1500	300	1800	600	−1200
20000	1500	600	2100	1200	−900
30000	1500	900	2400	1800	−600
40000	1500	1200	2700	2400	−300
50000	1500	1500	3000	3000	0
60000	1500	1800	3300	3600	300
70000	1500	2100	3600	4200	600
80000	1500	2400	3900	4800	900
90000	1500	2700	4200	5400	1200
100000	1500	3000	4500	6000	1500

The basic principle is quite straightforward. The fixed costs have to be paid even if Quickpack produces nothing. In this case they come to £1500 per day. The packaging sells at 6p per package but costs 3p to pack. So every time Iain's company sells a product they have 3p left after paying the direct costs. This money will be used to pay the fixed costs. It will take 5000 products to raise the £1500 needed to cover the fixed costs. Any products they sell above 50,000 will contribute 3p profit to the company.

As can be seen, Iain's breakeven level of output is at 50,000 units.

Output	Fixed Cost £	Variable Cost £	Total Cost	Total Revenue	Profit
0	1500	0	1500	0	-1500
10000	1500	300	1800	600	-1200
20000	1500	600	2100	1200	-900
30000	1500	900	2400	1800	-600
40000	1500	1200	2700	2400	-300
50000	1500	1500	3000	3000	0
60000	1500	1800	3300	3600	300
70000	1500	2100	3600	4200	600
80000	1500	2400	3900	4800	900
90000	1500	2700	4200	5400	1200
100000	1500	3000	4500	6000	1500

Figure 2.11 *Spreadsheet based on Quickpack Ltd data*

Lata's slide show includes a graph produced from a spreadsheet to show what is called a breakeven analysis.

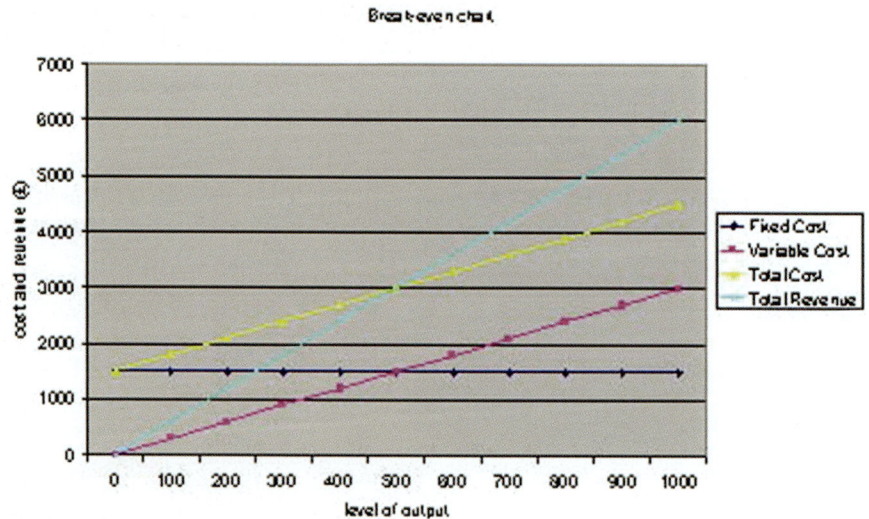

Figure 2.12 *Break-even chart*

Printing

PRODUCING TRADITIONAL PUBLICITY LEAFLETS

Iain has decided to have some new printed leaflets produced to supplement the new web site. Iain is not certain what he wants, but he has some sort of folded leaflet in mind. He has explored a range of folded leaflets used by his competitors.

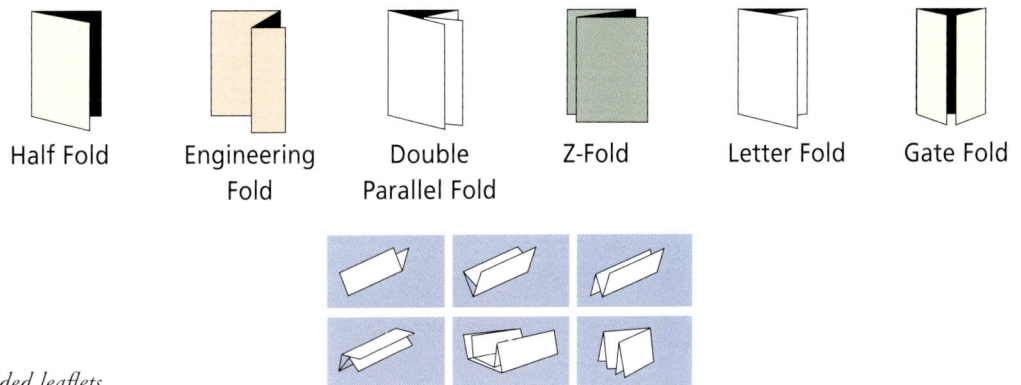

Half Fold   Engineering Fold   Double Parallel Fold   Z-Fold   Letter Fold   Gate Fold

Figure 2.13 *Range of folded leaflets*

He has also commissioned a group of graphic designers to design the new leaflet which is to be printed in full colour. Iain knows all about computer printers as he has three in the office: an old impact printer, a laser printer and a new inkjet. Printers provide output in the form of permanent copy, normally on paper. Many can also print on to acetate sheets that are used on overhead projectors.

The designers tell him that computer printers are too slow and costly to produce the finished leaflet and they are only any good for small print runs. Ian is introduced to the senior graphic designer named Zanna.

She tells Iain that first they will need to create a design he likes using a DTP package. Writers, graphic designers and artists will draw up detailed drafts of a suitable design together with the necessary illustrations and photographs. These designs will then be sent to her for page layout. She will have to make the difficult decisions about how best to fit the pieces of art and text into a very limited space. Finally, after the layout of every page has been completed, edited and proofread, a digital 'printer's file' will be created for the publicity leaflet. This will be done by burning a CD, or by sending it to a professional printer using File Transfer Protocol (FTP).

Iain is told by Zanna that there are eight main types of printing process they could use, not counting the original letterpress process which is not used much any more.

The processes are:

- engraving – for high quality stationery;
- thermography – to give raised printing, used for logos on stationery and business cards;
- reprographics – used in offices for copying and duplicating;
- digital printing – likely to grow in the near future but costly at the moment for his needs;
- screen – used for T-shirts, mugs and artistic work;
- flexography – usually used on packaging, such as can labels;
- gravure – used for huge runs of magazines and direct-mail catalogues;
- offset lithography – being the best for his leaflet.

They will use offset lithography for his leaflet. Zanna tells Iain that offset lithography works on the very simple principle that ink and water don't mix. His brochure will be colour separated first using the DTP software. This is because the leaflet will need to be printed four times, once for each colour black, cyan (blue), magenta (red), and yellow. He asks her how only four colours could give a full colour leaflet. Zanna tells him that colours mix, like in a colour monitor on the computer or in his bubble jet printer.

She goes on to describe the lithographic process. Each colour separation containing words and art will then be put on to what are called plates. Plates are like film negatives and are created from the digital files. She tells him that there are different materials for plates, including paper, but these produce a much lower quality. The best plates for Iain's leaflet will be made from aluminium. Images from the negatives are transferred to printing plates in much the same way as photographs are developed. The plates will then be dampened by water, then ink. The ink adheres to the text and pictures, the water to the rest of the plate. Then the image is transferred to a rubber blanket, and from the rubber blanket to paper. Zanna said that this is why the process is called offset.

Designing for commercial printing is therefore slightly different from designing for standard printers that are connected to a computer. Iain has three different types of printer in his office. These three standard types of printer are: impact printers, inkjet printers and laser printers.

Impact printers

The most common impact printer is a dot matrix printer.

Dot matrix printers were the first type to be developed for use in computer systems. They are impact printers, producing output by hammering pins or character patterns against a ribbon and the paper. This means that they are able to print multi-part stationery such as invoice sets used by Iain and many other companies, where a number of copies are required.

Dot matrix printers are noisy and produce a low quality of printout and, for these reasons, have largely been replaced by either inkjets or lasers.

Figure 2.14 *Dot matrix printer*

Non-impact printers

Inkjet and lasers are non-impact printers. They are quiet when working and produce high-quality output. They can all produce graphics and most types are capable of producing colour.

Laser printers

A laser printer uses a laser beam to build up an electrical image of a page on a light-sensitive drum in the same way as a photocopier. The primary principle at work in a laser printer is static electricity.

Laser printers and photocopiers use toner which is the equivalent of ink. The paper grabs the toner rather than the printer applying it to the paper. Toner is an electrically charged powder with two main ingredients: pigment and plastic. The pigment adds the colour, the plastic melts and fixes the image to the paper.

The image is built up from dots of toner. Early laser printers used 300 dots to the inch, but the latest printers use at least 600 dots to the inch (2.5cm) so that the individual dots cannot be seen.

Colour laser printers use three-colour toner cartridges – cyan, magenta and yellow – plus black.

Laser printers are fast and produce high-quality output. They are expensive, however, particularly colour laser printers. Toner cartridges have to be replaced as soon as they run out and may also be expensive. Some suppliers operate schemes for recycling used toner cartridges.

Figure 2.15 *Laser printer*

Inkjet printers

An inkjet printer is any printer that fires extremely small droplets of ink on to paper to create an image. Inkjet printers are often also called bubble-jets because they produce output by spraying tiny drops of ink on to the paper. Tiny resistors create heat, and this heat vaporises ink to create a bubble. The bubble causes a droplet to form which is ejected from the print head

The dots formed are smaller and more numerous (usually between 300 and 800 dots to the inch) than those produced by a dot matrix impact printer.

Inkjet printers are fairly inexpensive compared with laser printers, and much less expensive than colour laser printers. Inkjet printers normally take up less space than laser printers and are almost silent in operation. Inkjet printers are, however, slower than laser printers. Running costs are also usually higher than for lasers as quality specialised printing paper is costly. Ink cartridges, especially colour cartridges, can be expensive and do not last long if full colour pictures are being printed.

Standard inkjet printers have three-colour cartridges, plus a black cartridge. Inkjet printers designed to produce photographic quality output have five-colour cartridges, plus black.

Figure 2.16 *Inkjet printer*

Colour inkjet printers can produce images that are almost as good as photographs if they are printed on high quality paper. The inkjet system does not work well on any paper that is absorbent as the wet ink droplets tend to spread before they can dry.

▉ Networks

We have talked a lot about networks in this book, but what exactly are they?

All of the companies we have looked at use a computer network. The Oliver family have a network of friends and relations, some in Australia. A network is a group of people who know each other well and communicate together to share information often. A computer network is similar. It is made up of two or more computers that are connected so that they can exchange messages and share information. The computers on the Internet can talk to one another because they are networked.

To be networked, computers must be connected in some way so that they can exchange information with one another electronically. On the Internet, the connections take many different forms. Some computers are directly connected to others with wire or fibre-optic cables. Some are connected through local and long-distance telephone lines, and some use wireless satellite communications just like the human network formed by the Oliver family, complete with extended family, some in Australia. Satellite systems are used for long-distance phone calls to places like Australia and also used for some other long-distance phone services and cellular phones to communicate with other computers on the Internet.

There are a number of different types of network, the most common being: LANs (Local Area Networks) and WANs (Wide Area Networks). A LAN is confined to a small area, usually within a single building. The Oliver family members all live in the same house so networking together is easy. A WAN is not confined to one building. The computers and terminals forming part of the network can be spread around the world just like the wider friendship groups and family members in our family.

THE BASIC NETWORK

All networks need a means of communicating and are made up of the following:

- server or client workstation;
- Networking Interface Cards (NIC);
- cabling;
- networking operating system such as Windows NT;
- certain basic terms are used in networking, and it helps to be familiar with them;

- peer-to-peer: this is commonly two PCs connected together to share files or a printer;
- Local Area Network (LAN): this is probably the most popular in smaller applications;
- Wide Area Network (WAN).

Networks use nodes, another name for client computers or the computers using the network, and are set up in topologies: the geometric arrangement of the network. The word topology simply means 'type'.

Ring topology

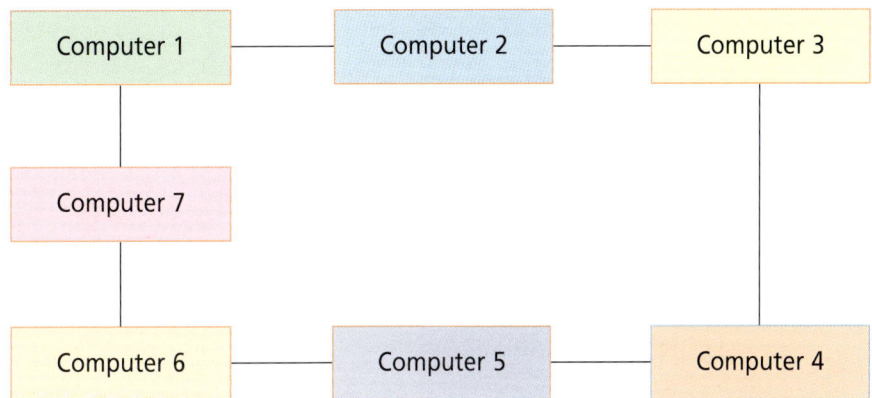

Figure 2.17 *Ring topology*

In a ring topology, all of the terminals or other nodes in the network are connected together in a circle, with no device having any more importance than any other. Gavin describes this as a game of ring-a-ring-of roses. All people, or in this case machines, hold hands. Although the computers are connected in a circle they do not need to be placed in one. An obvious disadvantage is that if there is a fault in any part of the circle, all of the nodes will be affected, or, as Gavin says, it all falls down.

Line (bus) topology

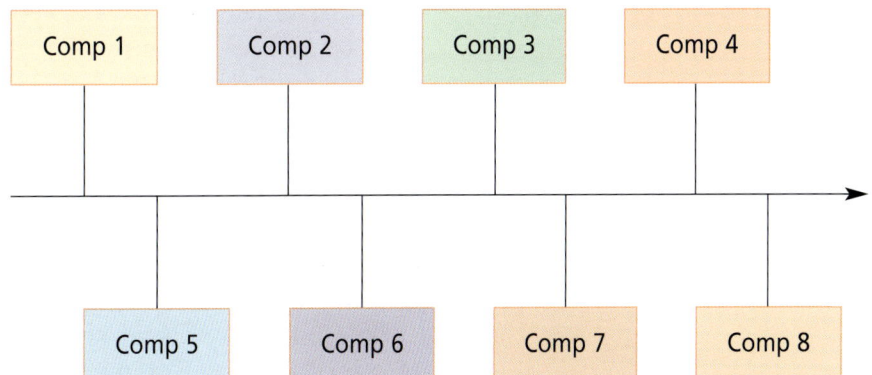

Figure 2.18 *Line (bus) topology*

In this system, data is sent to all nodes on the network at the same time. Devices are positioned along a line, rather like bus stops. Gavin calls this the Can-Can, all kicking together and in time with the music. As in the ring topology, each device has equal status, but the advantage here is that, if one terminal is not working correctly, the others are not affected (although the dance is not as good). This type of network is cheap and reliable.

Star topology

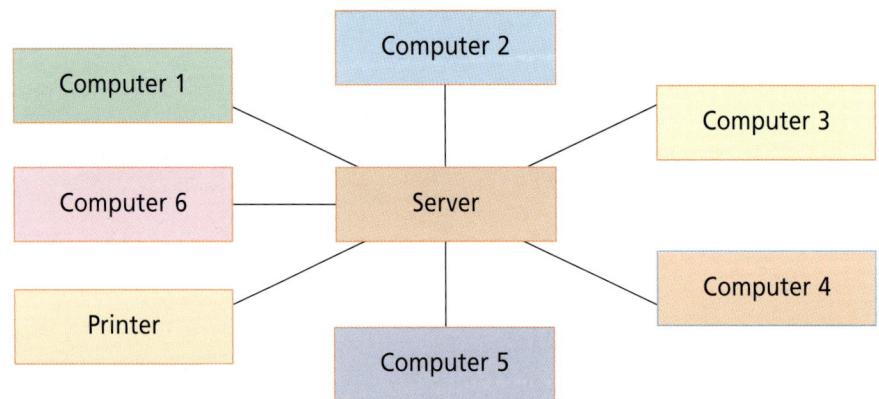

Figure 2.19 *Star topology*

In this type of network, a central controller forms the principal node, while the subsidiary nodes form the points of the star. As the central machine controls the whole system, the whole system will be affected if it breaks down. Gavin jokes that the stories his dad tells of how his father was the boss in the house and everyone did as they were told is a bit like a star topology. Star topologies use more cabling than other topologies, and this makes them more expensive. However, communication is fast because there is a direct path from the central controller to each terminal and all follow the instruction of the boss.

LANs – local area networks

So why have networks? ICT is about communication. The Oliver family work better because they work together and share things. If they did not communicate and help each other the family would not be able to do as much. Similarly there are a number of advantages to companies using a local area network of computers. Costly resources such as printers can be shared by all of the computers.

This means that better quality printing is available to everyone because one or two expensive, high-specification printers can be bought instead of several cheaper, lower specification models.

Of course part of being able to work together is the ability to speak the same language. Computer networks talk to each other via what is called a Protocol. This is the communication method for the network. Each computer on the network must have a protocol the others understand. Think of it as trying to speak French to an English person. Unless they knew French they would have a job to understand you. Rupa is learning English but she has a job to communicate with the younger members of the family. So computers all need a common protocol so they can understand one another.

When we speak we talk in sentences. A computer network uses data packets which are messages of data that can been sent over the network.

Let's examine a real network used by our case study family.

Veena's Health Centre uses a LAN with a central backing store so all the work carried out by the people who work there is saved together. A central backup takes place automatically at regular intervals. Veena is therefore usually able to retrieve work that has been deleted by mistake. She can load her work on any computer on the network. They all share the same software, and upgrading is easier too.

The data in the database has to be shared. Several people need to use the database at the same time, but they cannot edit the same record at the same time. When a record is opened by one user, it is locked so that other people cannot try to edit it at the same time. This avoids the confusion that would result if several people were trying to edit data at the same time. Once the first user has completed and saved the operation, the record is unlocked again.

Veena is not totally happy with the system. Because a lot of terminals are served by only two printers, long print queues sometimes develop, causing her to have to wait for printed output. The doctors at the practice are also paranoid about network security. They know that if a virus gets into one computer, it is likely to spread quickly across the network because it will get into the central backing store.

When the system was fitted the cabling was expensive to buy and to install. In a busy office situation like Veena's the, cabling had to be placed under the floor so that people would not trip over it. If connecting cables are damaged, some sections of the network can become isolated. They will not be able to communicate with the rest of the network.

WANs – wide area networks

WANs are set up differently. Because of the distances involved, external communication links such as satellites, microwaves or telecommunication links are used to connect the network. The connection must normally be paid for because the links are external.

The health centre LAN that Veena uses is connected to WAN via a special gateway. Many local area networks are connected to the Internet in this way. The Internet is an example of a vast WAN. Veena accesses the Internet via the LAN.

Using networks on the Internet

So far we have looked in detail at networks that have been set up together. They have been constructed so they can speak together. Just like the Oliver family, they all know each other. The Internet is different because you do not know all the people you are talking to or even how the network connects together. Unlike the topologies we looked at earlier, the Internet connects the networks together using a net framework, where each node is connected using more than one connection.

The name given to computers using the Internet to network together is an Internetwork. The Internet is the world's largest Internetwork. It includes computers linked together in networks, which in turn are linked together in Internetworks, and those Internetworks linked together in still bigger Internetworks to form one big net of connections. There are tens of thousands of networks connected to the Internet today. Because the Internet is an Internetwork, each computer is not necessarily directly connected to every other computer. In other words, any computer on the Internet can talk to any other, but the message may have to travel through several other computers or networks on its way there.

Think of it like air travel. From London, you can fly anywhere in the world. For some destinations, however, you can't get a non-stop flight. You have to fly to Germany, Spain or Singapore first, then from there to your destination. Information makes its way around the Internet in a similar way, stopping off at various places.

ICT and society

▌*Introduction*

This section of the book will help you understand how far ICT systems affect everyday life. It explores how individuals, as well as members of the extended family, join in with clubs and societies, work teams and community groups using ICT, in their personal, social and professional lives. Some individuals and groups do not have access to ICT, yet ICT still affects their lives.

As you have discovered in the other sections of the book ICT now plays an important part in all our daily lives. We have come to accept and trust computers to pay our wages, manage our car's engine, keep the central heating working and to transmit messages around the world. Much that we do is recorded in some way on ICT systems. Some people question why we trust computers so much.

A large number of people are also concerned about the power of ICT. They fear that computers hold information about them that they are not allowed to see. To overcome some of these concerns, laws have become necessary to help make sure that personal information held on computers is correct and is not misused in any way.

Yet new ICT products and applications are constantly being developed and the pace of development is very fast. Our lives would not be as comfortable without ICT. In this section of the book you will explore how and why ICT can have negative as well as positive effects.

You will already have knowledge of how ICT is used for:

- business;
- working styles and new employment opportunities;
- legislation;
- entertainment and leisure;
- personal communications.

In this section you will explore the wide variety of technology that is available to access and exchange information and carry out transactions. You will also learn about the development of the specialised hardware and software associated with a range of ICT needs including:

- Internet technologies, e.g. World Wide Web, e-mail, multimedia, encryption;
- Internet connections, e.g. modem, ISDN, ASDL, broadband;
- mobile telephone technologies, e.g. SMS, WAP;
- digital broadcasting;
- personal digital assistants (PDAs) and organisers;

- storage media, e.g. DVD, minidisk;
- touch screen technologies.

You will learn how ICT has changed the work styles and lives of the Oliver family. This section of the book also covers legislation that is enacted by Government to protect people from the harmful effects of ICT.

Databases: good or bad?

On the way home Iain was in a bit of a hurry. He had worked late at the office and knew he would be in trouble. Friends were coming round for dinner and he had to cook the main course. His mind was on other things and he went a little too fast in the car past a speed camera. Suddenly there was a flash of light. He knew within days he would have a speeding ticket. The police use computers for a variety of purposes. Large databases contain details of motor vehicles, criminals, DNA and fingerprints. All can be called up in a matter of seconds. Criminal records are kept for many years.

Figure 3.1 *Speed camera*

Police stations throughout the country use their own terminals that are linked direct to the Police National Computer. A police officer using a password can obtain information from the files held on the main computer database. By typing in a suspect's name and date of birth, the police officer will be able to read from the screen any records which the database holds on that person, where they were last known to be living etc.

If the registration number of a car is typed in, the name and address of the car's registered owner will appear on the screen in a matter of seconds. This information is used to send out tickets for speeding caught on speed cameras as in Iain's case. They are also used to track down the owners of stolen cars. The latest speed cameras use digital technology to automatically log the owner of the car instantly.

Iain's car number, address, and exact speed, time and place had now been captured by the system. Because computers can store such huge amounts of data, more and more information about people is being collected by the police and stored as data on computer files. Of course it is the job of the police to protect the public and the faster their investigations can be carried out, the sooner a criminal can be caught, but people are worried that the data could be inaccurate or be obtained by someone else. Iain should not have been speeding, but he was not happy about being caught.

PAYING THE GAS BILL

It is early Saturday morning, and Rupa gets up to find a gas bill has arrived in the morning post. She opens the envelope and finds that the bill is much higher than she had expected. Years ago in India, Rupa would have immediately visited the Gas Board office to find out if there was a mistake on her bill. She dials the customer service number given on the bill, expecting to talk to a person from the gas supplier who can answer her question about the bill. She is confused to hear an automated message, telling her to press one of a number of keys on the telephone, depending on what her query is about. Rupa has an old dial telephone and she likes to use this phone as she finds it easier to operate. The phone has no buttons to press. Rupa hangs on, hoping that an operator will answer her call finally. After a length of time, she is greeted by a different automated message, telling her it is a very busy time for the operators and suggesting she calls back later. As she still finds English quite difficult, especially on the phone, Rupa has to listen more than once to make sure that she understands the message.

WHAT IS A CALL CENTRE?

A call centre is an office that is set up by any company that expects large numbers of telephone enquiries from its customers, specifically to answer those telephone enquiries. The call centre is usually not linked in any way to the rest of the company and its staff may not even be employees of the company. They may be employed by another company that offers call centre services. Examples of companies that operate call centres are utility suppliers – gas, electricity, telephones – banks and building societies. IBM have set up a call centre just for staff. It is part of the personnel department and staff from all over the world can contact someone in a central location who can access their flies and speak their language.

Liz

I did a degree in Spanish and Portugese and then, because my ICT skills were limited, a training course with Pitmans. I then joined the Human Resources department located in IBM's Head Office in Portsmouth.

My section is basically a call centre within IBM that acts as a resource for IBM staff throughout Europe, the Middle East and Asia. We are divided into teams according to our language skills and spend our day answering telephone calls or emails from staff who have queries relating to their jobs. On average, we answer 50–100 calls each day. A notice board in the centre of our large, open office area displays how many people are available to answer calls from each geographical area, and it tells us the number of calls that are waiting to be answered. Team work is very important for us. If one person is very busy with a difficult call, or someone is off sick, other team members must share the workload.

Training is an important aspect of our working lives. When we join a team, we receive training that is specific to the skills that we need. For example, I answer calls from IBM staff in Portugal, so I need to know about employment legislation and human resources issues that relate to that country. Communication skills are really important. We join workshops to learn how to deal with people who are feeling very stressed, for example, or about how to be assertive without being aggressive. As we work in a large, open office space, we have a knowledge room where we can go to study and work on on-line training offered by IBM. We are encouraged to undertake about two classroom-based training courses, and three to four on-line courses per year.

Health and safety must always be observed in our working environment. We take regular breaks and are encouraged to move away from our monitors at these times. We have a quiet room where we can go to relax, and a loud room if we need to let off steam. IBM also provides a large canteen and coffee bar area. We can pay for food and drink with e-cash. E-cash is used both in vending machines and in the restaurant. There is a machine in the wall near the canteen to re-charge e-cards; this is important because there is only one bank branch on site (NatWest) serving 5,000 staff.

Most of the answers to callers' problems or queries can be found on-line. The IBM Human Resources Home Page is full of information and links to aspects of human resources work. If a person is about to retire from the company, for example, we can go to the section that deals with retirement benefits, or if a person needs to take some time off work because of a family problem, we can advise him or her about what to do.

To help our teams to function properly, and to co-ordinate work, we have monthly general meetings, and three-monthly team meetings. We receive feedback from team leaders about our performance and can discuss matters relating to our daily work. If someone has performed particularly well, or has been especially helpful to another colleague, he or she will receive a reward. Statistics about our performance, such as how many calls or e-mails are coming into our section and how many are being answered, are always available on screen too. If one of us needs to contact a team leader quickly, we have a special little connect screen that we can bring up on our monitors.

As we are dealing with personal information about IBM staff all the time, security is very important. Each of us has a password and log-in that gives us a certain level of access to confidential records. Team leaders can access more confidential information than their teams.

I find my job very rewarding. When I was at school and university, I would not have thought of choosing a job in an ICT industry, but the technology is really a powerful tool that I use to do my work in the best possible way. My work is all about communicating, researching and putting together information, and co-operating in a team. It is good to know that I am helping people by answering questions that are sometimes affecting their lives in significant ways. I meet new people all the time and always have opportunities for new learning. There is plenty of variety – two days are never the same.

So call centres are often seen by companies as a step towards offering customer service, while at the same time minimising costs. For a bank, for example, a call centre is about fifty times more expensive than a fully self-service operation on the Internet but much cheaper than a town centre bank branch. Call centres can use operators, although fully automated systems are now being used by some banks and other companies. For a call centre to be effective, the operator needs to access account details instantly when a customer telephones.

New telephone technology has enabled you to see who is phoning you. BT's fixed line system is known as a caller display. The automatic transfer of telephone numbers is called caller line identification (CLI). Call centres can use this automatic CLI system to link direct into a database. When Rupa phones the gas supplier's call centre, her file is automatically called up from the database. Of course she could be someone else using her phone number. To protect customers, passwords or reference numbers are usually issued, and the operator will ask you for your name and some of the letters of your password.

It is normal for banks to issue their customers with a password, or customers may be able to choose their own. For security reasons the operator of the call centre should not know the full password. When you phone the call centre, the operator asks your name and account name. The operator calls up your file, and before he or she can access the database, the program asks for two or three letters of your password. These letters are chosen at random and could be, for example, the second and fifth letters of your password. In this way, the operator does not learn your password but is able to access the database.

■ *What is an automated telephone answering system?*

Fully automated systems use interactive voice recognition (IVR) or the telephone keypad to access and control customer accounts. These automated centres are also referred to as automated non-personal call centres.

The industry name given to the integration of telephone systems with computers is computer telephone integration (CTI). CTI is very dependent upon effective databases containing information on customers and potential customers. Telephone receptionists need to be able to call up all relevant customer details, including letters, outstanding balances, savings accounts and credit status. Organisations using CTI usually issue their telephone operators with a written script to follow each time a customer phones. The telephone operator then selects a series of boxes on screen. As each box is completed, it leads to another box and the complete sequence carries out the customer's instructions.

The development of caller line identification (CLI), which automatically provides the recipient of a telephone call with the telephone number of the person making the call, has enabled banks to automate some of their processes, and to enhance security. Some banks, for example, Barclays, launched themselves as an ISP (Internet Service Provider). This provides closer links with their customers, and enhances security. Some banks use the telephone to check instructions given over the Internet. Telephone systems have enabled customers to achieve 'any time, anywhere' banking.

ADVANTAGES AND DISADVANTAGES OF CALL CENTRES AND AUTOMATED TELEPHONE ANSWERING SYSTEMS

- The use of call centres means that customer queries such as Rupa's can be answered at any time of day, any day.
- Where customers' money or personal details are involved, security systems in call centres protect against fraud or misuse of information.
- Grouping together a team of customer service operators in a call centre is much less expensive than employing customer service staff throughout a company.
- When a fully automated system is used, the cost is reduced further.

However, as Rupa finds, actually speaking to a helpful human being in a call centre is not always as easy as it should be, especially if the person making the call is not very comfortable with new technology, or has difficulty with language. Also, the fact that call centre operators are often not closely connected with the companies for whom they answer queries means that they are not always able to give detailed answers to queries.

A visit to the supermarket

Veena goes to the local supermarket once a week to do the bulk of the weekly shopping. She would like to be able to make more use of the small shops in the neighbourhood, and the market that is held on a Thursday morning but, with working full time, she cannot fit in this kind of shopping. Often Edward goes to the supermarket with her, to help out. It also gives him the chance to look in the supermarket's newsagent section for the computer and bike magazines that he likes to read.

The supermarket's ICT system will form part of the huge system that has its centre in the supermarket chain's head office. Each supermarket

Figure 3.2 *Shopping*

that forms part of the chain will be linked to the central office. The parts of the system that customers see are at the checkouts. They consist of scanners with bar-code readers (see section on scanners, pp. 72-4), and EPOS or EFTPOS tills.

Rupa does not like the big supermarkets. 'They are too bright, big and uncomfortable,' she says. 'Proper grocery shops have people who know what you want, like that nice Mr Singh. They also deliver shopping to you on a bicycle with a large basket on the front. That supermarket you visit expects you to go to them, pick up your own shopping, push it around in a trolley that does not go in the direction you want it to go. Then you take the shopping out of the trolley, pack it into bags and carry it home yourself. You even have to pay a deposit in case you steal the trolley'. 'Phu' she shouts. 'What do they do for the money you pay? Just sit there.'

Sunita used to work at a supermarket checkout. 'I did not just sit there!' she comments. 'It was not an easy job.'

'But you don't even have to look at any of the prices,' replies Rupa. 'All the products have bar-coded labels and you just pass them over a scanner that reads all the details of the product from the bar code into the computer. The display on the till even shows the customer the total cost'. 'You don't even need to add up. When you pay with real money, the display even tells you how much change to give.'

Veena tries to convince Rupa that this self-service approach leads to lower prices and a wider range of products, but she is not open for convincing. 'I am uncomfortable with all that technology,' she states. 'I like to visit "real" shops with people I can talk to.'

Veena and Edward go round the supermarket and fill the trolley with the goods that the family needs. Veena looks out for the week's discount and multibuy offers. There are often price reductions on popular lines, and opportunities to get an extra item free if you buy two that are on offer. Veena also has a store loyalty card and receives special offer coupons each month that can be used to obtain further price reductions on certain goods.

Every item for sale in the supermarket bears a bar code that carries information about the price of the product, and its identity for the supermarket's stock system. When Veena and Edward get to the checkout, they unload all the goods onto the moving belt so that the checkout assistant can scan the bar code on each item. Scanning will enter the price of the product into the supermarket's checkout computer system, and it will inform the stock system that the item has been removed from stock. As the system is constantly updated, any information about special prices or multibuys will also be registered.

The code represents a number, which is the data to be fed into the computer system. The bar code reader detects the amount of light reflected by the dark and light lines in the bar code, and many readers are now so sensitive that they can read a code from a distance of five metres or more.

In supermarkets and warehouse situations, the reading of bar codes allows computer systems to keep stock levels up to date so that goods can be re-ordered as soon as they are required.

Useful data about demand can also be obtained, for example, revealing which item in a particular range is selling best. In libraries, each book is marked with a code, and borrower tickets also have a code that allows the computer system to match borrowers with books and return dates. A similar system is operated with items of luggage and their owners at airports.

Veena and Edward notice the beeping sounds that indicate that each item has been successfully scanned. It *is* possible for a bar code reader to misread a bar code, for example if there is a dirty mark on the code. To avoid mistakes, a check digit calculated from all the other figures in the code is attached to the rest of the code when it is printed (see item on check digits in database section, above, p. 00). If the bar code has been damaged so much that the scanner cannot read it, the checkout assistant will have to type in the code using a keyboard. Veena finds that, even though the goods pass through the checkout very quickly, the multibuys and other special offers always seem to be correctly noted.

Pocket money

Watching the till clock up how much his mum is spending reminds Edward of a history project he is doing at school. Edward had been reading about the Romans and tells Veena that only two thousand years ago, Roman soldiers received cakes of salt as part of their pay. 'Roman solders would not have been interested in money, plastic credit cards, gold or silver,' he states.

'Does that mean we can pay you your pocket money in salt cakes?' replies Veena. 'Better go and fetch a few more bags of salt.'

'For something to be valuable, everyone must agree that it is worth having,' answers Edward. 'I prefer money rather than salt.'

Of course Edward was right in that early humans did not use what we would call *money* at all. People would exchange food, tools made from flint for other food, wood, jewellery and ornaments produced by others in a process called bartering. Edward regularly barters with his friends, swapping a music CD for another or swapping play station games.

Gradually, certain objects were accepted as being of value to everybody, and these became the first money. Metal became acceptable as money (in the form of bars) because it lasts and is easier to move around than earlier kinds of money, so it became more and more popular. Soon lumps of gold or silver became money, often with trader's marks on them. Now a plastic card with a magnetic strip on it is worth having.

When Veena offers her store card before she pays for the shopping, scanned information about what she has bought is linked to her customer reference in the supermarket's customer database. Having information like this enables the supermarket's management to target their purchasing and special offers to the buying patterns of their customers.

The process of actually paying for the shopping takes place by means of an EPOS or EFTPOS terminal. This acts as an input and output device. It receives all the scanned information from the shopping, and the details from Veena's store card, plus the bar codes of any special offer coupons that she has. Veena normally pays for the shopping with her bank debit card, and in this case, an EFTPOS terminal also receives information from the card about Veena's account. Its output is in the form of a receipt that gives details of every single item bought, any offers, use of the store card, and use of any coupons. When Veena pays with her debit card, the terminal also prints a payment slip that she must sign to authorise money to be taken from her account. If she is short of cash, she can ask for an amount of cash that the checkout assistant will give her when she has signed the authorisation. The amount will be deducted from her bank account, along with the value of the shopping. This is called Cashback.

Veena always pays for her grocery shopping with her debit card. On the front of the card is printed the name of Veena's bank, the sort code, which is a code to identify the bank in the national database, the account number, which is the key field in Veena's bank to identify her account, and the expiry date of the card. This information is also contained on a magnetic strip on the back of the card. The magnetic strip also contains a four-digit number to enable Veena to draw money out of a cash machine.

Figure 3.3 *A credit card*

Veena also has a credit card which she uses when she wants to delay payment of goods. Unlike a debit card, purchases made with the credit card are paid at first with money from the credit card company's account. At the end of the month, Veena has to settle her account with the credit card company, or they charge her interest on the amount she has not yet paid.

Veena also uses cheques occasionally, especially when she is paying people who do not have the facilities to accept payments via plastic cards. Paying by cheque gives her a few days before the money is taken from her account. Cheques are also useful when Veena needs to make a payment that must be sent by post. Cheques have magnetic ink numbers that can be read by machine. Cheques are now slowly being phased out and yet it was only at the start of the nineteenth century that banks began to issue cheque books. Veena uses a cheque book by putting money in the bank or by arranging to borrow from the bank. Each cheque in the cheque book is blank, and Veena can fill in someone's name and the amount of money to be paid to that person.

'It is easier to send a cheque for a million pounds through the post than to send that amount of money in notes,' says Veena.

'Have you really got a million pounds?' asks Edward. Veena just stares at him.

Veena tells Edward that before computer systems, banks were linked by a system called the 'clearing house'. Whenever a cheque was written, the bank involved needed to record in its books that one company now had more money and another had less. No movement of cash needed to take place. It was easy to settle accounts if the person writing the cheque and the person receiving the cheque used the same bank but if they had different banks, the process was much more complicated. Some people issued cheques for money they did not have.

The only other forms of payment Veena uses are for the family television licence, which is paid by standing order, and the telephone bill, which is paid by direct debit. A standing order is a written agreement that an exact amount of money will be transferred from the customer's bank account to a supplier's account (such as the television licence office) on a certain day.

A direct debit allows the supplier (such as the telephone company) to take an unspecified amount from a customer's bank account on a regular, set date, provided that the customer is notified first.

An EPOS (electronic point of sale) terminal is the type of cash register commonly found in retail outlets that also acts as a terminal to the main computer of the retail outlet. Data about goods being sold is fed into the terminals, normally via bar code readers, touch screens and keyboards. As well as providing customers with itemised bills, these systems also generate useful management information.

EFTPOS terminals are similar to EPOS terminals but with some additional features. They are able to transfer funds from a customer's bank account direct to a retail outlet's account after reading the customer's debit card. This provides a much faster method of payment than cheques and credit cards. In England it is normal at present for a customer to sign a payment slip to authorise payment from his or her account. In Europe, a different system is more common. The debit card is supplied with a PIN, and the customer must key in the PIN to a special input device linked to the checkout terminal, to authorise payment.

With all the money coming out of Veena's account, it is fortunate that she has a job that pays money monthly direct into her account. Using a system called BACS, her employer uses the same sort code and account number to credit Veena's bank account with her salary. All transfers that are made direct from one bank account to another use a system called EFT (Electronic Funds Transfer).

Veena uses a traditional bank. Her son Gavin keeps telling her to get an Internet bank account which will pay interest on her current account. Veena is very concerned about the security of Internet bank accounts. She thinks it is easy for Gavin, who has no worries about people accessing his money as he has very little in the bank. Gavin is always keen to try out new ideas and has even explored telephone banking and using digital television banking. The one big advantage of Gavin's bank is that he can access it 24 hours a day, 365 days a year.

FACSIMILE TRANSMISSIONS

Iain's office uses a facsimile (fax) machine to send hard copies of documents such as orders and invoices. A fax machine converts a printed document into digital data that can be transmitted across the telephone network. At the other end a fax machine will decode the data back into visual form and print a copy of the original document. In this way documents such as letters and drawings can be transmitted to a different location very quickly. Although the technology is different, the effect is the same as sending an e-mail attachment.

PHOTOCOPIERS

One of the most used pieces of equipment in Iain's office is the photocopier. Before photocopiers everything either had to be copied by hand or copied using a typewriter and carbon paper.

Photocopiers work using static electricity. Photocopiers use a basic physical principle: opposite charges attract. Inside the copier is a special drum. The drum can be selectively charged with static electricity. As with laser printers, very fine powder known as toner is attracted to all the parts of the drum charged with static electricity. You place your original on the glass plate and it is scanned with light. This is why it is called a photocopier. Where the sheet of paper you are scanning is black, static electricity is generated on the drum. Then a sheet of blank paper gets charged with static electricity and this pulls the toner off the drum making a perfect copy. Heat then melts the plastic in the toner, fixing the image to the paper, and you have a copy.

Figure 3.4 *A fax machine*

Changing shopping habits

On the way home Veena pops into Mr Singh's shop to buy a red school shirt. Mr Singh owns a small fashion shop where the Oliver family live. Rupa likes Mr Singh because he knows all his customers and always has a friendly smile and welcome for every customer. With his wife he decides which clothes they should buy from the manufacturers to sell in their shop. They have to try and buy the clothes that people want.

Mr Singh uses a computer system to monitor sales. He can say which colours, sizes and shapes are the best-selling items in his shop. The problem is that fashions change constantly. How can Mr Singh possibly decide what clothes people will want to buy next week, or next month? Not only must he decide which fashions to stock, but also how many of each item. Some very useful information can come from the computer system. He will know, for example, that the number of red shirts sold each week has been steadily increasing or decreasing. He could therefore assume that the popularity of red shirts should continue to rise in the near future. However, in order to make use of this information, Mr Singh needs to have the information quickly and it has to be easy to understand. He also needs to use the computer model outlined in the first section of the book to ask 'what if' questions.

The first stage is to get the information into the computer. There are a number of ways he can do this.

Method 1

Type the data in by hand. This would be time-consuming and could be inaccurate.

Method 2

Use cards with holes punched in them attached to each garment. These cards were called Kimball tags, a name still used today even though cards with holes in are mostly a thing of the past. They were once used in most shops although the majority now use bar codes. The holes contain data such as the type of item, together with its size and colour. When an item was sold, the tag was torn off and stored. A machine then read the pattern of holes and fed the data into a computer.

Method 3

Each garment carries a label with a magnetic stripe on it or barcode. Data such as price and colour is contained in the stripe or code. When a shop assistant sells an item, he or she scans the data. Data from the stripe is automatically recorded into the point of sale terminal. It looks like a till but there is a screen that displays details about the item being sold. In reality this is how most shops gather data about sales. Mr Singh is unusual in owning his small fashion shop. Most of our high street shops are parts of large chains. Some of these chains are global groups that monitor sales throughout the world. The point of sale terminals link to head office using a Wide Area Network like the one you studied earlier in the book.

By linking together, today's shops stock thousands of different items from all over the world to meet the needs of our growing country.

Gavin orders a large amount over the Internet. The growth in use of mobile phones is likely to extend the use of electronic shopping further. But even town centre shops rely more and more on new technology. All large shops are run electronically to make sure that things like re-ordering and stocktaking are done as quickly and efficiently as possible. The most successful shops have the type of organised system we talked about in the first section of the book. They are able to take on a wider range of products because their ICT systems are able to cope with a wider range of products. Having a good range of products in a wide variety of sizes, colours and styles is what attracts customers.

Mr Singh knows all of his customers personally. When it comes to the Internet, retailers have to get information in other ways. One of the main ways it to use cookies. Cookies are not nice chocolate chip biscuits but small Internet files that live on your computer and gather information. There are already over 100 million cookies scattered around the world. The information gathered includes who you are, what you have bought, which sites you have visited, how long you stayed there and how often you revisit sites.

Cookies are generated by a web server and stored in the user's computer, ready for future access. Web browsers often send out information via cookies to sites viewed without the user's knowledge.

Some cookies are useful for having the browser remember specific information such as passwords and user IDs. You could for example develop an online ordering system using cookies that would remember what a person wants to buy. If Gavin spends two hours ordering CDs at his favourite site, he could log off and return weeks or even years later and still have those items in his shopping basket.

Site tracking by means of cookies can show web site owners the places in their web site that people go to and then wander off because they don't have any more interesting links to hit. This helps web designers design better sites. It can also give more accurate counts of how many people have been to pages on their site; in other words, how many hits a page has had.

However, because cookies monitor your Internet use, a lot of people think they are an invasion of privacy. Gavin did not even know they existed. The main concern is that all this data has been collected on Gavin without his knowledge. Gavin does not believe that anyone should have the right to collect information about him without asking first.

HOW COOKIES WORK

A command line in the HTML of a document tells the browser to set a cookie of a certain name or value. Here is an example of some script used to set a cookie.

Set-Cookie: NAME=VALUE; expires=DATE; path=PATH; domain=DOMAIN_NAME; secure

Cookies are based on a two-stage process.

- First the cookie is stored in your computer without your knowledge or consent. The web server creates a specific cookie when you access a site. Your web browser receives the cookie and stores it in a special file called a cookie list.
- Second, the cookie is automatically transferred from your machine to a web server next time you log onto the Internet. It then transmits the cookie containing your personal information to the web server and from there to the company that set it.

You can access your cookie list from within the Windows directory.

A NEW COMMUNITY?

Gavin is having a bit of an argument with Rupa who has told him that the Internet is a waste of time.

'You can get all the same information in a book, and its cheaper,' she says.

'The Internet is not simply a source of information, it is a place to communicate, conduct business, learn and share ideas,' replies Gavin. 'The Internet is a growing learning community.'

'Books are still better,' she replies.

'But while paper and traditional printing can provide some sources of information,' replies Gavin, 'there is no way of refining the search, no way of telling which information is out of date, no way of limiting a search by geographical area.'

'I can do this with a CD-ROM,' replies Rupa, 'or even in a good library. What about people who can't afford computers?'

'First there are cyber cafes and other public places like libraries where they can access the Internet,' states Gavin. 'And what the Internet as a community can offer is much more than books and CD-ROMs, otherwise libraries would not want them. The Internet offers a way of interacting. There are discussion groups, pressure groups, lobby groups and much more. The Internet is a powerful enabling technology for the development of communities because it supports the very thing that creates a community, human interaction.'

'Full of pornography and rubbish so I am told,' retorts Rupa.

'OK, the Internet already includes all kinds of people, cultures, and communities found in a global society,' states Gavin. 'Like any community it has rules, but it also has ways we should behave even if no one forces us to. Some people break the rules just as they do in our own town. It does not make us all bad or the town no good. The Internet is a potential community for us all and has some unique advantages over more traditional communication methods. It takes away many of the logistical difficulties of space and time. We can talk and communicate all over the world, you can't do that with a book. I can visit museums and art galleries on the Internet and much more.'

Realising neither is going to win the argument they both settle down for a coffee.

LOCATION

All shops work on the basis that three things matter: location, location and location. The shops of the past that proved the most successful were located in places where people walked. Being located in large shopping centres ensured that you would pick up passing customers who would be attracted into your shop by attractive window displays.

Some traders would conduct extensive research into the best location for a shop. ICT is used to map shoppers' habits and find the best location. For example, if your shop is suited more to young, old or busy people you need to target this particular social economic grouping and put your shop where they go.

SHOPS AS CUSTOMERS

It is not just people like the Oliver family that need to buy products. Shops have to buy their stock from other suppliers called wholesale suppliers who in turn buy goods from manufacturers. Even manufacturers have to buy raw materials, components, machines, and packaging services as provided by Iain's company. This network of suppliers is called the supply chain. Unlike the general public, manufacturers do not go to the high street to buy their products. They use catalogues, manuals and visits from company representatives to select from different suppliers.

Manufacturers constantly have to keep up to date with new technology, find the best suppliers in terms of quality and price and arrange delivery at the correct time in the manufacturing process. All of these activities have changed as a result of the introduction of ICT-based systems.

Even the product catalogues that manufacturers, shops and wholesalers use themselves have changed as a result of ICT systems. As we explored in the last section of the book, updating and printing paper-based catalogues is expensive and time-consuming. Catalogues have to be regularly updated with new product details and prices. The introduction of CD-ROM and on-line catalogues has helped to enable suppliers to maintain and update catalogues.

■ *Dad's party*

Veena has asked Edward to design invitations to his Dad's fiftieth birthday party. The party is to be held at the local pizza and pasta restaurant.

Iain has lots of friends and colleagues and Veena is worried about the cost of inviting too many people. Edward suggests that he could use a spreadsheet to give Veena an idea of how much the party will cost, depending on how many people are invited. He also wants to design the invitations on the computer, and print them out using the school's colour printer.

The restaurant can offer a discount depending upon number of people attending, as long as they select food in advance from special menu. Edward draws up a spreadsheet model. He even encourages Rupa by looking for cheap flights on the Internet, so she could visit her daughter in Australia. Edward finds lots of useful travel information on the Web, even systems that can work out your itinerary.

Edward's text messages

Edward is planning a night out with his friends. He hopes that Sunita, who is in his class, will be able to come. He has managed to get her mobile phone number from one of her mates and wants to send her a text message that will make her laugh and attract her attention. He decides to search the Internet for an unusual picture to send Sunita.

Veena is not keen on anything to do with mobile phones. 'People who use them are so rude,' she states. 'And they even drive their cars using them. They should be banned in public places', she tells Edward.

Edward spends most of his life texting on his mobile phone. The proper name for this is the Short Message Service (SMS). It is defined within the GSM digital mobile phone standard that is popular in Europe, the Middle East, Asia, Africa and some parts of North America.

He can send a single short message of up to 160 characters of text in length to Sunita. Those 160 characters can comprise words or numbers or an alphanumeric combination. Non-text-based short messages (for example, in binary format) are also supported by his phone. He has learnt a new language of dashes, commas and brackets.

What he does not know is that the Short Message Service is a store and forward service. In other words, short messages are not sent directly from sender to recipient, but always via an SMS Centre instead. Each mobile telephone network that supports SMS has one or more messaging centres to handle and manage the short messages. Keen to make sure Sunita gets the message, Edward uses a feature called the confirmation of message delivery. This means that unlike paging, he does not simply send the message and trust and hope she gets it. Instead, he can receive a return message back notifying him whether the short message has been delivered or not. Mobile technology means that short messages can be sent and received simultaneously with GSM voice, data and fax calls. This is possible because whereas voice, data and fax calls take over a dedicated radio channel for the duration of the call, short messages travel over and above the radio channel using the signalling path. As such, users of SMS rarely, if ever, get a busy or engaged signal as they can do during peak network usage times.

Edward likes his cellular phone. With it he can talk to anyone on the planet from just about anywhere.

He also uses it to:

- store his friends' contact details;
- produce task and to-do lists;
- keep track of appointments and set reminders;
- use the built-in calculator for simple maths;
- send or receive e-mail;
- get news, entertainment and weather information;
- play simple games;
- integrate his other devices such as PDAs, MP3 players and GPS receivers.

What Edward does not know is that in essence, a mobile phone is a radio, albeit an extremely sophisticated radio.

The cellular system that Edward uses divides an area into small cells. This allows extensive frequency reuse across an area, so that millions of people can use cell phones simultaneously. Each cell has a base station that consists of a tower and a small building containing the radio equipment. Edward knows that the school has a tower very close to it.

All cell phones have special codes associated with them. These codes are used to identify the phone, the phone's owner and the service provider.

Cell phones are some of the most intricate devices people play with on a daily basis. Modern digital cell phones can process millions of calculations per second in order to compress and decompress the voice stream.

Figure 3.5 *The parts of a cell phone*

Edward's mobile is what is correctly called a cell phone. It has a number of input and output devices.

- an antenna;
- a liquid crystal display (LCD);
- a keyboard (not unlike the one you find in a TV remote control);
- a microphone;
- a speaker;
- a battery.

At the heart of the system is an analogue-to-digital and digital-to-analogue conversion chip that is used to change the audio signal from analogue to digital and the incoming signal from digital back to analogue. This first section of the book covered this in detail.

A mobile phone also has a microprocessor and Flash memory chips which provide storage for the phone's operating system and customisable features, such as the phone directory, tunes and display.

Edward uses a digital cell phone. It uses the same radio technology as analogue phones, but in a different way. Analogue signals cannot be compressed and manipulated as easily as a true digital signal. Edward's digital phone converts his voice into binary information (1s and 0s) and then compresses it.

Edward's phone uses the GSM system. GSM is the international standard in Europe, Australia and much of Asia and Africa. In areas covered, cell-phone users can buy one phone that will work anywhere where the standard is supported.

Veena is always worried about Edward using the phone as she has heard that it can cause cancer.

GPS

Mike, Gavin's friend, is very keen on sailing and has just purchased a Global Positioning System (GPS). It links to satellites orbiting the earth. His GPS means he can determine his precise longitude, latitude and altitude anywhere on the planet. With it he can know exactly where he is and where he has been.

'I just stop someone in the street and ask them where I am when I am lost,' jokes Gavin.

'This is not really possible when you are sailing,' replies Mike. 'Unless you can find a friendly mermaid.' At the heart of Mike's GPS receiver is the ability to find the receiver's distance from four (or more) GPS satellites. Once it determines its distance from the four satellites, the receiver can calculate its exact location and altitude on Earth.

'Is it the same satellite we get our digital TV programmes from?' asks Gavin.

'No, there are lots of satellites and other bits of orbiting junk,' replies Mike. 'A satellite is basically any object that revolves around a planet in a circular or elliptical path. The moon is a natural satellite. Of course there are many man-made satellites, most much closer to Earth.'

'Man-made satellites are not usually mass-produced. They are custom-built to perform their intended functions such as monitor the weather or broadcast digital TV. GPS satellites are different as they need lots of copies so my GPS can pick up at least four anywhere on the planet,' states Mike.

For the record, there are over 23,000 satellites or rather pieces of space junk, floating above Earth. GPS satellites send out radio signals that GPS receivers can detect. Mike's GPS receiver measures the amount of time it takes for the signal to travel from the satellite to the receiver and from this information can calculate where he is relative to the four satellites.

Figure 3.6 *Satellite*

Each satellite has an extremely accurate and synchronized clock. Mike's receiver bases its calculations on the speed of digital signals sent out at exact times.

One problem with measuring the time it takes for Mike's GPS system to receive a signal from a satellite is that electromagnetic signals travel through a vacuum at the speed of light but when they hit the earth's atmosphere, which is not a vacuum, they slow down. To make matters worse, different weather conditions can affect the speed of the signal. Mike's GPS receiver has to guess the actual speed of the signal using a complex mathematical model of a wide range of atmospheric conditions.

PDAs (Personal Digital Assistants)

Lata is fed up with carrying around a big filofax organizer that contained her address book, daily planner, to-do lists, memo pads, calendar, project lists and college reports 'It's bulky, heavy and full,' she says, 'but if you don't have it, you're lost.' She has just purchased a 'new toy' according to her mother, in the form of a personal digital assistant, or PDA. It is a remarkable, tiny, fully functional computer that she can hold in one hand. And unlike that paper organizer, a PDA can hold downloaded e-mails and play MP3 music.

Lata explains to her mother that it is not a toy and that PDAs fall into two major categories: handheld computers and palm-sized computers. The major differences between the two are size, display and mode of data entry. Compared to palm-sized computers, handheld computers tend to be larger and heavier. They have larger liquid crystal displays (LCD) and use a miniature keyboard, usually in combination with touch-screen

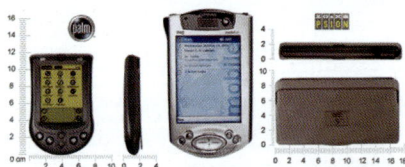

Figure 3.7 *PDA*

technology, for data entry. Palm-sized computers are smaller and lighter. They have smaller LCDs and rely on stylus and touch-screen technology. They also use handwriting recognition programs for data entry.

MEMORY

A PDA doesn't have a hard drive. It stores basic programs (address book, calendar, memo pad and operating system) in a read-only memory (ROM) chip, which remains intact even when the machine shuts down. Your data and any programs you add later are stored in the device's RAM. This approach has several advantages over standard PCs. When you turn on the PDA, all your programs are instantly available. You don't have to wait for applications to load. When you make changes to a file, they are stored automatically, so you don't need a Save command. And when you turn the device off, the data is still safe, because the PDA continues to draw a small amount of power from the batteries.

All PDAs use solid-state memory; some use Static RAM and some use Flash memory. Lata's has a SmartMedia card that is a removable form of memory. Due to this, the amount of memory in her PDA is upgradeable. Lata's PDA also has a colour LCD display screen. Unlike the LCD screens for desktop or laptop computers, which are used solely as output devices, Lata's PDA uses its screen for output and input.

Lata often downloads MP3s from the Web to play on the PDA. The MP3 format has completely rewritten the rules of music distribution. It has had a huge impact on how Lata collects and listens to music. The MP3 format is really a compression system for music. This helps to reduce the number of bytes in a song, without hurting the quality of the song's sound. The MP3 format can compress a CD-quality song by a factor of 10 to 14, without losing the CD sound quality. A 32 megabyte (MB) song on a CD compresses down to about 3 MB on MP3. This lets Lata download a song quickly from the Internet.

When Lata plays an MP3, her PDA extracts the song from memory byte by byte and then decompresses it. After running the decompressed bytes through a digital-to-analogue converter it simply amplifies the analogue signal so that Lata can hear it. The main difference between a portable CD player and an MP3 player is that the CD contains the bytes instead of memory, and on a CD the bytes are already decompressed so no decompression is needed.

Lata also downloads moving pictures using a system called MPEG. This is the acronym for Moving Picture Experts Group. This group has developed compression systems used for video data. DVD movies, digital TV broadcasts and satellite systems use MPEG compression to fit video and movie data into smaller spaces.

Lata must be very careful about copyright. Although she can find just about any song she wants on the Internet, copyright laws still apply. She knows that several manufacturers are working in conjunction with the music industry to embed copy protection in the digital music file. These encryption techniques require special code in the file and a means for the player to authenticate it.

Book of life

Edward has been reading about the latest research into DNA and how scientists are now creating the 'book of life' on a digital chip that people will carry with them everywhere they go. He can't wait to get a chip with all his DNA data on it, plus all the viruses and bacteria, DNA and RNA codes that could possibly make him ill. He tells his mother that all his life's data could be put on a chip, pager, CD player, genetic ID card, anything. He tells her that her job will not be needed as the technology will save time in pinpointing a patient's illness by allowing for nearly instantaneous tests.

'They would be able to make treatment decisions based upon your genetics, mum,' he says. 'The chip could determine that your child has been infected with a type of listeria that can cause meningitis. Your PDA computer will e-mail your doctor the test results along with a recommendation to prescribe an antibiotic. But not penicillin, since the device knows your child is allergic to that drug. It will then be sent automatically to the pharmacist who will send the correct medicines by courier.'

'Better buy yourself a faster motorbike then,' says his mother.

Not put off, Edward starts talking about another medical advance he has been reading about on the Internet, nanotechnology.

Nano comes from a Greek word meaning 'dwarf.' It is also a unit of measure equal to one billionth. Nanotechnology is about working with minuscule amounts or measurements. Chemists and engineers are working with computers and other tools to construct molecule-sized machines. Using the scanning tunneling microscope, scientists can see individual atoms.

'Imagine having an illness and being cured by a robot the size of a blood cell.' Edward says, 'or think of an army of machines the size of bacteria repairing a building damaged by a fire. They may even be able to clean up pollutants from the environment.'

'Perhaps you could enlist nanomachines to help you clean your bedroom or cook your dinner,' replies his mother.

The workplace and the law

A number of health problems have been identified as having a link to prolonged use of computers in traditional office settings:

- repetitive strain injury (RSI)
- backache

- eye strain
- headache
- skin rashes.

Repetitive strain injury

RSI is caused by the joints in the fingers and lower arms being constantly pounded by typing at high speed. It causes pain in the joints and can cause long-term disability if nothing is done about it.

Eye strain

Eye strain is quite common in many types of close work. A recent study of display screen operators indicated that nearly 70% of them suffered some sort of eye problem ranging from eye strain or irritated eyes to blurred vision.

Computer use and reproduction

There have been some reports that women who have used display screens for long periods have produced abnormal births. This is connected to the radiation given out by display screens when they are working. (Many other electrical appliances also give out radiation.)

Mobile phones and in-car communications systems

Increasingly often, mobile phones form part of information systems. The frequent use of these phones is also associated with certain health risks. They are believed to cause neck strain and headaches.

Many drivers also unwisely use mobile phones while they are driving. This distracts them from watching the road, and may contribute to causing accidents. A recent study carried out by the University of Toronto indicated that a driver using a mobile phone while on the move was four times more likely to be involved in a collision, and six times more likely during the first few minutes of a conversation.

All employees working with computer equipment are protected by a number of Acts of Parliament.

Health & Safety at Work Act 1974

This Act makes it the responsibility of all workers and employees to take care of the health and safety requirements of themselves and others. For example, you cannot trail computer leads where someone could trip over them. Employers have to take all reasonable steps to protect their employees.

Health & Safety (Display Screen Equipment) Regulations 1992

These regulations aim to protect workers who are using computer screens. Employers have to ensure that computer equipment meets minimum safety standards, that they assess the health and safety risks that might result from their employees using computer equipment; that they give workers regular breaks away from the computer; that they provide regular eye tests for workers who have to use a monitor as part of their job, and that they provide training on how workers can take their own actions to protect themselves and others.

The following chart shows some of the risks of using computer equipment, and preventative actions that should be taken:

Risk	Action
Eye strain from staring at a monitor	Fit a screen filter; light the area well; look away from the screen at a distant object regularly; take regular breaks; use large monitors; use flicker-free monitors; position the monitor far enough away; adjust the colour and brightness of monitor correctly; carry out regular eye checks
Back strain	Use a proper computer chair; sit at the computer correctly; take regular exercise; stand and walk around the office at regular intervals; use a foot rest
Repetitive strain injury (RSI)	Use an ergonomically designed keyboard; use a wrist rest; take regular breaks; position the keyboard correctly; do finger stretching exercises
Radiation	Remember that radiation is emitted from the back and sides of a monitor; keep mobile phone use to a reasonable level

Computer Misuse Act 1990

This Act was written to discourage people from hacking into computer systems and deliberately sending viruses via email. Anyone found guilty can face an unlimited fine and up to five years in prison.

Figure 3.8 *Health and safety for workers using computers*

Copyright, Design and Patents Act 1989

This Act makes it illegal to copy any computer file without permission of the owner. The Act prevents the copying of text and images from the Internet, and makes it illegal to use software without a proper licence. Workers cannot use software purchased by the company for company use at home without an additional licence. Anyone found guilty faces an unlimited fine.

Regulation of Powers Act (2000)

The Act allows the government to demand that a public telecommunications service intercepts an individual's communications for purposes of 'national security', 'preventing or detecting serious crime' or 'safeguarding the economic well-being of the UK'. The definition of public telecommunications services is broad and could apply to Internet services providers, phone companies, or even someone running a web site.

When an ISP is served with a warrant, it has to comply and it may not reveal this fact to anyone ever. While the interception warrants normally have to specify the communications of an individual or set of premises to intercept, under certain circumstances the Home Secretary can order that the 'external communications' of a telecommunications service be intercepted (e.g. all the Internet traffic flowing through a particular ISP's machines) if he deems it necessary for purposes of national security, preventing/detecting serious crime or safeguarding the UK's economic well-being. The government can demand that decryption keys be handed over in order to access protected information, where the person concerned has or has had the keys and does not have the information.

It is an offence not to hand over such a key on pain of two years' imprisonment.

Electronic Communications Act 2000

The Act allows the government to set up a voluntary approval scheme for bodies providing cryptography services (such as electronic signature and confidentiality services) to businesses and the public and makes clear that electronic signatures, certificates supporting them and the processes under which such signatures and certificates are issued and used can be admitted as evidence in court. This will give people more confidence in the use of electronic means to conduct business.

Data Protection Act

The Data Protection Act was introduced to control technological ability to transmit data and to protect people's right to privacy. The rapid growth in the power and coverage of information systems means that databases like that in Veena's Health Centre are able to hold huge quantities of data which could be distributed around the world in seconds. Much of this data relates to individual people, and may be of a personal nature. However, we all expect to have a right to privacy. We do not expect to have personal details such as our age, personal family details, medical records, financial data and our political or religious beliefs to be freely available to anyone.

The first Data Protection Act became law in 1984 but was replaced in 1998 by a new Act that included the Directive of the European Commission. The new Act also covered manual records, as well as those held on computers.

Under the terms of the Act, any person, organisation or company wishing to hold personal information about people must register with the Office of the Data Protection Commissioner.

The basic principles of the Data Protection Act 1998 are as follows: Personal data must:

- be processed fairly and lawfully (this principle contains the most details in the Act because, for the other principles, different conditions apply according to the type of data held);
- be obtained for specified and lawful purposes;
- be adequate, relevant and not excessive for the purpose;
- be accurate and up-to-date;
- not be kept any longer than necessary;
- be processed within the rights of data subjects;
- be kept secure against loss, damage and unauthorised and unlawful processing;
- not be transferred to countries outside the European Economic Area.

For the purpose of data protection, it is important to be clear about what 'personal data' means. The term is defined as: 'Data that can identify a living person, and allow an opinion to be expressed about that person.'

For example, a simple name and address is not considered 'personal data', but if it included a date of birth and bank account information, it would be 'personal data'.

Data about an individual can be further classified as 'sensitive' personal data and the use of this type of data is more restricted. 'Sensitive' personal data includes details of

- racial or ethnic origins;
- religious beliefs;
- political opinions;
- membership of trades unions;
- state of physical or mental health;
- sexual life.

The sixth basic principle of the Act refers to the **rights of data subjects**. A data subject is a person on whom data is held. The 1998 Act increased the rights of data subjects considerably. To summarise these rights, the individual can:

- ask for and be given a copy of data held;
- prevent processing of data if it is likely to cause damage or distress;
- prevent data being used for direct marketing;
- prevent automated decisions being made on the basis of data held;
- receive compensation for damage and distress caused by use of data;
- have data corrected, blocked or erased if it is inaccurate;
- make a request to the Data Protection Commissioner if he or she believes that the Act has been contravened.

The 1998 Act allows for exemptions to its provisions to be made under the following conditions:

- where national security is concerned;
- where crime or taxation are concerned;
- where data relates to health, education and social work;
- where data is used in regulatory activities by 'watch dog' organisations;
- where data is being used for research, history and statistics;
- where data is required by law and in connection with legal proceedings being disclosed;
- where data is held for domestic purposes, for example, for household, personal or family use.

Keeping up-to-date

Paco's company is always changing. New mobile phone technology changes components and production methods, jobs change and the skills people need to make telephones change all the time. 'The only constant thing here is change,' he says with real feeling. Monitoring the performance of the people who work for the company and then deciding what training should be given to enable them to improve and keep up to date is essential. ICT is used to record and monitor both performance and training. A careful record is kept of the training needs of every worker. Every one who works for the company must undertake at least five days' training a year.

First, when anyone starts at the company, they must follow what is called induction training. It shows them exactly what the company does and helps them settle into the new job. The induction programme is face to face with a trainer. Over three days PowerPoint presentations and practical tasks help them to get a feel for the job. PowerPoint slides are used to make them familiar with the company's rules and regulations, health and safety requirements and to generally make them feel at home. They are also given a special presentation folder containing lots of useful information on the company.

Once they are in the job they have to undertake development training. It enables them to develop the skills and qualities they need in order to perform their job better and prepare for promotion. It also keeps them up-to-date with new technologies. Some of this training is Internet based and workers can study at home or in the special training centre provided by the company. Other training is sometimes provided by external training organisations. The name for this is off-the-job because workers go to college or to specialist training centres.

Of course most people now have to continue with learning. Even Rupa undertakes external training when she goes to college to learn English. Iain has tried to get her to use the Internet, and has purchased lots of CD-ROMs with training programmes on but she does not feel happy with the technology. Paco's company are very keen on Internet training as there are lots of up-to-date courses and they can be delivered at the most convenient time and location.

Mediacom also provide some training that is carried out by people who work for the company. This is called in-house training. The benefit of in-house training is that the company can offer training that is directly relevant to the jobs that people will do. The disadvantage is that the company has to take people off other jobs to provide the training or to employ specialist trainers. This can prove to be expensive. To overcome this problem the company has started to use publishing software to produce their own training materials. They have also purchased commercial training materials. Both their own materials and the purchased ones use videos, books and computer software such as CD-ROMs and computer-based assessment materials.

The company has also started to use computer-based assessment, where the worker is asked to perform a number of tasks using a computer. These may be multiple choice questions or simple activities that can be used to assess the trainee and then direct them to a learning strategy

Paco's company provides training that takes place where the workers are working. The name for this is on-the-job training. The main benefit is that workers receive relevant training whilst production continues.

ICT to assist people with disabilities

Gavin's friend Mike is in a wheelchair after a motorbike accident. He finds it hard to move around the university and is always saying the problem is not his, but the university's. 'It's not my wheelchair that's a problem, it's all those stairs,' he points out at regular intervals. Gavin and Mike are both very interested in Assistive Technologies, the name often given to devices aimed at giving full access to ICT resources for all.

Gavin is always keen to point out that all of us have some disabilities. His disability is his writing. He cannot spell and his sentence structure is poor. Writing barriers for people with mild disabilities include:

- mechanics: spelling, grammar and punctuation errors;
- process: generating ideas, organizing, drafting, editing, and revising; and
- motivation: clarity and neatness of final copy, reading ability, and interest in writing.

Gavin uses grammar and spell-checkers, dictionaries and thesaurus programs to assist him with his written assignments.

He also uses macros, an option mentioned in the first section of the book (see page 88). A macro allows keystrokes to be recorded in a file that can be used over and over. Gavin uses macros for spelling difficult engineering words, for repetitive strings of words, and for formatting paragraphs and pages. Macros also save time for Gavin as he has cognitive and motor (keyboarding) problems.

Gavin also uses word prediction software. It works in a similar way to macros. If he has difficulty with word recall or spelling and cannot easily use the dictionary or thesaurus feature, word prediction software offers him several choices of words that can be selected.

Information and communications technology (ICT) can be used to support people with all types of disabilities to live full productive lives. Assistive productivity tools can be hardware-based, software-based, or both. Calculators, for example, can be the credit-card type or software based, which can be popped up and used during word processing. Spreadsheets, databases and graphics software also offer productivity tools, enabling workers to calculate, categorise, group and predict events.

Productivity tools can also be found in small, portable devices called personal digital assistants (PDAs) (see pages 152–4). Newer PDAs can be used as notetaking devices via a small keyboard, microphone or graphics-based pen inputs. PDAs can even translate words printed with the pen input device to computer-readable text, which can then be edited with the word processor and transmitted to a full function computer.

The workplace in the twenty-first century will reflect a diverse employment population exposed to a high level of technology. Like all employees, people with disabilities will need the tools in work environments to be competitive in what is called the 'new age workforce.' While some of these tools or job accommodations may be different from those traditionally used, they will provide those with mental and physical disabilities with the opportunity to become productive and competitive members of the workforce.

As stated earlier, any item, piece of equipment or product system (whether acquired off the shelf, modified or customized) that is used to increase, maintain or improve functional capabilities of individuals with disabilities can be described as assistive technologies.

AT devices may be categorised as high technology and low technology.

LOW-TECH DEVICES

Many low-tech devices can be purchased at a local hardware store, selected from a catalogue, or fabricated using tools and materials found in home workshops. Examples of low-tech devices are note-taking cassette recorders, pencil grips, NCR paper/copy machine, simple switches, picture boards, taped instructions or workbooks.

One illustration of a use of a low-tech device is for an assembly employee in Paco's company, who has attention deficit disorder. This means that he is very easily distracted and has difficulty remaining on task. The low-tech solution is that Mediacom provides a tape player with headphones to drown out outside noises that could distract him. Another illustration is for a secretary in Iain's office, who is hard of hearing but must answer the telephone at various times through the working day. Iain has purchased an amplified telephone receiver, and now the secretary can adjust the volume of the telephone as needed

HIGH-TECH DEVICES

High-tech devices frequently incorporate some type of computer chip, such as a handheld calculator or a 'talking clock.'

Examples of high-tech devices include optical character recognition (OCR), calculators, word processors with spelling and grammar checking, word prediction, voice recognition, speech synthesizers, augmentative communication devices, alternative keyboards or instructional software.

For example, a worker in Iain's office with a visual impairment must now access the computer to enter and extract information. To solve the problem Iain has provided a high-tech solution in the form of a Braille and Speak device that attaches to the computer and provides full access to the computer. A clerk with cerebral palsy in the local hospital must deliver volumes of mail to various offices. The hospital services purchased a computerised three-wheel motorised scooter with basket for delivery of mail.

Examples of other technology adaptations

- For people with visual impairments – screen reading program and speech synthesizer, Braille embosser and printer.
- For people with motor impairments – alternative keyboard such as trackball or joystick, ultrasonic pointer device, voice recognition for input.
- For people with hearing impairments – visual icons that replace sound cues on the computer, video captioning.

HOW ICT HELPS PEOPLE WITH DISABILITIES

For workers who struggle to form letters, who tire easily or who have limited motor control, computers may be their only way of getting their thoughts on to paper. Using specialist input devices can help the people with poor motor control or arthritis to gain confidence and hold down a job. There is a wide range of software and hardware available as alternatives to using the traditional keyboard and mouse. This type of technology includes:

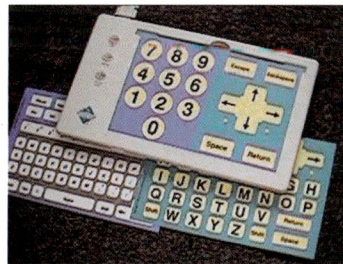

Figure 3.9 *Overlay keyboards*

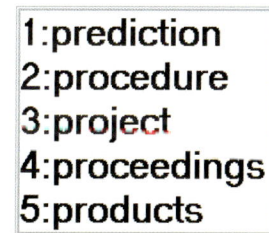

Figure 3.11 *Predictive word processors*

Figure 3.10 *Touchpads*

Figure 3.12 *Specialist keyboards*

Figure 3.13 *On screen keyboards and mice*

It is important that the user feels comfortable and confident in using the support system, as this has an effect on the usefulness of the item(s).

HARDWARE

In most cases a desktop machine is better for people with disabilities than a laptop or PDA, as it has relatively larger keys, a separate mouse and is quite robust. But Mike's wheelchair and need to access ICT facilities in several places in the university mean that a laptop is better. He has a particular model of laptop that was designed for use by people in wheelchairs. It is more robust that a conventional laptop and has attachments for fixing in place on the arm of the wheelchair.

For moving around at home, Mike also has a lightweight word processor which has a normal size keyboard, word processing software and a built-in display, a thesaurus, spell-checker, calculator, calendar and personal information manager. Extras such as a built-in disk drive, infra-red port for printing and facilities for connecting to a network or the Internet may also be added, but Mike cannot afford these yet. The small screen size can be an issue with this sort of device, but Mike has no problems with his sight, just his legs.

As Mike and Gavin are training to be engineers they are very interested in engineering solutions to some of the problems people have accessing the power of ICT. With most computers, navigation around the screen is generally controlled by using a mouse and a keyboard for inputting characters. However, both of these can be a barrier to ICT access for some people.

Mike and Gavin have been exploring a number of variations of the traditional keyboard. Some, with larger keys, can withstand hard use and offer both ABC and Qwerty layouts. They have explored small keyboards with built-in trackerballs and wrist rests, which can be ideal for users with limited hand movement. Mechanical keyguards are available for a range of keyboards and can help people with a tremor to locate the correct key.

Mike particularly likes the overlay keyboards that can be used for a wide range of activities, including controlling the screen pointer, because they tend to be relatively cheap options for individuals with difficulties in using standard keyboards. With an overlay, keyboard keys can be designated to carry out a sequence of operations, such as starting a particular application and entering words rather than letters into word processors.

They find lots of other mechanical assistive technologies, such as touch pads, joysticks and tracker balls, all helpful for those who do not have the motor skills or dexterity to operate a conventional mouse. The touch pad on Mike's laptop is easy to use as it requires only the lightest touch to operate, which can benefit people with restricted movement and stamina. They even find head pointing devices which can pick up a signal from a sender attached to the user. The movement of the user is then converted to mouse movement on the screen.

So recent advances in computer interface design and accompanying hardware, such as menu-based, graphically oriented bitmap displays, mice, tablets and touch screens have made interacting with the computer less intimidating for most users and both easier and more efficient for everyone, from novice to professional, or have they? The computer's power, versatility and ease of use have made its predecessors in almost every field all but obsolete. Gavin's misspelled words or other typos in anything he writes from a single business letter to a hundred-page university paper can be located in a matter of seconds, and he no longer has to retype the entire page. But Gavin and Mike want to see devices made to give everyone this capability.

As an engineer who lives in a wheelchair Mike is convinced that you should not take for granted 'normal' motor functions and coordination. Mice and touch screens are a nice improvement over keyboard for some tasks, but can hardly be utilised by those in the advanced stages of degenerative muscular disorders, and much less so by the quadriplegics he regularly meets on his trips to hospital. Yet it is these physically disabled people that Mike thinks have the most to gain from and the greatest dependence on computer and electronic aids for work, recreation, environmental control, or even for their most basic communication needs. He is concerned that although several hardware and software interfaces have been devised for the handicapped computer user, there are no inexpensive systems that deliver the true power and ease of today's computers.

One of the devices Mike likes can track the movement of the pupil in an operator's eye. The doctor at the hospital told Mike that there are estimated to be over 150,000 severely disabled persons able to control only the muscles of their eyes. Gavin and Mike like the idea of mapping eye movements as deliberate eye control actions can convey all sorts of useful information in basically two independent ways: through the six muscles that control absolute eye position, speed and direction of movement, or through the eyelid by measuring blinking and blink duration.

Some devices measure movement through surface electrodes placed on the skin around the eyes.

Other people can move the mouse but cannot manage to control the buttons. Gavin finds on the Internet a mouse interface which allow the mouse buttons to be switched off and replaced by external switches. Mike finds the joystick particularly useful as it is familiar to him, as he uses one to control his wheelchair and play computer games at home. His new games machine has super graphics, thanks to DVD and digital technology. It is almost like real life.

All of these devices can be connected in the same way as a standard mouse, and the use of a universal serial bus (USB) means they work without any additional adjustment other than the alteration of the mouse speed settings in the control panel. A USB port has the advantage of allowing up to 128 interchangeable devices to be plugged into one computer and the connections are quite sturdy with no pins to bend. The operating system software automatically recognises the devices when they are plugged in without the need to restart the computer.

SOFTWARE AND SETTINGS

Both Gavin and Mike use the many facilities available as part of the standard Windows environment. Many of the options available can improve access for disabled learners. This includes slowing the mouse speed down and using the 'sticky keys' option, which allows the user to hit one key after the other to carry out an action instead of holding down two keys at the same time. These are found in the control panel under accessibility options.

Slowing down the keyboard 'character repeat' speed can help users who have a tremor so that they do not end up with strings of unwanted letters. Alternatively, the filter key setting in the 'Accessibility' options on Windows stops the letters repeating themselves. There are similar settings available on Apple Mac computers. As explained earlier in this section of the book, they also both use keyboard shortcuts to make it easy to carry out many of the required functions such as saving or copying a file, or deleting a section of highlighted text. Apart from the hundreds of standard shortcuts, they create their own for actions or sequences they find difficult, using macros.

Gavin finds it hard to put text together, and as he types so slowly, he loses track of his ideas. He uses Microsoft Word, although other word processors provide the same facilities, and the AutoText facility to help. Although it is designed to aid mistyping or misspelling words, Gavin has set up a list of abbreviations for technical words used in his engineering degree which the computer recognises and expands into words and, in some cases, sentences. He set up the required abbreviations when he started his course and they now save him time and improve the quality of his work.

He has created word lists and grids in all the software he uses. He can simply type in the first letter of the word he requires, and suggestions appear on the screen for him to select. The more often a word is selected, the quicker the software learns the core vocabulary he has set up. This type of software is extensively used on SMS messaging systems employed by mobile telephones. It makes it much easier to type on a mobile handset.

There is also software which displays the keyboard on the screen so that words can be written by clicking with the mouse on individual letters. This can be useful for people who find that the effort of pressing a key limits the amount they can write, or for users who are unable to use any type of physical keyboard.

Speech recognition can be invaluable to many workers with different disabilities or learning needs. This technology would seem to be ideal for people who can speak but do not necessarily have good motor control.

However, many users with physical problems find that it can be a frustrating experience for them. Sometimes they have problems with the physical effort of speaking loudly enough for the machine to hear them and, often, the pattern of their speech varies depending on the time of day and levels of fatigue. To improve performance rates, a microphone volume booster is an optional extra which could help. This is a small box that links the microphone to the machine to boost the volume and is essential for laptops and some desktops.

How ICT has affected personal communications

Rupa's own daughter, Meera, lives in Sydney, Australia. Rupa likes to keep in close contact with her. Before the family had access to the Internet, Rupa used to write traditional letters to Meera, and these took several days to reach her daughter on the other side of the world. Occasionally, Rupa would telephone Meera, but this was expensive, and she always had to remember the time difference in Sydney. When Rupa was getting up, it was already evening for Meera, and when Meera got up next morning, her mother was asleep in bed. Now that the family has access to the Internet, Rupa can e-mail Meera whenever she wants to. Meera does not have to be awake when Rupa sends the messages, but Rupa can ask for a read receipt, so that she knows that a message has reached Meera's computer.

At first, Rupa found it difficult to remember the steps to send an e-mail, but now she finds it easy, although she is not very fast at typing. She always makes sure that she types out her message with the system off-line, to avoid running up the telephone bill unnecessarily.

E-mail is an important facility offered by the Internet, and its use is increasing every day.

As with all other computer functions, you must have the appropriate software. Rupa's family must also have an e-mail account, which is supplied by the Internet service provider that they use. Each member of the family has an e-mail address, which must be different from anyone else's address. To send a message, Rupa must also know the e-mail address of the person she is sending it to.

The software provides the interface for writing and addressing the message. It also displays messages received, and provides functions such as an address book and diary. Rupa does not find much use for these functions, but Lata, Gavin and Edward fill the address book with the names, e-mail addresses and mobile phone numbers of all their friends, and the diary helps keep track of where each member of the family is during the week.

Messages can be written, and any documents attached to them, while the computer is off-line. This helps to keep costs down. Telephone charges are only incurred while actually sending and receiving messages.

When Rupa finishes writing her message, she presses Send to send it to an Outbox in the family's computer, which is acting as the source computer. Rupa could send the same message to many different people, simply by adding their e-mail addresses to the address box. She finds this facility useful on special celebration days, when she wants to send a greeting to several members of the family around the world.

The communications software and modem then connect to the ISP's file server. Once connected, Rupa can tell the system to transmit the message, and to receive any incoming messages, which will go into an Inbox. She is always excited when the Inbox indicates that she has mail to read.

Rupa's sent message is placed in a mailbox on a main computer.

As soon as Meera logs on (connects her computer system to the Internet), she can access her mailbox and, when the incoming message has been transmitted to the Inbox, read the message.

Electronic offices

Veena looks at the time shown at the bottom right corner of her computer screen. 'Almost one o'clock,' she thinks. 'I'll just save this letter on to my hard drive and then finish when I get back from lunch.' She saves the file using a password.

Veena has arranged to meet Julie for lunch. Veena and Julie used to work together four years ago. They still meet regularly to exchange news. Their lives have followed quite different paths over the last few years. Veena has continued to work for the health centre while Julie has opted to give up her job to look after her two young children. They communicate with each other regularly by telephone. They go to the restaurant and order two sandwiches and coffees. 'Everything is done by computer now,' states Veena as the woman serving them touches graphic pictures on a concept keyboard before swiping Veena's credit card through a swipe machine.

Over lunch, Julie tells Veena that she is now looking for a job. She wonders how much office life has changed over the last few years. Veena tells her that communication is now a vital part of her job, and that the Internet is now used to exchange a large amount of data between the health centre and local hospitals.

'We often have to send information quickly to other health centres, hospitals and sometimes other countries,' she says. 'Sometimes a telephone call will do, but more often the information has to be in writing, or it contains X-ray pictures, or the person you want to speak to is not there when you telephone them. If the person is on the other side of the world, time differences often mean that he or she is asleep when you call.'

'Doesn't all that electronic stuff keep going wrong?' asks Julie. 'I have trouble working the microwave.'

'We have telephone help lines, technicians, support networks and software engineers,' replies Veena. 'When it was first introduced I thought ICT would reduce employment opportunities. It doesn't, it just changes the types of jobs people do, and the skills they all need.'

'We now use telephones, fibre optic cables, satellites and computer networks everyday,' states Veena. 'All designed and maintained by someone. All this technology was supposed to save paper, but we seem to generate even more of it.'

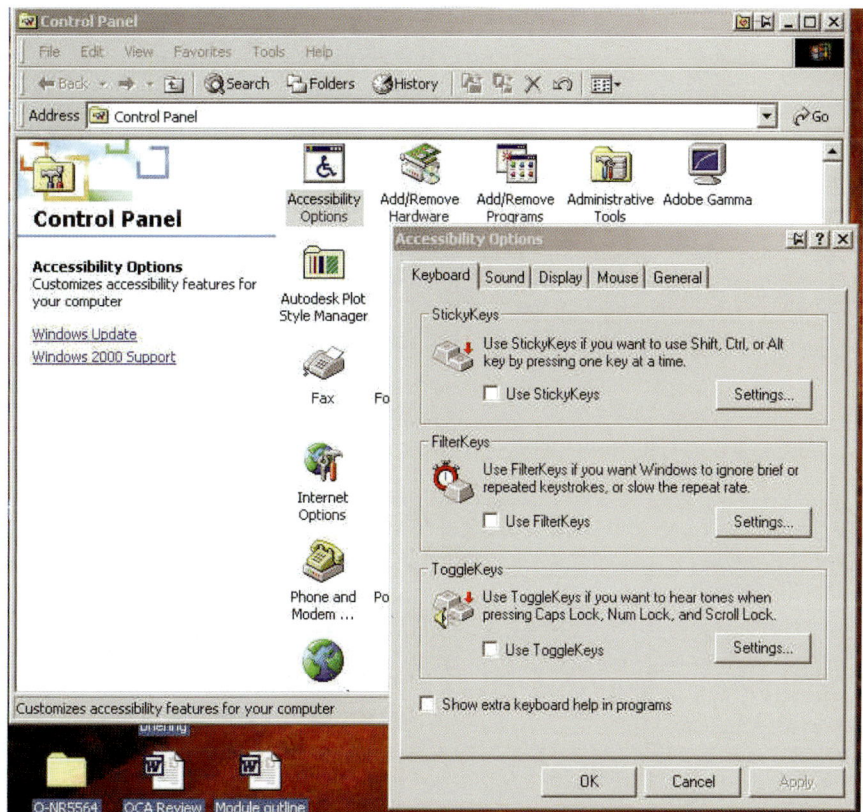

Figure 3.14 *Windows Accessibility Options*

'If people can work from anywhere, why go to the office?' asks Julie.

'Even the two of us need to meet up sometimes,' says Veena. 'I know you are worried about the skills you don't have but with the speed of change in ICT we are all learners.'

The use of CAD/CAM in designing the London Eye

As a special treat Veena decided to take Edward on the London Eye. Gavin decided to go too. 'With a particular interest in the engineering side,' he claims. The British Airways London Eye is near the Houses of Parliament; it is capable of carrying 4500 riders per day and on a clear day you can see for over 25 miles. Gavin is interested because the Eye was designed, manufactured and installed in only 16 months, thanks largely to ICT. This short timescale meant that the companies building it had to use a large number of cutting edge technologies. Good communication between the companies involved in the design and manufacture of the Eye was essential.

Over the past 30 years, the design and manufacture of manufactured items has seen a large number of changes. The use of CAD (Computer Aided Design) and CAM (Computer Aided Manufacture) has changed working practices and the type of skills workers need. Companies can also use new technology to work together in the design and manufacture of products.

Companies used to employ a large number of skilled staff, each member of staff having one particular role and one main skill. Nowadays many companies employ a smaller number of multi-skilled personnel. New jobs supporting new technologies have also been created. Retraining and learning new skills are now an important part of work.

The Dutch engineering company contracted to manufacture parts for the London Eye has developed many strategies for manufacturing complex steel structures. When they built the London Eye they had new challenges. The London Eye is more than 135 metres high. This is over 30 metres taller than Big Ben and over 60 metres taller than the first Ferris wheel invented by George Ferris Jr. The structure weighs 1900 tonnes.

CAD/CAM was an invaluable tool to the company, as it enabled the design, manufacture and testing of the components to be shared between companies that were not geographically close, while maintaining quality.

As we know from earlier in the book, the first step in the design process is a feasibility study. This involves a number of calculations to see if designs could work. It enables the manufacturing companies to start developing procedures for making the components.

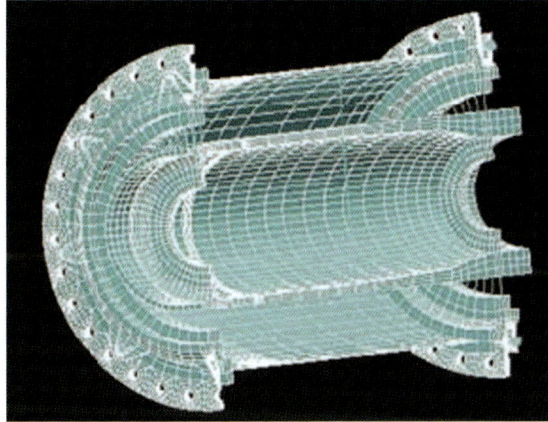

Figure 3.15 *Using the computer to model the complex structure of each component*

The two-month feasibility study for the Eye investigated five main issues that would determine how the final structure was designed:

- overall stability;
- whether extended use would weaken the components to a dangerous level;
- how the components would stand up to differing loads;
- how the structure would behave in different wind conditions;
- static strength of the steel.

Once the feasibility study established that the project could be completed successfully, the team began building a complete computer model of the structure. The model was complicated because it was made from many different elements and designed to be in constant motion.

Once the model was built, calculations were undertaken to decide how long the structure was likely to last in constant use. The movement of the rim made these calculations very difficult. The computer model was set up to simulate imperfections in every position of the wheel. To predict the life of the structure, consultants plotted the stress against the number of turns of the wheel. Given that the wheel turns twice an hour and that the designers planned for it to last 50 years, they had to base their calculations on 438,000 turns.

Figure 3.16 *Testing the model components for fatigue and strain*

Another major factor in the analysis of the London Eye was the question of how the structure would behave in different wind conditions. The company also wanted to ensure the ride was as comfortable as possible for the visitors, especially as they were concerned that some people might feel motion sickness.

Because of the complexity of these calculations the designers had to use dedicated software, which speeded up the process considerably.

The software was used to test the effect of wind on every one of the 32 capsules. This calculation was enormous because the load on each capsule is different during one revolution of the wheel, so the investigation covered 6,400 loadings on each one over a period of 320 seconds. This provided the data to determine the behaviour and comfort of the structure.

Figure 3.17 *Complete design for the Eye*

Communication between the different companies involved in the Eye relied heavily on the use of new technology. The main structure was built in Holland, using tubular steel provided by British Steel, now called Corus; the hub and spindle were cast in the Czech Republic; the bearings,which allow the rim to turn, were made in Germany; the cables were made in Italy and the capsules were made in France.

Each of these elements was manufactured using the most up-to-date processes.

Sheet materials were cut and formed using computer controlled presses, the panels were then transferred to welding jigs using robots, where the welding process was carried out using other robots.

Figure 3.18 *Spot welding robot*

Each weld had to be precisely positioned to ensure that each component functioned as expected when the wheel was erected. This meant that the robots had to run through a cycle of testing and self-maintenance as well as the process of welding. Each robot was programmed to weld a number of joints, then carry out a cycle of regrinding its welding tip, and checking the size and accuracy of its own welding. If the weld had moved outside the set tolerances the tip would be discarded and a new tip automatically fitted.

Figure 3.19 *A robot loading components onto pallets*

All of this enabled the quality of the manufacture to be monitored by the computer system. The components were then transferred to a dispatch location ready for sending to the manufacturing point.

The use of EDM (electro-discharge machining) machines was also a significant factor in the precision and quality of the manufacture of components. These machines can produce holes in components much more accurately than standard drills. The data is translated from the computer model into codes that the EDM can then use to move an electrode that erodes the material.

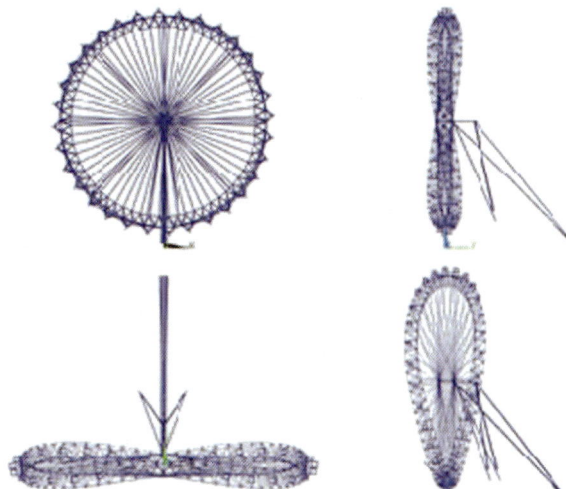

Figure 3.20 *Electro discharge machine*

All of the international cooperation came together through the use of integrated CAD/CAM to produce the now famous landmark on the River Thames. Veena, Gavin and Edward thoroughly enjoyed their trip.

Figure 3.21 *The London Eye from Westminster Bridge*

The Oliver family's new digital TV

Iain Oliver has had an analogue TV for about 40 years. It shows pictures taken on a video camera at a frame rate of 30 frames per second. The camera turns the picture into rows of individual dots called pixels. Each pixel is assigned a colour and intensity. It is the resolution in a monitor or TV that gives the picture its crispness and detail. The resolution is determined by the number of pixels shown on a screen or monitor. The rows of pixels are combined with synchronization signals, called horizontal sync and vertical sync signals, so that the electronics inside a monitor or TV set can display the rows of pixels. All of the Oliver family have much higher resolution pictures on their computer monitors than they have on the analogue TV. The lowest-resolution computer monitor displays 640 × 480 pixels. The worst computer monitors therefore have a higher resolution than the best analogue TV sets.

Iain has just bought a new digital TV. It gives much better quality pictures because digital cameras work at a much higher resolution than analogue cameras and the TV can show pictures at a much higher resolution, like the computer monitors. The signal is also transmitted and received digitally. As you read in the first section of the book, digital signals are much better than analogue in terms of quality. Digital displays are also of much higher resolution. With ten times more pixels on the screen, all displayed with digital precision, the picture on their new digital TV is incredibly detailed and stable and the sound quality is excellent.

'What's on telly tonight?' asks Gavin. Iain picks up the remote control on the TV, switches on the TV, presses the text button, then types the numbers needed to find out. After a few seconds, the television screen shows him what is on. There is nothing very interesting. 'Nothing you would like to watch,' replies Iain.

As we explored earlier in the book, the moving pictures you see on a television set are simply a series of still pictures or frames that change very fast. It is called animation. Although it all happens very quickly, there is time between each frame to transmit some extra signals. This is how teletext screens are received, in between the bursts of picture transmission. When Iain keyed in the page number, the TV waited for the page to be transmitted, captured the page and displayed it on the screen.

Digital TVs can be connected via phone lines so that they can send and receive text. With the advent of digital television, television banking and shopping are likely to grow dramatically. 99% of households have televisions and you do not need a PC and a modem to use them. There are hundreds of digital television channels, some of which are devoted to banking and shopping services. Sky uses its interactive teletext service via the television.

With Internet searching available through the television, new microprocessor controlled digital television and the further integration of communication and computer technologies, it is difficult now to state where the computer stops being a computer and the digital television stop being a television.

Figure 3.22 *Old analogue TV*

■ *Digital photography*

Edward wants to take a picture of his cat and e-mail it to his friend. The first step is to create a digital version of the image, so his computer can process it. As he only has a normal 35mm camera, he first has to take a photograph using a film, take it to the chemist so that it can be processed chemically, have it printed on to photographic paper and then use his digital scanner to sample the print.

Gavin tells him it would be much easier using a system that could sample the original light that bounces off the cat to create a digital image in the first place. This device is called a digital camera.

The main difference between a digital camera and a film-based camera is that the digital camera has no film and takes digital pictures. You learnt about the differences between digital and analogue signals in the first section of the book. Rather than have a film, digital cameras have a sensor that converts light into electrical charges. In order to get a full colour image, the sensors in digital cameras use filtering to look at the light in its three primary colours just as in the printing process explored in the last section of the book. Once all three colours have been recorded, they can be added together to create the full spectrum of colours.

Digital cameras also have an LCD screen, which means that you can view your picture right away. This is one of the great advantages of a digital camera: They are also small and easy to use; a digital camera is ideal for creating pictures that Edward can e-mail to friends or post on the Internet.

Edward can use a digital camera in the same way as he would his conventional film camera. Most digital cameras are simple automatic point-and-shoot cameras. They generally have auto-focus, and they can adjust for brightness, shutter speed and aperture automatically.

To get the pictures out of the camera you can link the camera to a computer via a cable or use a removable solid state storage device such as CompactFlash, SmartMedia and Memory Sticks. These solid state storage devices talked about earlier in the book are sometimes called digital film when used in a digital camera.

Of course it takes a very large amount of memory to store a high-quality digital picture. Edward is told that the resolution depends on the number of pixels, just like in a computer monitor and digital TV.

Cheap digital cameras use 256×256 pixels. He is told that this resolution is so low that the picture quality is almost always unacceptable. Real digital cameras start with a resolution of 640×480 pixels (307,000 pixels in total). This resolution is ideal for Edward's cat picture as it is about right for e-mail and a web site. The better cameras start with 1216×912 pixels (1,109,000 pixels in total). You need at least this if you are planning to print your images, and want them to look good. Cameras that start at this resolution are called 'megapixel' cameras. Some cameras have much higher resolution. 1600×1200 pixel cameras can produce images that can be printed in larger sizes with very good results. This is almost 2 million pixels in total with some cameras recording over 4 million pixels.

Edward decided to draw up a chart to compare digital cameras with normal film cameras.

Of course files of this size take up a large amount of space. A camera's memory will hold more images at low resolution than at higher resolutions and it will take less time to move the images from the camera to your computer. Low resolution images also take up less space on the computer.

Almost all digital cameras use some sort of data compression to make the files smaller. There are two features of digital images that make it possible to compress a picture. For example, in Edward's picture, blue sky takes up 40% of the photograph. The compression method will take advantage of these repeat patterns. Edward can also set the resolution of the picture. Lower resolution means smaller file sizes. As he wants to send the file by e-mail he is willing to give up some quality for a smaller file size.

Edward is told that if he takes the pictures in JPEG format at 640×480 resolution, he will be able to download them to his computer and e-mail them to friends without having to do anything to the picture.

What are the advantages of normal film cameras?	What are the advantages and disadvantages of digital cameras?
Very good print quality	The ability to view images as soon as they have been recorded
Easier to show his friends	Unsuitable pictures can be deleted and therefore do not have to be processed
Cheaper to buy than good digital cameras	The camera memory can be re-used
Don't need to buy a computer and a quality printer to produce prints	Panoramic views can be produced by 'stitching' images
Film is cheaper than photographic-quality paper and ink cartridges for printing purposes	Pictures can be edited and manipulated
Cheap on batteries	Pictures can be downloaded and printed as soon as they have been shot
Less delay between shutter release and image capture	The digital environment enables the whole process from recording images to viewing, printing
Better for action shots	E-mail and creating web pages can be carried out quickly and efficiently
Have interchangeable lenses	There is no need to purchase films, and third-party processing is eliminated
No delay between storing the image from one shot and being ready to take the next	There is a saving in physical storage space, as photographs are stored electronically
No need for compression, reducing picture quality and causing jagged edges	Audio commentary is available with some software

Using image-editing software, Edward could change the picture if he wants to. He can:

- crop the picture to capture just the part he wants;
- add text to the picture;
- make the picture brighter or darker;
- change colours;
- stretch part of the picture;
- change the contrast and sharpness;
- apply filters to the picture to make it look blurry, painted, embossed etc.;
- resize pictures;
- rotate pictures.

He could even cut someone or something out of one picture and put them into another.

Edward's friend David likes buying things from auctions. Edward thinks that a digital camera would be excellent for selling things. David could take a picture of an object and post it to the auction site very quickly and without having to pay for film or developing. It would have been very useful when he purchased his motorbike as you could post pictures on the Web to help potential buyers see what they are getting.

'Just think what would happen if estate agents used digital cameras,' said David. 'They could use the software to make the pictures look better, add a bit of sun, remove the lamppost, touch up the paint.'

From e-commerce to m-commerce

We have recently seen a quite astonishing rate of development in the provision of access to the Internet through handheld terminals, especially mobile telephones, and this is changing the way businesses function. Digitalisation is changing every aspect of our lives. Edward's idea of using digital cameras at auctions is a reality and pictures can be sent direct from and to handheld terminals.

Edward uses text messaging (*often known as SMS for Short Message Service*) extensively to talk to his friends. He can type messages to his friends, even with the mobile held behind his back. Edward can also read e-mails over his handheld terminal and on his mobile telephone. But speed has been a problem and the idea that a device with a small low-resolution monochrome screen, limited memory, a numeric keypad and reliant on wireless technology could be used to access the WWW and look at digital pictures initially seemed impracticable, and rather like science fiction to Edward.

Certainly a bandwidth of 9.6kpbs used on Edward's phone makes it inadequate for all but the short text messages he uses to talk to friends. He has started to download pictures and tunes but they are very crude.

Edward has been reading an article by Martin White on new technologies and mobile telephones. The article talks about UTMS technology and how it can offer bandwidths of at least 512k, which is four times as fast as his present land-based computer at home. Edward is not convinced that General Packet Radio Service (GPRS) technology which provides a 115kbps bandwidth is that much better than what he has now. His screen is too small anyway. His friends have better displays, but telephones that have been getting smaller for years are now starting to get bigger.

The article Edward has been reading states that it is highly likely that there will be more mobile devices accessing the Internet than PCs within a couple of years. It states that in Japan, mobile phones are already the most popular way to access the Internet. Edward is excited by the fact that soon he will be able to access the Net and the experts online from his mobile faster than the desktop computers sited in the school building.

The article states that advances are the result of a number of different factors, all coming together at an opportune moment. Analogue mobile telephone services have recently changed to second-generation digital services (often referred to as GSM). The most advanced mobile telephones use a new, faster system called the Universal Mobile T elecommunications System (UTMS). These new phones can display HTML pages, based upon a subsct of the extensible mark-up language (XML) called Wireless Mark-up Language (WML). The link between the handset and the web server is then managed by the Wireless Application Protocol (WAP), which is the wireless equivalent of the HTTP server protocol.

The article says that there is no need to have a new URL for websites to be displayed on mobile phones. The WAP technology ensures that the HTTP server recognizes that the call is coming from a WAP device, and routes the request to the section of the site that has been created in WML. It is also possible to translate HTML pages through the WAP server, although it is likely that not all pages will display properly. Edward is convinced people will need to design special web sites for the new technology due to the types of screens mobiles have. Edward thinks that it will only work properly when mobile screen technology moves towards the pixel-level displays that are used on PC screens.

Global marketing

Gavin buys lots of CDs and DVDs over the Internet. The Internet allows retailers to sell their goods to a world audience. A number of large banks are negotiating deals with manufacturers of major brands to by-pass shops altogether and sell goods through the banks themselves.

Taxation has become a major problem in Internet sales. Internet shopping is a free-for-all, with few regulations. One of the big problems in the UK is Value Added Tax. When goods are purchased outside the European Union, VAT is paid only on goods that cost more than £18.00. This means it is cheaper to buy two CDs separately than together. Prices of goods vary all over the world. Timberland shoes, for example, are half the price in the USA that they are in the UK. This makes purchases considerably cheaper outside Europe. There is also a problem in who collects the tax on a purchase that originates outside the European Union. At present, the Post Office or courier company acts as an agent to collect duty and collects it through the delivery person or Post Office itself. This system could not cope with increasing Internet sales.

Another big issue on taxation is that Lata and Gavin buy MP3 music files and software and download them over the Internet. There is no mechanism for levying taxes or import duties on purchases like these, and at present, they avoid paying any tax whatsoever.

Index